Richard Belcher walks us th~~
in ways that go beyond what
firm belief in the authority of Scripture and in the relevance of
its teaching sets this commentary apart from others. He offers
timely insights into recent scholarly challenges to traditional
Christian approaches to the book. He devotes himself to pointing
out how Genesis should be applied to modern Christian living.
This commentary will serve pastors well as they preach and
teach. It will serve lay people well as they seek to understand the
implications of Genesis for their lives.

Richard Pratt,
President,
Third Millennium Ministries, Orlando, Florida

The meaning of creation (and/or evolution) has taken its place at
the front of the intellectual/cultural stage for over a century and
a half, and shows no sign of moving from the center of discussion
and debate. Secularists and Christians – both liberal and conservative – instinctively understand the high significance of the issue,
and hence, the intensity of the continuing debate. Whether God
is real and Scripture is true are both tied up in the foundational
text of the Bible: Genesis chapters one to three. Richard Belcher's
Genesis is a clearly written and judiciously researched guide to the
entire question of the meaning of the book of Genesis (not just to
its first three chapters, pivotal though these are). I found his discussion of such issues as the meaning of 'Day' in Genesis one and
two; whether these early chapters are poetry or prose, and other
related questions, calmly discussed, in a fair and charitable man-
ner, but also with incisive critique, where called for. His interaction with recent works of C. John Collins and John Sailhamer was
perceptive, and makes a real contribution to current discussions
of the early chapters of Genesis. His summarization of the world
view that is provided us by a believing reading of Genesis is most
helpful, without being long and tedious. His survey of the lives
of the Patriarchs with their virtues and vices is a guide to God's
people in all ages, and constantly brings to the fore the victorious
grace of God in the lives of sinners who believe.

Douglas F. Kelly,
Richard Jordan Professor of Theology,
Reformed Theological Seminary, Charlotte, North Carolina

Richard Belcher's commentary focuses on the big picture of
Genesis, tracing God's story of redemption through the biblical

narrative. His careful exposition shows how Genesis reveals God's intentions for his creation and his unstoppable purpose to bless his people and redeem them out of slavery, bringing good out of evil. God's people can live with confidence that God will be faithful to his promises to redeem and restore the broken and the suffering. He is alb to take what people mean for evil and turn it into good. This commentary deserves a wide appreciation, as it will help pastors, leaders, and Christians see how Genesis proclaims the deepest message of the Bible: the grace of God for sinners and those who suffer.

Justin Holcomb,
Executive director of the Resurgence,
Lead Pastor of Mars Hill Church, U-District, Seattle, Washington,
& adjunct professor at Reformed Theological Seminary

It is hard to think that more material was ever packed into a brief compass, or with greater clarity, helpfulness and ease of reading than Dr. Belcher has managed in this commentary. The words 'thoroughness', 'fairness' and 'lucidity' spring to mind to describe the whole work. Indeed, I cannot think of an important 'stone left unturned'! The treatment, for example, of the creation narrative ranks among the fullest and fairest I have ever read, but, without exaggeration every page has its quota of good things, problems solved, and truths illuminated. In a word, I enjoyed this book from beginning to end and warmly commend it. I would have been personally helped by tying the comment more clearly down with verse references, but, within Belcher's chosen method of working, his excellent analysis of Genesis is followed through by accurate subdivision, and helpful study questions Ten out of ten!

Alec Motyer,
Well-known Bible expositor and commentary writer,
Former principal of Trinity College, Bristol

It is not often that the Christian community is provided a commentary which is both scholarly and practical. Richard Belcher's commentary on Genesis is rigorously faithful to the content of the book, thoughtfully responsive to the issues of the day and easily as well as enjoyably navigated by any and all who have the privilege of opening its pages. It is my privilege to commend it to you without reservation.

Harry L. Reeder, III ,
Pastor Teacher,
Briarwood Presbyterian Church, Birmingham, Alabama

GENESIS

The Beginning of God's Plan of Salvation

Richard P. Belcher, Jr.

CHRISTIAN
FOCUS

Dr Richard 'Dick' Belcher is the Professor of Old Testament at Reformed Theological Seminary, Charlotte, North Carolina. He graduated from Covenant College, received his MDiv from Covenant Theological Seminary and his PhD from Westminster Theological Seminary. He is an ordained minister in the PCA and pastored an urban church in Rochester, New York, for ten years.

Unless otherwise indicated all Scripture quotations are taken from *The Holy Bible, English Standard Version*, copyright © 2001 by Crossway Bibles, a division of Good News Publishers. Used by permission. All rights reserved.

Scripture quotations marked 'NIV' are taken from *The Holy Bible, New International Version*®. NIV®. Copyright © 1973, 1978, 1984 by International Bible Society. Used by permission of Zondervan. All rights reserved.

Scripture quotations marked 'NASB' are taken from the *New American Standard Bible*®, Copyright © 1960, 1962, 1963, 1968, 1971, 1972, 1973, 1975, 1977, 1995 by The Lockman Foundation. Used by Permission. www.lockman.org

Scripture quotations marked 'NRSV' are taken from the *New Revised Standard Version Bible*, copyright 1989, Division of Christian Education of the National Council of the Churches of Christ in the United States of America. Used by permission. All rights reserved.

Scripture quotations marked 'KJV' and 'NKJV' are taken from *The King James Version* and *The New King James Version*. All rights reserved.

ISBN 978-1-84550-963-7

10 9 8 7 6 5 4 3 2 1

Published in 2012
in the
Focus on the Bible Commentary Series
by
Christian Focus Publications Ltd.,
Geanies House, Fearn, Ross-shire,
IV20 1TW, Scotland, UK.
www.christianfocus.com

Cover design by Daniel van Straaten

Printed and bound by
Bell & Bain, Glasgow

MIX
Paper from responsible sources
FSC® C007785

Contents

Preface

There are many good commentaries on Genesis available today. In fact, the reader will notice that this commentary references several other commentaries quite frequently. I have found Matthews, Waltke, Currid, and Hamilton to be good companions and guides as I have progressed through the book of Genesis. The focus of this commentary is to help the reader get the big picture in the book of Genesis. This approach is accomplished by seeing the development of the progress of redemptive history through the flow of the narrative. God is clearly at work in history to accomplish His purposes. Genesis lays out the purposes of God for His creation and how He is at work to accomplish those purposes. The fascinating thing is that the purposes of God have not changed and that He is still at work today fulfilling those purposes. Thus the book of Genesis is not just an ancient document that has no relevance to modern-day life, but it is the Word of God which speaks a message that is important for God's people today. Genesis is the book of beginnings that lays a foundation for understanding the rest of Scripture. Keep the Bible open as you read through this commentary, for it is the Word of God that is living and active, sharper than any two-edged sword. May God use His Word to enrich your life.

The Introduction to this commentary covers certain questions that arise when one studies the book of Genesis. Although many of these questions are important questions which have significant implications for the interpretation of the Bible, one could skip the Introduction and begin with the Commentary section. Or one could read sections of the Introduction that are of interest. If the authorship of Genesis does not excite you, then maybe a review of the different approaches to the meaning of 'day' in Genesis 1 would be more interesting. There are study questions for the Introduction which could lead to some spirited discussions if this commentary is used for a group Bible study.

I would like to thank Christian Focus for the opportunity to write this commentary on Genesis. I would also like to thank Reformed Theological Seminary for the opportunity to teach there and for the wonderful working environment they provide for professors. I am especially grateful for my colleagues in Biblical Studies at the Charlotte campus (Drs. Robert C. Cara, Michael J. Kruger, and John C. Currid), who are more than colleagues but are truly friends and brothers in the Lord. I have been blessed by three excellent teaching assistants in the last several years who have helped me directly or indirectly to write this commentary. Thanks to Mark James, William Hunter, and Brent Horan. I am very thankful for my wife Lu whose daily assistance is such a blessing. I dedicate this book to my three daughters Nicole, Danielle, and Alisha. Your lives have always been affected by your father's calling, from pastoral ministry in urban Rochester, New York, to doctoral studies in Philadelphia, Pennsylvania, to teaching at RTS Charlotte. Thank you for your flexibility. We are grateful for God's work of grace in each of your lives.

Richard P. Belcher, Jr.
September 2011

Abbreviations

AUSS	*Andrews University Seminary Studies*
BibSac	*Bibliotheca Sacra*
CT	*Christianity Today*
CTM	*Concordia Theological Monthly*
ESV	English Standard Version
EQ	*Evangelical Quarterly*
GKC	Gesenius, Kautzsch, Cowley Hebrew Grammar
JAOS	*Journal of the American Oriental Society*
JETS	*Journal of the Evangelical Theological Society*
JSOT	*Journal for the Society of the Old Testament*
NASB	New American Standard Version
NIV	New International Version, 1984
NJPS	A New Translation of the Holy Scriptures according to the Traditional Hebrew Text (1985)
NIDOTTE	*New International Dictionary of Old Testament Theology and Exegesis*
NRSV	New Revised Standard Version
PTR	*Princeton Theological Review*
TynBul	*Tyndale Bulletin*
TWOT	*Theological Wordbook of the Old Testament*
WCF	Westminster Confession of Faith
WTJ	*Westminster Theological Journal*

Introduction

Genesis is the book of beginnings. Its author assumes God's existence because He does not have a beginning (1:1), yet everything else does have a beginning. Genesis gives an account of the beginning of the 'heavens and the earth', the beginning of light and life, the beginning of the role of human beings in God's creation, the beginning of the covenant relationship, the beginning of marriage, the beginning of sin in the fall, the beginning of hope in one to come, the beginning of strife and division, the beginning of civilization, and the beginning of death. One could say that Noah represents a new beginning after the flood, but the old sinful patterns remain, so God, in a sense, begins anew with Abraham to bring blessings to the earth and to the nations.

Genesis is a foundational book because it is a book of beginnings. It is foundational to life in general because an understanding of the first few chapters of Genesis explains basic issues concerning life in this world. Genesis is foundational to the Pentateuch: try reading the early portions of Exodus without understanding the promises made to the patriarchs. Genesis is foundational to the rest of the Old Testament because the concepts and ideas set forth in Genesis are further developed in the rest of the Old Testament. The hope in God's promises is kept alive. Genesis is also foundational to the New Testament, for the promises of hope set forth in Genesis are fulfilled in the New Testament. In this way Genesis is more than foundational; it is itself forward-looking. The history laid out in Genesis is not random but it has a purpose according to God's plan. In Genesis 1–11 sin is not able to hinder God's purposes for humanity. God makes certain promises to Abraham in chapter 12 which will be fulfilled even if Abraham and his descendants are not always trusting in those promises or acting faithfully toward God. At the end of his life, Jacob announces what will happen to his sons in the future (literally 'in the last days' in 49:1). At the end of Genesis, Joseph affirms that even though his brothers meant evil against him in selling him into slavery, God was able to bring good out of the situation (50:20). Thus it is not surprising that the one announced in Genesis 3:15 is eagerly awaited by those suffering under the curse of sin (5:29). There is also development in the identification of this one who will crush the serpent's head, from a son of Adam (3:15), to a son of Abraham (12:1-3), to a king who will come from the tribe of Judah (49:8-12). At the end of Genesis, the story is not finished because the one promised had not yet come.[1]

The Question of Authorship

Genesis is not just an ancient history book; it is also a message for God's people in every age. Understanding how God communicated this message to His people will help one better understand the message itself. Several topics are important for understanding how God communicated it.

God used Moses as the primary human instrument to reveal His message to His people Israel. Moses occupied a special place within God's redemptive program. He had more direct access to God than all other prophets because God spoke to Moses face-to-face, but to the other prophets He spoke in dreams and visions (Num. 12:6-8; Deut. 34:10-12). Moses laid a foundation for the people of Israel in the Pentateuch so they could understand who they were and their role in the world. Genesis identifies Israel's God as the God of Creation and sets Israel's place among the nations as a prelude to the blessing that will come to the nations through Israel (Gen. 1–11). The sin of human beings cannot hinder the redemptive purposes of God as God chooses Abram as the person through whom His blessing to the nations will come (Gen. 12–50). Moses also laid a foundation for the prophets in

---

1. For further discussion on the forward-looking nature of Genesis, see Warren Gage, *The Gospel of Genesis: Studies in Protology and Eschatology* (Winona Lake, Ind.: Carpenter Books, 1984) and John Sailhamer, *The Pentateuch as Narrative* (Grand Rapids: Zondervan, 1992), pp. 34-38.

the sanctions of the Mosaic covenant, which are presented in the blessings and curses of the covenant (Lev. 26; Deut. 27–28). The message of salvation in the prophets is connected to the blessings of the covenant and the message of judgment in the prophets is connected to the curses of the covenant. Part of the ministry of the prophets is to preach the blessings and curses of the covenant to the people. Also, the major institutions of Israel are either established or explained in the Pentateuch. Not only is the law given to God's people, but the priests and their work at the tabernacle is laid out in Exodus 25–40. The future leaders in the land of Canaan and their function are discussed, including judges (Deut. 17:8-13), prophets (Deut. 18:15-22), and even a future king (Deut. 17:14-20). It is clear that the Old Testament and the New Testament cannot be understood without understanding the first five books of Moses.

The Documentary Hypothesis

The view that Moses is the fundamental author of the Pentateuch has not been universally accepted among scholars, especially since the Enlightenment. Julius Wellhausen[2] popularized a view called the documentary hypothesis that dominated Old Testament studies for over 100 years. His basic argument is that originally there were four separate documents (J, E, D, P) that were woven together by an editor (called a redactor) into one document, which is the Pentateuch as it now exists. Each of the separate documents J, E, D, and P has certain characteristics. It becomes apparent in reading the Pentateuch, according to this view, that a redactor was at work because there are seams or fractures where sections are stuck together. Thus a scholar is able to pull out the four original, independent documents from the Pentateuch and reconstruct them. Document P is the priestly document, and it is the latest document. In this view, the Pentateuch was not complete until after the exile. Thus Moses could not have had anything to do with writing the Pentateuch.

Although a few conservative scholars over the years have argued against the documentary hypothesis (such as

---

2. Julius Wellhausen, *Prolegomena to the History of Israel* (Atlanta: Scholars Press, 1994 [1885]).

Hengstenburg, Pusey, Cassuto, Allis, and Young), it has only been fairly recently that critical scholars themselves began to call into question this theory.[3] The literary character of parts of the Pentateuch began to be explored with the conclusion that some of the stories, such as the Joseph narrative, were literary masterpieces.[4] It became difficult for some to hold that certain parts of the Pentateuch were the results of a redactor, who was seen by many as being rather clumsy in the way he put the sources together, and that those same stories were literary works of art. Thus there was a move toward examining the final form of the text as we have it without being concerned with the historical process of how the text came into existence. Brevard Childs developed canonical criticism which was concerned with the theology of the text and with how the text functioned in an authoritative way within the community of God's people. Theology and authority, which had been omitted from the interpretation of the Bible during the Enlightenment, took on greater importance. However, such a move did not mean a move toward Mosaic authorship. Moses was viewed as the canonical author of the Pentateuch because the Pentateuch presents him as the author, but not the real historical author of the Pentateuch.[5] Thus critical assumptions still stood as judge over Scripture instead of allowing Scripture to be the final authority.

Moses as the Fundamental Author

If a person is willing to take seriously what the Pentateuch and other Scriptures state, there are good reasons for affirming that Moses was the fundamental author of the Pentateuch. Most ancient Near Eastern works do not name the author, so it is not unusual that Moses is not specifically named as the author of the Pentateuch; however, there are references in the Pentateuch to Moses' writing activity as he receives revelation and is a witness to redemptive acts. He records historical acts

---

3. R. N. Whybray, *The Making of the Pentatuech: A Methodological Study* (Sheffield: JSOT Press, 1987).

4. See John Barton's discussion of the conjuring trick of the disappearing redactor in *Reading the Old Testament: Method in Biblical Study* (2nd ed.; Louisville: Westminster John Knox Press, 1996), pp. 56-58.

5. Brevard Childs, *An Introduction to the Old Testament as Scripture* (Philadelphia: Fortress Press, 1979), pp. 132-35.

concerning the Amalekites (Exod. 17:14) and the stages of Israel's wilderness journey (Num. 33:2). Also, Moses writes down the laws that God had given to His people (Exod. 24:4); for example, 'Moses had finished writing the words of this law in a book' (Deut. 31:24), which book was then placed in the ark of the covenant. Moses also wrote the Song of Moses (Deut. 31:22). Further, the perspective of the text is important. This includes places of which there are eyewitness accounts, such as Exodus 15:27, which gives the exact number of palm trees and springs of water. The book of Exodus also reflects accurate knowledge of Egyptian customs.[6] And sometimes overlooked, the perspective of the Pentateuch is that the people of God have been delivered from Egypt (the book of Exodus), they are on their way to the land of Canaan (Numbers), and they are on the verge of entering the land of Canaan under the leadership of Joshua (Deuteronomy). The primary perspective of the text fits the time period and the events of Moses' life.

It is also significant that other Scriptures affirm that Moses was involved in the writing of the Pentateuch. The law is not only identified as the law of Moses (Dan. 9:11-13) and called the book of Moses (Ezra 6:18; Neh. 13:1; 2 Chron. 25:4), but there are also specific statements that Moses wrote portions of the law. For example, Joshua is encouraged to do 'according to all the law that Moses my servant commanded you' (Josh. 1:7). The commands of Moses may have included verbal words spoken to Joshua by Moses, but it also includes the imperatives of the law written by Moses. The Book of the Law is mentioned in Joshua 1:8 in terms of 'all that is written in it'. The New Testament also affirms that Moses wrote the law. For example, in Matthew 19:7 the disciples ask Jesus, 'Why then did Moses command one to give a certificate of divorce and send her away?' which comes from Deuteronomy 24:1. And Jesus himself affirms in Mark 7:10, 'For Moses said, "Honor your father and your mother," and "Whoever reviles father or mother shall surely die",' which is a quote of Exodus 20:12 and 21:17.[7] It is dangerous to try to blunt the force of these affirmations by arguing that Jesus really knew that Moses

---

6. John Currid, *Ancient Egypt and the Old Testament* (Grand Rapids: Baker Books, 1997).

7. All Scriptural quotations are from the English Standard Version.

did not write the Pentateuch but that He accommodated Himself to the views of His audience.[8] This approach would call into question His integrity and perfection by having Him teach a view that is false if Moses did not really write the Pentateuch. Plus, the characteristic of Jesus' ministry was to speak the truth to people even when it was difficult (John 6).

There are good reasons to affirm that Moses wrote the Pentateuch. However, such a view is not without a few problems that need to be addressed. There are certain statements in the Pentateuch that appear difficult to reconcile with Mosaic authorship. When the authority of Moses is questioned by Miriam and Aaron in Numbers 12:1-3, the statement in verse 3 seems to be a comment about Moses: 'Now the man Moses was very meek, more than all people who were on the face of the earth.' One wonders if the most humble man who ever lived could make such a comment about himself.[9] Also, Deuteronomy includes the account of Moses' death. Although these two incidents could be explained as from the hand of Moses on the basis of divine inspiration, there may be another explanation that makes sense of these statements. It is clear that the Hebrew text of the Old Testament was entrusted to the scribes and was kept by them over a long period of time. If one accepts Mosaic authorship, the Pentateuch would have originated around 1400 B.C., but the Old Testament writings do not come to an end until 400 B.C. Language would change over a thousand-year period so that the text would need to be grammatically updated. Geography also changes over such a long period of time. Thus the names of two cities, the Ur of the Chaldees (Gen. 11:28; 15:7) and Dan (Gen. 14:14), were not known by these names until much later than the time of

---

8. Peter Enns, 'William Henry Green and the Authorship of the Pentateuch: Some Historical Considerations,' *JETS* 45:3 (2002): pp. 385-403.

9. However, see E.J. Young, *My Servants the Prophets* (Grand Rapids: Eerdmans, 1952), pp. 42-46, who argues that Numbers 12:3 is integral to the passage and should not be seen as an interpolation. He notes that Moses is not praising himself because he is writing in the third person. Young seems to be arguing against the critical view that the text is a composite text more than the view that is set forth here that advocates minor scribal changes. Also, John Currid (*Numbers* [North Darlington: Evangelical Press, 2009], p. 21) makes the argument that Numbers 12:3 is from the hand of Moses based on the fact that the literary technique of writing about oneself in the third person is common in ancient Near Eastern literature.

Moses. So how can all this evidence be explained in terms of Mosaic authorship?

Based on the evidence set forth above concerning Moses' role in producing the Pentateuch, Moses can be called the fundamental author of the Pentateuch. The events in Genesis were before his time, so he would have been dependent on oral tradition, written sources such as genealogies, and information revealed to him by God. Near the end of the Pentateuch is the statement that when Moses had finished writing the words of this law in a book he gave it to the priests and Levites who had the responsibility of teaching the people the law of God (Deut. 31:9-13, 24-26). It is possible that Joshua added the death of Moses to the Pentateuch, but perhaps later scribes were responsible. They would have wanted to ensure that the law was understandable to the people and would have been concerned to study and preserve the ancient texts, especially during the monarchy. They would have been responsible for updating the text grammatically and geographically, which does not entail major content changes, but does ensure that the text can be understood.[10] Ezra is presented in a similar role in Nehemiah 8:8. So what does Mosaic authorship mean? It means that he is the *fundamental author* and that the majority of the Pentateuch comes from his hand.

There are recent trends among conservatives, however, that have expanded the material in the Pentateuch which is not from the hand of Moses. Moses is seen by some as the *substantial author,* with extra additions such as Numbers 12:3 and the account of his death as being only the tip of the iceberg of other additions that were made to the Pentateuch.[11] Others talk about the Mosaic origin of some of the material of the Pentateuch, but believe that the *final author is unknown* because the final form of the Pentateuch was not until the exile.[12] Such views minimize the perspective of the Pentateuch as being on

---

10. Michael A. Grisanti, 'Inspiration, Inerrancy, and the Old Testament Canon: The Place of Textual Updating in an Inerrant View of Scripture,' *JETS* 44:4 (2001): pp. 577-98.

11. Ray Dillard and Tremper Longman III, *Introduction to the Old Testament* (2nd ed.; Grand Rapids: Zondervan, 2006), pp. 42, 50-51.

12. T. D. Alexander, 'Authorship of the Pentateuch,' in *Dictionary of the Old Testament Pentateuch* (Downers Grove, IL: InterVarsity Press, 2003), pp. 61-72, and Bruce Waltke, *An Old Testament Theology* (Grand Rapids: Zondervan, 2007), pp. 56-58.

the verge of taking the promised land and goes against the evidence that connects the Pentateuch with Moses.

The Role of Narrative and Poetry in Genesis

In order to understand a work of literature it is helpful to understand what type of literature is being examined (called genre), which focuses on the content, mood, and structure of a work. Most of Genesis is narrative, which tells a story driven by conflict and its resolution.[13] For example, much of the Abraham narrative is driven by the tension between the promises that God makes to Abraham in Genesis 12 and the fulfillment of those promises in Abraham's life.

There are also sections of poetry at key places in Genesis and at key places in the rest of the Pentateuch.[14] Early on in Genesis there are short poems that come near the end of sections. These poems are spoken by a central character as a reflection on the events that have occurred and often are followed by a short epilogue bringing the section to a close. For example, the words of Adam when Eve is presented to him (Gen. 2:23) are in poetry. His statement is followed by an epilogue in 2:24-25, which draws out a lesson and brings the section to a close. Other short poems that function in the same way occur in Genesis 3:14-19, 4:23-24, 5:29, and 9:24-27. Each of these poems is followed by an epilogue.

There are also larger poetic texts found in the Pentateuch that are inserted into the narrative near the end of sections. These larger poems are also found in the mouth of a central figure (Genesis 49, Numbers 23–24, and Deuteronomy 32). What is significant about these larger poems is that they all give an account of what will happen in the future, with Genesis 49:1 using the phrase 'in the days to come', which can be literally translated 'in the latter days'.

It is also important that both the smaller and the larger poems contain references to the development of the seed concept introduced in Genesis 3:15. It is clear from Genesis 5:29 that people are looking for the one who will bring comfort

---

13. For a discussion of how to interpret narrative, see Richard L. Pratt, Jr., *He Gave Us Stories* (Phillipsburg: P & R Publishing, 1990).

14. For a discussion of how Hebrew poetry works, see Mark D. Futato, *Interpreting the Psalms: An Exegetical Handbook* (Grand Rapids: Kregel, 2007).

from the curse. The rest of the poems develop the seed concept through the line of Shem (Gen. 9:27), a king from the tribe of Judah (Gen. 49:8-12), who will conquer all his enemies (Num. 24:17). The last major poems, Deuteronomy 32–33, focus more on the LORD as king of his people whom he will vindicate and save. Moses had called together the elders to announce the trouble that would happen 'in the end of days' (Deut. 31:29).[15] Already in Genesis there is a looking to the future in light of God's promise of deliverance in Genesis 3:15.

Genesis in the Context of the Ancient Near East[16]

Although Genesis is a message from God to His people through His servant Moses, it also reflects its ancient Near Eastern setting. Genesis is a book written to God's people in a particular cultural context. One should not be surprised that some of the practices of the patriarchs reflect those of the ancient Near East. A few examples would include granting additional privileges to the eldest son (Gen. 25:5-6), the custom of adopting one's own slave (Gen. 15:2), and the gift of a female slave as part of a dowry (Gen. 29:24).[17] Some have argued that Genesis, and other books of the Old Testament, are so much a part of the setting of the ancient Near East that the world view of the ancient Near East is also reflected in Scripture.[18] However, it would be wrong to conclude that the world view of Genesis is limited to its particular cultural setting because the Bible is also a message from God. Scripture reflects God's world view because it is His revelation. The character of Israel's God as the true and living God ensures that the literature and world view of Genesis is not culture-bound to its particular setting. The character of Israel's God

---

15. Sailhamer, *Pentateuch*, pp. 35-37.

16. The term 'ancient Near East' refers to early civilizations and cultures that include Mesopotamia, Canaan, and Egypt, which is where the events of Genesis occur.

17. For a discussion of the history of the debate over the historicity of the patriarchal narratives and an examination of individual ancient Near Eastern customs and the methodology employed in the comparisons, see M. J. Selman, 'Comparative Customs and the Patriarchal Age,' in *Essays on the Patriarchal Narratives* (eds. A. R. Millard and D. J. Wiseman; Winona Lake: Eisenbrauns, 1983), pp. 93-138.

18. Peter Enns, *Inspiration and Incarnation* (Grand Rapids: Baker Academic, 2005), p. 53, where the statement is made that God 'adopted the mythic categories with which Abraham – and everyone else – thought'.

over against the gods of the ancient Near East means that Israel's view of history, law, hymns, etc., is distinct from the view of the other cultures of the ancient Near East. For example, in a polytheistic setting the possibility of sovereign control over history is eliminated because individual deities may be at odds with one another. The plans of the gods may not be carried out because of opposition from other gods. But there is no rival to Israel's God because He is the sovereign God and is thus able to carry out His sovereign plans.[19]

One area where world view has been a source of discussion is the area of creation. Some argue that the human authors of Scripture must have been bound by the typical view of the cosmos that is reflected in the ancient Near East.[20] In this view the universe is understood as having three tiers composed of the heavens, the earth, and the underworld. The earth was thought to be composed of one continent that had mountains at its perimeters to hold up the sky. The sky was understood to be a solid mass or dome, which separated the earthly seas from the heavenly sea that was just above the dome. The heavens were where the deities dwelt and they were composed of three or more levels with pavements of different kinds of stone. The earth was thought to be surrounded by waters and supported by pillars.[21] Such a view is supposed to be reflected in Scripture, such as when Genesis 1:6 uses the term *rāqîa'* for the firmament or expanse, which is thought to refer to a solid dome, or when Psalm 24:2 speaks of the earth being founded upon the seas, or when Psalm 75:3 speaks of God keeping the earth steady on its pillars. However, if the Bible reflects a mistaken, mythological view of the cosmos, then it is hard to maintain a high view of the truth or the authority of Scripture.

---

19. John H. Walton, *Ancient Israelite Literature in its Cultural Context* (Grand Rapids: Zondervan, 1989), pp. 120-22.

20. P. H. Seely, 'The Firmament and the Water Above, Part 1: the Meaning of rāqîa' in Gen 1:6-8,' *WTJ* 53 (1991): 236-38, and Enns, *Inspiration and Incarnation*, pp. 54-55.

21. John Walton, *Ancient Near Eastern Thought and the Old Testament* (Grand Rapids: Baker, 2006), pp. 165-66, gives a summary of the ancient Near Eastern view of the world and then lists a series of texts that he believes shows that the Biblical text operates with a similar view. Walton also argues that the ontology of the ancient world emphasized function more than substance, which would mean that actual events are not being described in Genesis 1 but that only how certain things function in the cosmos is in view (for a brief critique of this view, see Vern Poythress, 'Appearances Matter,' *World* 24.17 [2009]).

Several things can be said in response to the argument that the authors of Scripture operated with an ancient Near Eastern view of the cosmos. First, poetry must be distinguished from narrative. Poetic descriptions use pictures and metaphors to describe things. The descriptions of the world in the psalms are poetic. A reference to pillars may be a way to describe the stability or the permanence of the earth. Genesis 1, on the other hand, is narrative and its descriptions of the cosmos and the creation of the world are very different from the way the Psalms describe the cosmos and creation. The idea that Genesis 1:6 sets forth a view of the sky as a solid dome is based on the meaning of the term *rāqîa'*. Several things argue against such a view. If the Israelites and other ancient peoples observed that the sun, moon, and planets move across the sky at different rates, then they would not have drawn the conclusion that the planets were implanted in a solid dome. Also, in several places in Scripture, such as Isaiah 42:5 and 44:24, the term *rāqîa'* describes something that is spread out and transparent. The verb form (*rq'*) is used to refer to the hammering out of gold into gold leaf (Exod. 39:3), but the emphasis seems to be on the spreading out of the substance rather on the solid nature of the substance. Thus the best understanding of *rāqîa'* in Genesis 1 is a transparent expanse, which is a reference to the sky.[22] One should also be cautious in thinking that there was a monolithic view of the cosmos in the ancient Near East.[23]

Second, the authors of Scripture use phenomenological language to describe the cosmos. In other words, they describe the cosmos primarily from the perspective of an observer on the earth. For example, someone today will describe the sun as rising and setting, which is the way humans on earth observe the sun. Such language can be used without making a scientific statement concerning whether the sun or the earth is at the center of the universe. In fact, by using ordinary language God speaks through Genesis to every culture. The expanse (*rāqîa'*) in Genesis 1 would be a description of the

22. G. K. Beale, *The Erosion of Inerrancy in Evangelicalism* (Wheaton: Crossway, 2008), pp. 198-99.
23. Othmar Keel, *Symbolism of the Biblical World* (Winona Lake: Eisenbrauns, 1997), p. 56.

sky as the place from which rain comes (the waters above the heavens) and where the lights are placed (Gen. 1:15).[24] Thus the language of Scripture is not naïve or unscientific, but is phenomenological.

Third, the descriptions of the cosmos may also be theological expressions that describe the world as a huge temple for God's dwelling. Connections can be drawn between Israel's temple and the heavens and the earth, which makes Israel's temple a microcosm of the heavens and the earth. The outer court of the temple represents the habitable world where humanity dwells. All Israelites could enter the outer court, where they would see the altar of earth and the washbasin, called the sea (1 Kings 7:23-26). The second section of the temple, the Holy Place, represents the visible sky with the lampstand associated with the light sources visible to the naked eye. Then, the Holy of Holies represents God's throne room where He dwells. In this place are the cherubim and it is off-limits to human beings. This represents God's unseen heavenly dwelling.[25] In this approach the expanse (rāqîa') is not only the sky but it also represents an aspect of the temple. For example, in Psalm 150:1 the term sanctuary (qōdeš) is used in parallel with expanse, showing the close connection between the two. But what part of the temple does the expanse represent? Beale argues that it separates the observable sky from the invisible heavenly temple, so that it may overlap with both the earthly and heavenly dimensions. Thus the expanse is the bottom part of the heavenly temple.[26]

Finally, it is important to view the description of creation in Genesis 1 as a polemic against the false views of the cosmos prevalent in the ancient Near East. First, any notion of an opposing force that stands over against God in combat is completely absent from the creation account in Genesis. The great sea creatures (tanînîn) in Genesis 1:21 are presented as created by God, which means they are not pre-existent rivals of the Creator that need to be conquered, as in Canaanite

---

24. Vern S. Poythress, *Redeeming Science: A God-Centered Approach* (Wheaton: Crossway Books, 2006), pp. 92-96.

25. Beale, *Erosion of Inerrancy*, p. 161.

26. Beale, *Erosion of Inerrancy*, pp. 168-69. Beale goes on to show how the reference to the four corners of the earth and the founding of the earth on the seas is related to temple concepts (pp.208-12).

mythology. Second, the normal terminology for the sun and the moon is not used in Genesis 1. Instead, the sun (*šemeš*) and the moon (*yārēach*) are called the greater light and the lesser light (1:16) to clearly show that they are not gods. Also, the emphasis on God sending rain to bring about fruitful vegetation (Gen. 2:5) and on the power of life to replenish itself given to each kind (Gen. 1:11), undercuts the necessity for the fertility cults and shows that Baal is not the source of rain. These differences demonstrate that Genesis 1 not only makes a complete break with the ancient Near Eastern mythological cosmologies, but that it is also a deliberate anti-mythological polemic meant to undermine the prevailing mythological cosmologies.[27]

The Days of Genesis 1

Even if one argues that Genesis 1 is a polemic and that it uses phenomenological language, there is still debate concerning how to understand the event of creation itself. The dominant view among secular scientists is not creation but Darwinian evolution, which is based on the theory of natural selection. This theory argues movement from simpler to more complex forms of life that take place through random mutations, which are purely the product of chance. Some argue for theistic evolution, which accepts that macro-evolution is the process used to bring about this world and life, but they argue that God was behind the process.[28] Others argue that there is evidence of design in the universe, which can be empirically detected. The complexity of life, such as DNA, argues against the evolutionary process because all the parts have to be present for there to be life.[29] The following discussion is going

---

27. Gerhard F. Hasel, 'The Polemic Nature of the Genesis Cosmology,' *EQ* 46 (1974): 81-102.

28. Henry J. Van Till, *The Fourth Day: What the Bible and the Heavens are Telling Us About the Creation* (Grand Rapids: Eerdmans, 1986), pp. 249-58, and Waltke, *Old Testament Theology*, p. 202. There has been a push recently among evangelicals to accept the view of theistic evolution, such as the book by Denis Alexander, *Creation or Evolution: Do We Have to Choose?* (Monarch, 2008). For an analysis and critique of theistic evolution, see Michael A. Harbin, 'Theistic Evolution: Deism Revisited?' *JETS* 40.4 (1997): 639-52, and Norman C. Nevin, ed., *Should Christians Embrace Evolution?* (Phillipsburg, NJ: P & R, 2009).

29. Michael J. Behe, *Darwin's Black Box: The Biochemical Challenge to Evolution* (New York: Free Press, 2006), and Phillip E. Johnson, *Darwin on Trial* (Downers Grove, IL: Inter-Varsity Press, 1993).

to focus more narrowly on the meaning of the word 'day' (*yom*) in Genesis 1, as discussed in the Day-Age view, the Literary Framework view, the Analogical Day view, and the Regular Day view. Other issues that are important to this discussion are the relation of general revelation to special revelation, the literary character of Genesis 1, and the effect of the fall in Genesis 3 on how the world functions.

The Day-Age View

The Day-Age view argues that the word 'day' (*yom*) in Genesis 1 represents a long period of time.[30] This view is concerned with the scientific evidence which the majority of scientists believe supports an old earth. The Biblical account of creation then is not in conflict with this scientific view if 'day' represents a long period of time, for it allows for the lengthy development of the geological record and it helps solve the problem of the travel time of light. Genesis 1 is understood as presenting real history rather than an allegorical or poetic account, and it is a history that is verified by science. Thus, what is presented in Genesis 1 is later confirmed by science so that there is a strong emphasis on the scientific verifiability of the creation account.[31]

The creation days are defined as six sequential long periods of time that appear in correct sequence and in scientifically definable terms.[32] The word *yom* is used in Scripture to refer to periods of indefinite length, such as its use in Genesis 4:3 (*yom* = process of time), Genesis 30:14 (*yom* = wheat harvest time), Joshua 24:7 (*yom* = a long season), and Isaiah 4:2 (*yom* = a future era). There is also evidence in Genesis 1 that *yom* should be understood as a long period of time. For example, Genesis 2:4 states, 'These are the generations of the heavens and the earth when they were created, in the day that the Lord God made the earth and the heavens.' In this verse the word

---

30. The following summary is taken from Hugh Ross and Gleason Archer, 'The Day-Age View,' in *The Genesis Debate: Three Views on the Days of Creation* (ed. David G. Hagopian; Mission Viejo, CA: Crux Press, 2001), pp. 123-64, and Hugh Ross, *Creation and Time* (Colorado Springs: NavPress, 1994).

31. Ross and Archer ('Day-Age View,' p. 139) assert, 'The unique beauty of the day-age creation model is its ability to accurately predict advancing scientific discovery. The ability to predict is the hallmark of any reliable theory.'

32. Ross (*Creation and Time*, p. 80) distinguishes the Day-Age View from both naturalistic and theistic evolution.

yom is used to refer to the whole process of creation, which clearly is longer than a regular day. Also, the seventh day in the creation account does not have a morning and evening, which demonstrates that the seventh day is not a normal day; in fact, the seventh day of God's creation week still continues.[33] Thus the 'days' of Genesis 1 should not be understood as regular days as we would experience them (twenty-four hours), but as days from God's perspective, which can refer to long periods of time (Ps. 90:4).

If the six 'days' of Genesis 1 represent a very long time, then certain implications follow. First of all, millions of generations of life predate human life. Different species arose at different times in response to the changing environment, with many of them becoming extinct. Thus God had to continually intervene in the creation process to replace extinct species. This direct intervention by God ceases after the sixth day.[34]

Secondly, this view teaches several things concerning death. Death was a part of existence before human life was created by God and before sin entered the world. Death includes both plant and animal life so that carnivorous activity was a part of the world as it was originally created. Natural death must be distinguished from spiritual death because even though natural death was prevalent before the fall, sin produced spiritual death (Rom. 5:12).

Third, this view argues that the law of decay (the second law of thermodynamics) has operated from the beginning of creation with the inevitable consequences of death, extinction, and disorder as a part of the original creation. It is this law of decay which Romans 8:19-21 has in view.

Each creation view has its own set of questions and problems. There are several related to the Day-Age view. First of all, although yom can be used to refer to a longer period of

---

33. In the Day-Age View, 'evening' and 'morning' refer to the beginning and ending components of 'day', however 'day' is used.

34. For a different view of God's intervention during the six 'days' of creation, see W. L. Bradley and Roger Olson, 'The Trustworthiness of Scripture in the Areas of Natural Science,' in *Hermeneutics, Inerrancy, and the Bible* (eds. E. D. Radmacher and R. D. Preuss; Grand Rapids: Zondervan, 1984), pp. 283-317. They argue that God created by using a combination of miracle and process (progressive creationism). God intervened miraculously to create the major types of animal and plant life and then worked in His customary way through process to develop the variety of plant and animal life. This took place over a period of six 'days'.

time than a regular day, that is not necessarily the case with its use in Genesis 2:4. The word *yom* in Genesis 2:4 occurs in a prepositional phrase (*bet* plus *yom* followed by an infinitive), which is an idiomatic expression that means 'when' something occurs. Thus the word *yom* in Genesis 2:4 gives no information on the range of meanings of yom outside of this idiomatic expression.[35] This means the necessity for understanding 'day' as a long period of time comes from outside the account of Genesis 1–2, namely, from the scientific evidence.

Secondly, the long periods of time before the appearance of human life affect the way one views the existence of that life. One must conclude not only that there was natural death before the fall, but also that when God declared His creation good He was pronouncing natural death a good thing.[36] Plus, if the law of decay, as defined by Ross, was at work from the beginning of creation, then God also declared death, suffering, and disorder to be good. Although Ross argues that Romans 8:19-21 says little about when bondage to decay began,[37] it seems evident that the subjection of creation to decay took place at a particular point of time beyond the event of creation itself. The negative character of the terminology fits better with the event of the fall into sin than it does with the original creation, which God declares to be good. The terms 'futility' (*mataiotes*) and 'bondage to decay' are used in other places of the New Testament where folly and sinfulness are in focus (2 Pet. 2:18-19). The presentation in Romans 8 supports this meaning, for creation is subjected 'not willingly', but in

35. C. John Collins, 'How Old is the Earth? Anthropomorphic Days in Genesis 1:1–2:3,' *Presbyterion* 20/2 (1994): 109-30. The fact that the expression bet plus yom plus the infinitive construct in Genesis 2:4 is followed by the proper name Yahweh could be seen as evidence that the whole expression is definite or determined, which would mean that 'day' is referring to a single, regular day and should be translated 'in the day'. However, for that to be the case the phrase would be translated 'in the day of the making of Yahweh', which is not what the text means. Rather, Yahweh acts as the subject of the infinitive construct. Plus, the definite article could be placed on the infinitive to make it clear that the phrase is definite, as in Genesis 21:8.
36. For an excellent discussion of the definition of life in Scripture, which excludes plant life, see James Stanbaugh, 'Whence Cometh Death? A Biblical Theology of Physical Death and Natural Evil,' in *Coming to Grips with Genesis: Biblical Authority and the Age of the Earth* (eds. Terry Mortenson and Thane H. Ury; Green Forest, AR: Master Books, 2008), pp. 373-98. He also defines the process of decay as including digestion, friction, and water erosion, but ageing and death did not exist until the sin of Adam.
37. Ross, *Creation and Time*, p. 66.

hope to be set free, which suggests that such subjection is not a good thing and that it occurred after creation. Thus the fall is a better option for when such subjection to the bondage to decay took place.[38] The effect of the fall on creation is a major point of the discussion, and views which emphasize the results of science downplay the significance of the effect of the fall on creation.[39] In other words, many argue that the created world operates very much the same before and after the fall, which is supposed to ensure the integrity of the scientific enterprise.

The Literary Framework View

Another view of the days of Genesis 1 is the literary framework view.[40] This view understands Genesis 1 to be an artistic, literary presentation of creation that is not to be taken literally or chronologically. A key text for this view is Genesis 2:5 which states, 'When no bush of the field was yet in the land and no small plant of the field had yet sprung up – for the LORD God had not caused it to rain on the ground, and there was no man to work the ground.' This view argues that Genesis 2:5 is looking back to Genesis 1 and shows that in Genesis 1 normal providence was at work because the earth was without vegetation due to the fact that it had not yet rained.

There are several implications to the view that normal, divine providence is at work in Genesis 1. First, Genesis 1 cannot be seen as *only* fiat creation (God speaking and things coming immediately into existence). Rain and the growth of plants take time. Secondly, the days of Genesis 1 cannot be chronological without running into major problems. If ordinary providence is at work in Genesis 1, then you cannot have light on Day 1 before the sun on Day 4, nor can you have vegetation on Day 3 before the sun on Day 4. A different way

---

38. Charles Hodge, *A Commentary on Romans* (London: The Banner of Truth Trust, 1972 [orig. 1835]), pp. 273-74.

39. Ross understands general revelation to be on the same level as special revelation (*Creation and Time*, p. 56). For a critique of this view, see Richard Mayhue, 'Is Nature the 67th Book of the Bible?' in *Coming to Grips with Genesis*, pp. 105-29.

40. The following summary of the literary framework view is based primarily on the following works: Meredith Kline, 'Because It Had Not Rained,' *WTJ* 20 (1958): 146-57; Mark Futato, 'Because It Had Not Rained: A Study of Gen. 2:5-7 with Implications for Gen. 2:24-25 and Gen. 1:1–2:3,' *WTJ* 60 (1998): 1-21; and Lee Irons with Meredith Kline, 'The Framework View,' in *The Genesis Debate*, pp. 217-304.

of reading the days of Genesis 1 must be at work other than a chronological sequence of days. Third, Genesis 1 should not be understood as a straightforward, historical account of how God created the world. In other words, Genesis 1 should not be placed in the hard science category of how it happened, but should be placed in the social science category, which is concerned more with who created the world.[41]

If a chronological presentation of the days in Genesis 1 runs into insurmountable problems, then the days of Genesis 1 must relate to each other in a different way. Some of the days have connections with each other, which can be demonstrated in a literary relationship that presents the work of creation in an artistic way. The light of Day 1 should be related to the sun of Day 4. Both deal with light and darkness and use the language of separation. Thus both days accomplish the same purpose. The sky and seas of Day 2 should be related to the fish and birds of Day 5. The dry land and vegetation of Day 3 should be related to the land animals and human beings of Day 6. There is no correlation with Day 7 which makes it unique as it presents the Creator King enthroned in His heavenly Sabbath rest over all creation. This yields the following literary framework:

Day 1	Light	Day 4	Luminaries
Day 2	Sky, Seas	Day 5	Sea creatures, winged creatures
Day 3	Dry land, Vegetation	Day 6	Land animals, Man

These two triads of days have a particular relationship with each other. Days 1–3 represent creation kingdoms and Days 4–6 represent creation kings who exercise dominion over the creation kingdoms. Thus the luminaries of Day 4 rule over the day and the night (1:16). The fish and birds of Day 5 rule over the spheres established on Day 2 (1:22). The same can be said for the relationship between the creature kings of Day 6 and

---

41. Bruce Waltke, 'The Literary Genre of Genesis, Chapter One,' *Crux* 27.4 (1991): 2-10. In his *Old Testament Theology*, Waltke comes out in favor of theistic evolution (p. 202).

the creation kingdoms of Day 3, except that human beings have a broader dominion over all creation.

There are several problems with this view of the days of Genesis 1.[42] First, the presentation of the days of Genesis 1 as an artistic, literary framework affects the way Genesis 1 is viewed. Not only are the days of Genesis 1 not chronological, but Genesis 1 is seen as 'semi-poetic' with the creation week presented as a poetic figure.[43] This presentation of Genesis 1 goes against the character of the text itself as historical narrative. Hebrew historical narrative is identified by the use of the imperfect waw consecutive, which dominates Genesis 1. Genesis 1 is not Hebrew poetry, but is historical narrative like the rest of the book of Genesis. One of the major functions of the imperfect *waw* consecutive is simple, chronological succession.[44] If the intent had been to teach a non-chronological view of the days, it seems strange that the author goes out of his way to emphasize chronology and sequence. On this basis the days in Genesis 1 should be seen as part of the historical narrative and as presented in chronological sequence. It is a false dichotomy to say that Genesis 1 is not concerned about how creation happened, but is only concerned with who did the creating.[45]

Second, the literary framework position is based on the view that Genesis 2:5-6 refers back to Genesis 1 so that it can be

42. For critiques of the literary framework view, see E. J. Young, *Studies in Genesis One* (Philadelphia: Presbyterian and Reformed, 1964); Noel Weeks, *The Sufficiency of Scripture* (Carlisle, PA: The Banner of Truth Trust, 1988); Joseph A. Pipa, Jr., 'From Chaos to Cosmos: A Critique of the Non-Literal Interpretations of Genesis 1:1–2:3,' in *Did God Create in Six Days* (Taylors, SC: Southern Presbyterian Press, 1999), pp. 153-98; and Robert V. McCabe, 'A Critique of the Framework Interpretation of the Creation Week,' in *Coming to Grips with Genesis*, pp. 211-50.

43. Kline ('Because It Had Not Rained,' pp. 156-57) specifically uses the phrase 'semi-poetic' and calls the week a figurative week.

44. Bruce K. Waltke and M. O'Connor, *An Introduction to Biblical Hebrew Syntax* (Winona Lake: Eisenbrauns, 1990), p. 547, quote S. R. Driver concerning the imperfect *waw* consecutive (also called the *waw* relative and *wayyqtl*), 'The most obvious and frequent relation is that of simple chronological succession.' They go on to state that the form and not the words signify succession (p. 548).

45. If Genesis 1 is not concerned about the how of creation, then the same could be argued for the account of the creation of Adam in Genesis 2. Does it matter how God created Adam, or that there was a real, historical Adam? In fact, it is no surprise that some who have adopted theistic evolution have also argued that it is not necessary to believe in a real, historical Adam. (See Peter Enns, *The Evolution of Adam: What the Bible Does and Doesn't Say about Human Origins* [Grand Rapids: Brazos Press, 2012]).

established that ordinary providence is at work in Genesis 1. However, there are other ways of understanding Genesis 2:5.

Some argue that Genesis 2:5-6 refers back to Genesis 1 but that it does not establish that ordinary providence is at work in Genesis 1. John Frame states that Genesis 1:11 gives the impression that once rain was available, the land miraculously produced mature plants at God's command, just as mature plants were produced at His command on other days.[46] McCabe argues that Genesis 2:5-6 does not describe the entire creation week but that it describes Day 6 when God formed mankind to rule on the earth. Thus it provides a setting for the formation and placement of man in the garden in Genesis 2:7.[47]

It is also possible that Genesis 2:5 looks forward rather than backward. Based on the grammar of Genesis 2, some argue that Genesis 2:5 does not refer back to the creation-in-process described in Genesis 1 (Kline's view), but that it refers to the completed creation ready for man to inhabit and subdue. Genesis 2:5-6 gives the setting for the primary narrative that starts in verse 7 with the creation of man.[48]

Others argue that Genesis 2:5 looks forward to the garden of Eden so that the plants in view are cultivated plants that will grow in the garden.[49] In this view there is a distinction between the plants in Genesis 2:5 and the plants in Genesis 1, based on the qualifying phrase 'in the field' in Genesis 2:5. The emphasis on the need for rain and human beings demonstrates that these plants are plants that will grow in the garden cultivated by human beings.[50]

---

46. John Frame, *The Doctrine of God* (Phillipsburg, NJ: P & R, 2002), pp. 304-5.

47. Robert V. McCabe, 'Critique of the Framework Interpretation,' pp. 229-30.

48. The grammatical basis for this view is that Genesis 2:5-6 is composed of the conjunction *waw* attached to a non-verbal form, which gives background to the main narrative of 2:7, where the imperfect waw consecutive is used. See the discussion in McCabe, 'A Critique of the Framework Interpretation,' pp. 229-231, and C. John Collins, *Genesis 1–4* (Phillipsburg, NJ: P & R, 2006), p. 133.

49. Keil and Delitzsch, 'Genesis,' *Commentary on the Old Testament* (10 vols.; Grand Rapids: Eerdmans, 1980 reprint), 1:76-78; R. Laird Harris, 'The Mist, the Canopy, and the Rivers of Eden,' *Bulletin* (now *JETS*) 11 (Fall 1968): 177-79; and Pipa, *From Chaos to Cosmos*, pp. 157-64.

50. Although 'field' (*śādeh*) can refer to open country, it can also refer to cultivated land (Michael A. Grisanti, שָׂדֶה/שָׂדַי in *NIDOTTE* (5 vols.; Grand Rapids: Zondervan, 1997), 3:1217-19. See Keil and Delitzsch ('Genesis,' 1:77) who also discuss the difference between 'beast of the earth' in Genesis 1 and 'beast of the field' in Genesis 2.

Others argue that Genesis 2:5 is a foreshadowing of Genesis 3 and events after the fall. In God's word of curse to Adam the references to the plants parallel what is said in Genesis 2:5. The exact phrase 'plant ('*ēśeḇ*) of the field' is used in both passages, and the phrase 'thorns and thistles' in Genesis 3:18 is a particularization of the general concept of 'shrub of the field' in Genesis 2:5.[51]

The point is that there are many ways to make sense of Genesis 2:5 without understanding it as a description of the whole creation week. If Genesis 2:5 does not refer to the whole creation week of Genesis 1, then a major foundation plank of the literary framework approach is removed.

Finally, the literary framework itself is suspect because the parallels do not match up well. The light of Day 1 and the luminaries of Day 4 (the sun, moon, and stars) do not work well with the scenario of creation kingdom (Days 1–3) and creation kings (Days 4–6). The light of Day 1 is not a creation kingdom over which the luminaries rule. For this to work, the creation kingdom would need to be the expanse in which the luminaries are placed, but the expanse is not formed until Day 2. The parallel between the birds of Day 5 and the expanse of Day 2 is also weak. Although birds fly in the sky, their habitation is land, which they need to survive, but land is not created until Day 3. It is interesting that Genesis 1:22 states, 'let birds multiply on the earth' (emphasis mine). The parallels between the sea creatures of Day 5 and the seas of Day 2 also do not match up. The waters of Day 2 are mentioned in connection with the formation of the expanse that divides the waters. The seas are not formed until Day 3. Plus, nothing in Day 6 fills the seas of Day 3. Thus, a close look at the literary parallels shows that the parallels are really non-existent.

---

51. U. Cassuto, *A Commentary on the Book of Genesis: Part 1 From Adam to Noah* (Jerusalem: Magnes Press, 1961), pp. 101-02; Sailhamer, *Pentateuch as Narrative*, p. 97; Kenneth A. Matthews, *Genesis 1:1–11:26* (Nashville: Broadman & Holman, 1996), pp. 193-94.

The Analogical Day View

Another approach to the days of creation is the analogical day view.[52] This view basically says that the days of Genesis 1 are not ordinary human days, but are God's days, which are both similar to our days and also different from them. This view is supported by a number of factors. The seventh day of Genesis 1 does not have the refrain of evening and morning, which means that it is not an ordinary day. In fact, the seventh day has not yet come to an end. Also, Exodus 31:17 presents God as being refreshed with His rest, but God does not get weary like humans do. This shows that the days are not identical to human days but are analogical to human days. These days are different from human days even though there may be some similarities. Although Exodus 20:8-11 sets forth the pattern of God's working and resting during the creation week, this pattern is an analogical pattern and not an identical pattern because the days are not human days. Human work and rest are not identical to God's work and rest. The point of similarity is the analogy that during the creation week God was working and resting. However, length of time, or the length of the days, has no bearing on the analogy because the days are not identical to human days. Thus Genesis 1 describes God's workdays, which are not identical to human workdays but are analogous to them.

Several other features of the analogical day view are important to notice. First, similar to the literary framework view, Genesis 2:5 shows that ordinary providence was at work in the creation week of Genesis 1. The cycle of rain, plant growth, and dry season had been going on for some time in the creation week, which means it cannot have been an ordinary week.[53]

---

52. The following discussion interacts mainly with C. John Collins' view because he has written the most recently on this particular view of the day; see 'How Old is the Earth? Anthropomorphic Days in Genesis 1:1–2:3,' *Presbyterion* 20.2 (1994): 109-30; *Science & Faith: Friends or Foes?* (Wheaton: Crossway Books, 2003); *Genesis 1–4: A Linguistic, Literary, and Theological Commentary* (Phillipsburg: P & R, 2006). Older authors who hold this view include William Shedd, *Dogmatic Theology* (Grand Rapids: Zondervan, 1971), 1:463-77; Herman Bavinck, *Reformed Dogmatics, Volume 2: God and Creation* (Grand Rapids: Baker, 2004), pp. 479-85; and Franz Delitzsch, *A New Commentary on Genesis* (Minneapolis, MN: Klock & Klock, 1978 reprint [orig. 1878]). However, Delitzsch understands many of the details of Genesis 1 much differently than Collins does.

53. Collins, *Science & Faith*, pp. 87-89.

Second, the character of Genesis 1 is not myth or poetry, but it is not regular prose either. Rather, it is exalted prose, which means that a literal hermeneutic should not be applied to the text and that the author of Genesis 1 is not that concerned about the processes that were used to create. Even with the more normal prose of Genesis 2:7 one should not press too far the process of how man was formed because the text may be presenting a literary convention of the potter forming clay.[54]

Third, the days in Genesis 1 are to be understood as occurring in chronological sequence. They are successive periods of undefined length, although there may be overlap between them.[55]

Fourth, there is concern with the scientific method and whether creation truly speaks, which leads to the assertion that any view of creation that argues for the appearance of age must be deceptive; it would also question whether science is possible for human beings.[56]

Fifth, Collins refrains from asserting the fallen nature of creation. The ground is not cursed but is the arena in which the curse is worked out. In Romans 8:18-25 the creation groans because it is the arena in which the curse is carried out, not because it has been corrupted itself.

Finally, the age of the earth cannot be answered from Genesis 1, but must be answered from other factors, such as science and geology. There is nothing in the creation account that hinders the view that the earth is old.[57]

In the Analogical Day view Genesis 1 can be understood in the following way. Genesis 1:1-2 provides background information for the narrative of creation which begins in verse 3.[58] These opening verses describe the creation of everything in the universe from nothing. Everything is created and in place but the earth itself is described as uninhabitable in verse 2 ('formless and void'). There is no time indication in Genesis 1:1-2, so many years could have passed by before God began to make the earth inhabitable in verse 3. The sun is

54. Collins, *Genesis 1–4*, p. 252.
55. Collins, 'Anthropomorphic Days,' p. 120.
56. Collins, *Science & Faith*, pp. 147-60.
57. Collins, *Science & Faith*, pp. 247-55.
58. The narrative account begins in verse 3 with the first imperfect *waw* consecutive (Collins, *Genesis 1–4*, pp. 42-43).

already in place but its light is not reaching the earth because of the darkness that covers the earth. On the fourth day the function of the lights is described in relationship to the earth as the clouds clear and the light from the sun reaches the earth. The days in Genesis 1 are long periods of time that may overlap with each other. They are God's workdays and not the workdays of human beings.

Several issues are important in evaluating the analogical day view. First, Collins is very concerned about the relationship between the validity of the scientific method and faith. He writes that good faith and good science need sound critical thinking and that conclusions are good only if they follow sound reasoning. Faith is good if it follows the rules of rationality. This is not necessarily a problem unless the rules of rationality override what the text says. For example, Collins argues that it is a problem if God created with the appearance of age. But why is that a problem when the text presents God as creating Adam and Eve as fully mature, functioning human beings? Is it a problem because science does not operate with that presupposition? Yet, one can legitimately argue that the Bible presents God creating with the appearance of age because He creates fully grown plants and animals. Thus it appears that aspects of science control parts of the interpretation of Genesis 1. This is also demonstrated in the denial that the creation itself is cursed. If creation is fallen, it might affect how science is able to 'read' creation scientifically. However, Genesis 3:17 clearly says the ground is cursed, which means the fall does affect how the world operates. It follows that Collins' view of the days in Genesis 1 is affected by certain things he believes are important in science. He states that he has no way of knowing whether the technical details of the Big Bang theory are sound, but he has no problem with the amount of time the theory needs. He also acknowledges that he is not able to assess the technical details concerning radiometric dating methods, but that he has no reason to disbelieve the standard theories of the geologists.[59] He is

---

59. Collins, *Science & Faith*, pp. 233, 250. See the evaluation by Terry Craigen, 'Can Deep Time Be Embedded in Genesis?' in *Coming to Grips with Genesis*, p. 207. Collins also comments that if the geologists are wrong, it is not because they have improperly smuggled philosophical assumptions into their work; however, see the

willing to accept as certain basic assumptions from science. It appears that these presuppositions from science have affected his exegesis to the extent that he denies what the text clearly states.

Second, no one affirms that God's days and human days are identical. Virtually nothing between God and humans is identical. Almost every aspect of our relation to God takes on an analogical character to some extent. Thus, to employ analogy to explain the days of Genesis 1 does not seem necessary, unless one wants to highlight the differences between the days of Genesis 1 and regular human days. It is significant that the point of analogy is basically limited to the aspect of God's working and rest and it has nothing to do with length of time, which is the major point of contention. Why omit time from the analogy when the other descriptions of the days in Genesis 1 use language that points to regular days?

Third, the identification of Genesis 1 as elevated prose and not normal prose allows this view to move away from understanding the text as describing what God actually does in creation. Collins mentions the possibility that the days in Genesis 1 may overlap with each other.[60] He also raises the question concerning whether everything narrated on a given day may have actually occurred on that day. Instead, the author might have grouped things together on certain days based on logical reasons.[61] He notes that these questions should be considered on the basis of the style of the account and how much Genesis 1 is supposed to be confirmable by scientific research. He then argues that Genesis 1 is not a scientific account of creation and that the style is elevated prose, which means we should not read the account too literally.[62] Thus Genesis 1–2 should not be pressed to argue for the sequence of events. These chapters are also not concerned about the processes of creation, or how God actually may

---

article by Terry Mortenson ('"Deep Time" and the Church's Compromise: Historical Background,' in *Coming to Grips with Genesis*, pp. 79-104), which shows the historical development of the science of geology and how philosophical assumptions did affect their conclusions on time in relationship to the Bible.

60. The possibility that the days may overlap is mentioned in the article 'Anthropomorphic Days', p. 120.

61. Collins, *Science & Faith*, p. 69.

62. Collins, *Genesis 1–4*, p. 253.

have created the world. Rather, the main issue concerns the truth value of the account. In other words, the important thing is what the account is trying to teach us concerning God and our relationship to Him and the world. This approach is dangerous because it no longer understands the text to be saying what it is actually saying, or that God actually created the world in the way that Genesis 1 describes it.

In this view Genesis 1 is not concerned with how God created because it is elevated prose, which should not be taken too literally. However, the way God created Adam in Genesis 2:7 has been considered important. Collins himself has argued that 'dust' in Genesis 2:7 refers to loose soil and that it does not refer to a living creature that God used to form Adam. Thus, Adam was a fresh creation rather than an upgrade of an existing model.[63] However, in a recent work on the historicity of Adam, Collins is more open to relinquishing how God created in Genesis 2. In fact, he argues that Genesis 1–11 should be read as non-literal, pictorial, and symbolic so that we are left with only an historical core in Genesis 1–11. The effect this approach has on Genesis 2:7 is that one should not read this text too literally in describing a physical and biological account of human origins. Genesis 2:7 does teach us that the process was not a purely natural process and that the special origin of man sets him apart from other animals. However, since Genesis 2:7 should not be read too literally, the way is open to entertain other scenarios as to how God set apart the first couple, including the fact that God took two hominids that already existed and acted upon them to set them apart as the first human beings.[64] These different scenarios are being driven by genetic science, in conjunction with theistic

---

63. Collins, *Science & Faith*, p. 268.
64. C. John Collins, *Did Adam and Eve Really Exist?* (Wheaton: Crossway, 2011), pp. 17, 20, 35, and 154. Collins prejudices the argument by narrowly defining the traditional view of God's creation of Adam and Eve to the fact that they are a special creation, which means that God intervened to set apart the first couple as human beings. In other words, the traditional view does not include the view that God formed Adam of the dust of the ground. This limitation allows newer scenarios, such as God acted on hominids in a special way to set them apart, to be placed with the traditional view, but this bypasses the main argument, which is what does Genesis 2:7 says about how God created Adam and Eve.

evolution, which has concluded that there is no way that one couple could produce the current genetic situation.[65] In light of this scientific evidence of genetics, Collins is open to conceiving of Adam and Eve as the king and queen of a larger population.[66] Again, other things become more important than what Genesis 2:7 actually states concerning the way God created Adam and Eve. The implications of this view are significant. Not only does God not create Adam from the dust of the ground, but He also does not create Eve from Adam's side. If God set apart two hominids as the first human couple, is Paul mistaken when he argues that God created Adam first, then Eve? The affirmation of a core of historicity in Genesis 1–2 is not enough to keep key theological truths from crumbling.

Finally, the fact that the seventh day does not have the 'evening and morning' statement does not necessarily mean that it is not a regular day. In Days 1–6, a description of the next day followed so that the phrase 'evening and morning' closes the day in view and introduces the next day. If no eighth day is described, there is no need to add the 'evening and morning' statement to close the seventh day and to introduce the eighth day.[67]

Variations of the Regular Day View
The next several views argue that the days in Genesis 1 are regular days, but the way they understand Genesis 1 is very different. The first view will be briefly mentioned here. The gap theory, also called the ruin-restitution view, argues that

---

65. Karl W. Giberson and Francis Collins, *The Language of Science and Faith* (Downers Grove, IL: Inter-Varsity Press, 2011). Francis Collins is also behind the Biologos Foundation, which sponsors the Biologos Forum, a website devoted to the promotion of theistic evolution.

66. C. John Collins is quoted in Richard N. Ostling, 'The Search for the Historical Adam,' *CT 55.6* (June 2011): 27.

67. Pipa, 'From Chaos to Cosmos,' p. 168. For other reasons regarding how to understand the seventh day as a normal day and not as an unending day, see McCabe, 'Critique of the Framework Interpretation,' pp. 241-46. Vern Poythress (*Redeeming Science*) too takes the analogical day position. He also puts a lot of emphasis on the fact that the seventh day is not a regular day. Poythress is not as hostile as Collins to the view that God created with the appearance of age because he recognizes that science starts with the assumption that things started from an immature state (*Redeeming Science*, pp. 116-20).

Genesis 1:1 presents a full and complete creation.[68] However, between Genesis 1:1 and 1:2 a terrible catastrophe occurred, bringing about the condition of the earth as formless and void. This catastrophe refers to the fall of Satan. The rest of Genesis 1 describes a recreation of the judgment-ridden earth in seven regular days (the sun is already in place) in preparation for the creation of humanity. This view became popular when the old-age view of the earth became prominent among scientists. It allows for a long period of time for the age of the earth and for fossils to develop. There are several problems with this view. Genesis 1 says nothing about the fall of Satan or some other catastrophe that caused the earth to become formless and void. Thus, the premise of this view is based on an argument from silence.[69] Plus, the words used in Genesis 1 mean to create and to make, not to remake.

Another view that understands the days of Genesis 1 as regular days is Historical Creationism, argued by John Sailhaimer, who takes a very distinct approach to what Genesis 1 is describing. This view is a literal and realistic account of how God created the universe. The title of his book, *Genesis Unbound*,[70] stresses that people bring certain assumptions to the words and concepts of Genesis 1 that keep them from understanding what Genesis 1 is trying to describe. Genesis 1:1 describes the creation of everything in the universe out of nothing so that the universe is complete, including plants and animals. The word 'beginning' in Genesis 1:1 does not refer to a moment in time, but it refers to an indefinite period of time. He argues this partly on the basis of the use of 'beginning' in the reign of kings, where the beginning refers to a period of time before the start of the first year of the king. Thus Genesis 1:1 allows for an extended

---

68. The gap theory is associated with Thomas Chalmers, a Scottish theologian of the early 1800s, and the 1917 edition of the Scofield Bible. It was also popularized by G. H. Pember, *Earth's Earliest Ages* (New York: H. Revell Co., 1900). An academic presentation of the view can be found in A. C. Cunstance, *Without Form and Void* (Brookville, Canada: published by the author, 1970). See also Merrill F. Unger, 'Rethinking the Genesis Account of Creation,' *BibSac* 115 (1958): 27-38. He argues that already in Genesis 1:1 the refashioning of a judgment-ridden earth is being described.

69. See the Appendix in O. T. Allis, *God Spake by Moses* (Phillipsburg, NJ: Presbyterian & Reformed, 1951), pp.153-59.

70. John Sailhamer, *Genesis Unbound* (Sisters, Oregon: Multnomah Books, 1996). This book has been out of print but a new edition was listed for March 2011.

period of time before the events described in Genesis 1:3, which makes room for an old earth and the formation of the fossil record. In Sailhamer's view, a significant transition takes place from Genesis 1:1 to 1:2 concerning the meaning of the term 'ereṣ. In Genesis 1:1 it means 'earth', but in Genesis 1:2 it means 'land' because the focus of the remainder of Genesis 1 is not on the earth as a whole but is on the land which God is preparing for humanity. In other words, Genesis 1 really describes the preparation of the promised land. This land is also equivalent to the Garden of Eden, which is described in Genesis 2, and is prepared by God for the habitation of humanity in six regular days. The promised land, however, is formless and void, which means it is uninhabitable for humanity. The remainder of Genesis 1 describes how God makes the promised land, which is also the Garden of Eden, habitable for human beings, who are not created until the sixth day. Thus, the plants and the animals in Genesis 1 are describing the plants and animals that are in the promised land because the focus of Genesis 1 is not on the earth as a whole, but on the special place God made for human beings.

There are several problems with Sailhamer's view of Genesis 1. First of all, the word 'beginning' (rēšît) in Genesis 1:1 cannot carry the weight that he places on it in this context. None of the Hebrew lexicons argue that 'beginning' can refer to an extended period of time. The use of 'beginning' in reference to the reigns of kings is not a parallel with the way 'beginning' is used in Genesis 1:1. Sailhamer argues that Genesis 1:1 is describing creation out of nothing, which means he takes 'beginning' in Genesis 1:1 as absolute ('in the beginning God') and not as a construct phrase specifying a temporal clause ('in the beginning when God'). However, the use of 'beginning' in relationship to the reign of kings is used in a construct chain specifying a temporal clause (Jer. 28:1).[71]

---

71. It is also significant that 'beginning' in Genesis 1:1 is followed by a finite, perfect verb, but the word 'beginning' in relationship to the reign of kings is followed by a preposition and a noun. Andrew Kulikovsky argues that even if Sailhamer's view concerning 'beginning' were correct, it would not support the idea that billions of years could be included in the phrase. If 'beginning' includes a few years in relationship to a king's reign, then 'beginning' would include only a few days in relationship to the six days of creation (see 'Unbinding the Rules: A Review of Genesis Unbound by John Sailhamer,' Technical Journal [now Journal of Creation] 14.3 [2000]: 35-38 for other problems with Sailhamer's view).

Secondly, the transition from earth (*'ereṣ*) in Genesis 1:1 to land (*'ereṣ*) in Genesis 1:2 is not obvious. In fact, the natural reading of these two verses is that the *'ereṣ* in Genesis 1:2 is referring back to the *'ereṣ* in Genesis 1:1, so that the *'ereṣ* (earth) that was created in Genesis 1:1 is now described as formless and void. Thus Genesis 1:2-8 is describing the condition of the earth. The use of *'ereṣ* for land does not occur until verse 9 when the dry land appears.[72] There is no obvious reason to take *'ereṣ* as 'land' until verse 9. Thus, Sailhamer's whole argument that Genesis 1 is describing the promised land has no basis.

Another variation of the regular day view is argued by Gorman Gray.[73] There are similarities between the way Gray, Collins, and Sailhamer understand Genesis 1:1 as describing the full creation of the universe. Gray argues that everything is created in Genesis 1:1 but that the earth is in an uninhabitable condition covered with water and a dark cloud. It is possible that many years transpire between the original creation of the universe in Genesis 1:1 and God's work in six regular days to make the earth a habitable place for humanity. In fact, billions of years could transpire between 1:1 and 1:2. Thus Gray argues for an old universe, which solves the problem that the light people see today took a very long time to reach the earth. However, Gray also argues that God worked on planet earth for six solar days to make it inhabitable for humanity. The statement in 1:3, 'let there be light,' is not the original creation of light but it describes the fact that God removes the dark cloud over the earth so that the light reaches the earth for the first time. The fourth day also does not describe the original creation of the sun and moon, but it describes their appointment to function as light bearers for the earth. The fact that God works for six solar days to make the earth inhabitable for humanity means that the earth itself is young. He also argues that the earth's geology is best explained by a worldwide flood.

---

72. Kulikovsky ('Review of Sailhamer') also points out that until Day 3 there is no dry ground at all.

73. Gorman Gray, *The Age of the Universe: What are the Biblical Limits?* (Washougal, WA: Morning Star, 2000).

It is interesting to compare Gray's view with Collins' view because they are very similar in several respects. Both see Genesis 1:1 as describing the creation of the whole universe out of nothing (ex nihilo). Both argue for a long period of time between Genesis 1:1 and 1:3. Both understand that Genesis 1:3 is not the original creation of light but is the account of light first reaching the earth. Both view the sun and moon as appointed as light bearers for the earth on Day 4, but Day 4 is not a description of their original creation. They differ significantly in the fact that Gray understands the days of Genesis 1 as regular days because the sun is already functioning on Day 1, whereas Collins does not understand the days as regular days. Collins argues for an old earth whereas Gray argues for a young earth, even though the universe is old. If the sun and moon are already present on Day 1, it makes more sense to understand the days of Genesis 1 as regular days because the phrase 'morning and evening' is describing real morning and evenings determined by the sun. Arguing for analogical days that represent long periods of time when the sun is already functioning as it normally does seems to be special pleading.

There are also questions concerning the way that Gray and Collins understand Genesis 1. First of all, they argue that the jussives in 1:3 ('let there be') and 1:14 ('let them be') do not refer to bringing light and the heavenly beings into existence, but they refer to appointing them to their purpose or function. Second, they understand the meaning of ʿāsāh, which historically has been translated 'to make' in Genesis 1:14, as 'to appoint'. Although the verb does have a variety of nuances, including 'to appoint', the meaning that best fits the context of Genesis 1 is 'to make'. Genesis 1 is full of God's creative activity, so the most natural meaning of ʿāsāh in this context is 'to make'. There is also a pattern in the chapter that establishes that the verb ʿāsāh means 'to make' and that the jussives mean to bring into existence in the sense of create. The pattern is that a statement using a jussive is followed by the statement 'God made' or 'God created'. For example, verse 6 has the jussive statement, 'Let there be an expanse in the midst of the waters', which is followed by the statement in verse 7 that 'God made the expanse'. Then verse 20 has the statement by God, 'Let the waters swarm with swarms of living creatures', which is followed by an assertion using the term 'create' (*bārā'*): 'So God created the sea creatures and every living creature that moves, with which the waters swarm.' Then verse 24 has the statement by God, 'Let the earth bring forth living creatures ... livestock and creeping things and beasts of the earth,' which is followed by an assertion using the verb 'make' (*'āsāh*): 'God made the beasts of the earth.' In verse 21 the verb 'create' is used, and in verse 25 the verb 'make' is used, which shows that they are parallel to each other and thus overlap in meaning. This is the pattern that is also used in relationship to the lights on Day 4. In verse 14 God states, 'Let there be lights in the expanse of the heavens,' which is followed by the statement, 'God made the two great lights.' Thus, the context of Genesis 1 supports the view that the verb *'āsāh* means 'make' and not 'appoint'. If God truly makes the two great lights in Genesis 1:14, then the sun was not in existence on Day 1. This pattern also supports the view that the jussive in 1:3 means that light was brought into existence at that time. The following chart demonstrates the pattern and the parallel between 'create' and 'make':

> Let there be light and there was light (1:3)
>
> Let there be an expanse and God made the expanse (1:6-7)
>
> Let there be lights in the expanse and God made the two great lights (1:14-16)
>
> Let the waters swarm with swarms of living creatures, so God created the great sea creatures and every living creature with which the waters swarm (1:20-21)
>
> Let the earth bring forth living creatures and God made the beasts of the earth (1:24-25)

Finally, there is the issue that Genesis 1:1-2 may represent a long period of time before God begins to work on the earth in Genesis 1:3. In this view, Genesis 1:3 is not the first day of the creation of the universe but is the first day that God began to work on the earth to make it inhabitable for humanity. However, it is not obvious that Genesis 1:1-2 represents a long period of time. In fact, Exodus 20:11 connects the six days of Genesis 1 with the creation of the 'heaven and the earth, the sea, and all that is in them.' Thus, if the creation of the heaven and the earth is included in the six days, then there is not a long period of time before Genesis 1:3, and Genesis 1:1-2 does take place on Day 1.[74] These issues raise serious questions concerning the way Collins and Gray have understood Genesis 1.

The Regular Day View

The final view of the days of Genesis 1 can now be set forth.[75] Some of the following issues have already been mentioned, but they will be restated here to show how they fit into this particular view. This view states that in a very short period of time God created the universe by the word of His power and then fashioned and formed the elements of the universe, also by the word of His power, so that at the end of six regular days the universe was functioning properly. Genesis 1:1 states the absolute creation of all things (time, space, matter, and energy) out of nothing and also gives the broadest possible picture of God creating the whole cosmos.[76] Genesis 1:2 describes the condition of the world right after God's original act of creation in 1:1. The original, created elements of verse 1 were not yet differentiated, separated, or organized, which is described in verses 2-31 where God takes that which is a desolation and waste, and makes it into a functioning universe. God creates light in Genesis 1:3, the first of a series of three separations that are essential for the formation of a cosmos (the separation of day and night, the separation of the waters above and below by the firmament, and the separation of the seas from the dry land). The distinction of day and night and the use of evening and morning are the basis of distinguishing the first day, which

74. Even Collins (*Genesis 1–4*, p. 74) argues that Exodus 20:11 uses an accusative of time for 'six days', which expresses the extent of time over which the work is finished. The significant point is that Exodus 20:11 includes the creation of the heaven and earth within that time frame.

75. Recent proponents of this view include Henry M. Morris and Gary E. Parker, *What is Creation Science?* (rev. ed.; Green Forest, AR: Master Books, 1987); Noel Weeks, *The Sufficiency of Scripture* (Edinburgh: Banner of Truth Trust, 1988); Douglas F. Kelly, *Creation and Change* (Ross-shire, UK: Christian Focus, 1997); Benjamin Shaw, 'The Literal Day Interpretation,' in *Did God Create in Six Days?* pp. 199-220; J. Ligon Duncan III and David W. Hall, 'The 24-Hour View,' in *The Genesis Debate*, pp. 21-66; and many of the articles in *Coming to Grips with Genesis: Biblical Authority and the Age of the Earth*.

76. Kelly, *Creation and Change*, p. 79.

is based on an established cyclical succession of periods of light (day) and periods of darkness (night).[77] Through a series of divine commands God fashions the universe and makes the earth a place that is inhabitable for humanity. The sun and the moon, called the two great lights, are created on Day 4 by God and are appointed to function in relationship to the earth (Gen. 1:14-19). The formation of light before the sun is not a problem if Genesis 1 is not describing natural processes but is describing divine, supernatural activity. Scripture represents God, not the sun, as the source of light (Ps. 104:2), and the end of the world will also have light without the sun (Rev. 22:5).

The exegetical basis for understanding the days in Genesis 1 as regular days consists of several points. First, the text represents God as creating this universe by the word of His power. God speaks and things happen.

Second, whenever the word 'day' is used in Scripture with a number, it always refers to a regular day.[78] Even Bradley and Olson, who are proponents of progressive creationism (see footnote 34), recognize that the use of 'day' with a number, which occurs over 200 times, refers to a regular day.[79] This exegetical point is usually denied because Genesis 1 is describing something so unique that this use of day with a number in the rest of Scripture does not carry its normal weight in Genesis 1. It is also significant that whenever morning and evening are used together outside of Genesis 1 the reference is to a normal day.[80]

Finally, the genre of Genesis 1 is historical narrative, which is no different than the narrative in the rest of Genesis. The consistent use of the imperfect *waw* consecutive in Genesis 1 shows that it is narrative and that the normal way of understanding the passage would be chronological

77. Kelly, *Creation and Change*, p. 85.
78. Kelly, *Creation and Change*, p. 107; Pipa, 'From Chaos to Cosmos,' p 183; and Andrew E. Steinman, 'dxa as an Ordinal Number and Genesis 1:5,' *JETS* 45.4 (2002): 577-84.
79. Bradley and Olson, 'The Trustworthiness of Scripture,' p. 299.
80. Gordon Wenham, *Genesis 1–15* (Waco: Word Books, 1987), p. 19. Robert Reymond comments that 'evening and morning' occurs outside of Genesis in 37 verses (such as Exodus 18:13 and 27:21) and in each case the reference is to an ordinary day (*A New Systematic Theology of the Christian Faith* [Nashville: Thomas Nelson Publishers, 1998], p. 393).

sequence.[81] Historical narrative is not inconsistent with the use of patterns or refrains.[82] Thus the genre of Genesis 1 is not poetry, semi-poetic, or elevated prose. These terms have been used to argue that Genesis 1 should be taken in a figurative way instead of a literal, straightforward way. The use of historical narrative, however, emphasizes a literal, historical view of the account of creation.

The Structure of Genesis

There are a number of ways that Genesis can be divided. A simple outline would be (A) Primeval History (1:1–11:9), (B) Patriarchal History (11:10–37:1), and (C) Joseph's History (37:2–50:26). Section A covers a fairly long period of time, from creation to the tower of Babel and is geographically set in Babylon. Section B covers a much shorter period of time and focuses on one family, Abraham. It is geographically set in Palestine. Section C is one story with a connected plot that focuses on one person, Joseph. It is geographically set in Egypt. Genesis is truly a book about world history.[83]

The book of Genesis has its own internal structuring device that uses the word *tôlĕdōt*, which is translated 'these are the generations of' or 'this is the account of.' This word comes from the verb *yālad* which means 'to beget'. It functions as a heading for what follows[84] and is used in two different ways in Genesis. In the first use the toledot phrase is followed by the ancestor of an important person, which is then followed by a narrative of the account of the life of that important person. For example, Terah is the ancestor of Abraham, so the Toledot of Terah (11:27–25:11) is a narrative account of the life of Abraham. There are five uses of the toledot formula that function this way. The Toledot of Isaac (25:19–35:29) is an account of the life of Jacob and the Toledot of Jacob (37:2–50:26) is an account of

---

81. It is worth repeating that Waltke and O'Conner (*Hebrew Syntax*, pp. 547-48) quote S. R. Driver concerning the imperfect *waw* consecutive: 'The most obvious and frequent relation is that of simple chronological succession.' They then comment that the form and not the words signify succession.

82. E. J. Young comments that just because something is put forth in a structured, schematic arrangement does not mean it is not chronological or that it is not straightforward history (*Genesis One*, p. 66).

83. Victor P. Hamilton, *The Book of Genesis* Chapters 1–17 (Grand Rapids: Eerdmans, 1990), p. 10.

84. Hamilton, *Genesis*, pp. 2-11.

the life of Joseph. The first use of toledot in Genesis, which is the Toledot of the Heavens and Earth (2:4–4:26), is the only one that is not followed by the name of a person. Rather, what follows is a narrative account of what became of the heavens and the earth. Also, the Toledot of Noah is followed by a narrative account of what happened to the family of Noah in the flood (6:9–9:29).

The second use of the toledot phrase consists of toledot followed by the name of an important person which leads to a genealogy of the descendants of that important person. For example, the Toledot of Adam (5:1–6:8) is followed by a genealogy of Adam. Five of the toledot phrases are used in this way, including the genealogies of Shem, Ham, and Japheth (10:1-32), Shem (11:10-26), Ishmael (25:12-18), and Esau (36:1–43).

The toledot phrase primarily serves as a structuring device for the book of Genesis. Not only is it a heading for what follows, but it also functions as a linking device that ties sections together. Many times the name of a significant person from the previous account is picked up and becomes the focal point of the next section. For example, Adam is an important person in the first toledot account (2:4–4:26) who becomes the focus of the next toledot account, The Toledot of Adam (5:1–6:8), which is the genealogy of Adam. Noah is highlighted in the genealogy of Adam (5:1-32) and he becomes the focus of the next toledot. Finally, the phrase also serves a narrowing function as the story of Genesis focuses on the righteous line through which God will accomplish His purposes of blessing for all the nations. The Toledots of Ishmael (25:12-18) and Esau (36:1-37:1) each deal with an important person from the non-elect line before the elect line is covered. They also demonstrate the fulfillment of God's promises to Abraham that many nations would come forth from him.

The following is a basic outline of Genesis using the toledot phrase. The 'G' stands for genealogy and the 'N' stands for narrative which describes the character of the text that follows the toledot phrase.

I. Primeval History   1:1–11:9

    A) Prologue: Creation   1:1-2:3
    B) The Fall and its Results   2:4-11:9

        1) Toledot of the Heavens and the Earth   N   2:4–4:26
        2) Toledot of Adam   G   5:1–6:8
        3) Toledot of Noah   N   6:9–9:29
        4) Toledot of Shem, Ham, and Japheth   G   10:1–11:9

II. Patriarchal History   11:10–37:1

    A) Toledot of Shem   G   11:10-26
    B) Toledot of Terah   N   11:27–25:11
    C) Toledot of Ishmael   G   25:12-18
    D) Toledot of Isaac   N   25:19–35:29
    E) Toledot of Esau   G   36:1–37:1

III. Joseph's History: Toledot of Jacob   N   37:2–50:26

STUDY QUESTIONS FOR THE INTRODUCTION

1   How is Genesis foundational to all of Scripture? In what way should it be foundational to your life?

2   How does understanding the way the Pentateuch was formed (the questions of authorship) affect your view of God's Word? Can you explain what the church means when it says that the Scriptures are 'inspired'?

3   Is it surprising that Genesis speaks so much of the future? How can that be explained?

4   Does the fact that Genesis often reflects the cultural context of the ancient Near East mean that Genesis

operates with the overarching worldview of the
ancient Near East? Why or why not? What does this
tell us about the church's relationship to the culture
around us?

5   Discuss how one's scientific presuppositions might
    affect a reading of Genesis 1–2. Why is the question
    of how God created in Genesis 2 so important?
    What other Scriptural teaching could be called into
    question if the way God creates Adam and Eve in
    Genesis 2 is denied?

6   If one holds to the Regular Day view, is it possible
    for that person to do good science? Discuss.

7   What is the significance of the fact that Genesis has
    its own internal structure? How does this help refute
    those who hold to such views as the documentary
    hypothesis?

I

Laying the Foundations for Correctly Understanding the World
(Genesis 1)

Primeval History (Gen. 1:1–11:9)

The book of Genesis was written to show that Israel's God is the sovereign Creator whose purpose to establish His covenant rule upon the earth will not be hindered by the sinfulness of humanity. The first major section of Genesis, called Primeval History, covers the creation of the world, the fall of mankind into sin, and the triumph and progress of sin through to the flood and the Tower of Babel. Foundational truths about mankind and this world are set forth in this section. Human beings learn their identity and their role within God's good creation. The power of sin and its devastating effects are clearly laid out. One also sees, however, God's proactive response to sin in order to establish His purposes in fulfillment of His covenant promises. Whenever sin seems to be getting the upper hand, God moves to hinder its effects and to establish His sovereign rule. When sin triumphs in chapter 4 through the murder of Abel and there is the escalation of sin in Lamech's boast, the godly community worships God and God moves to replace Abel with Seth. When sin and violence dominate the whole world, God moves to preserve a family through the judgment of the flood. When human beings seek to establish a name for themselves at the Tower of Babel, God scatters them and calls Abram, whose name will become great and through whom God will establish His covenant in order to bless the world. Thus, Genesis 1:1–11:9 sets forth foundational truths concerning the character and role of human beings within the world God has created.

These chapters are vital because if people do not understand the basic truths laid out here then they will operate from a world view that is distorted. Without understanding the goodness of God's creation, people will either conclude that material things are bad, or they will pursue material things as the highest good without recognizing the boundaries God the Creator has established for His creation. Without recognizing the nature of sin, people will not be effective in living with other human beings, in establishing policies to deal with human behavior, and in understanding God's solution to the problem. And finally, without understanding the character of God, people will conclude that God is unjust in His judgment and they will not see His gracious pursuit to establish His people through the fulfillment of His promises. If people do not understand Genesis 1–11, they will be operating with a distorted view of their own life and the world in which they live.

Prologue: Creation (Gen. 1:1–2:3)

The Character of God and Creation

The account of creation establishes the character of God, the character of His creation, and the place of mankind within creation. Genesis 1 assumes God's existence 'in the beginning', establishing His transcendent priority and separation from His creation. The name for 'God' in Genesis 1 is Elohim, which is used over 35 times in Genesis 1. It is actually a plural noun, which in some contexts could be translated 'gods', but when used of Israel's God, the God of creation, it is always translated with the singular 'God'.[1] The plural is explained as an intensive plural, which means that the individual or thing is thoroughly characterized by the qualities of the noun. Thus,

---

1.   In Genesis 1:1 the plural Elohim is used with the singular verb 'create' which shows that Elohim should be translated as 'God'.

Israel's God fully partakes of the character of deity. In fact, Israel's God is the true definition of deity. The aspect of deity that is emphasized in Genesis 1 is God's sovereign, majestic power as Creator. God is so powerful, that He merely speaks to bring things into existence and to make things happen (the verb translated 'said' is used ten times in Genesis 1, with each day beginning with God speaking, except the seventh day).

The power of God is also demonstrated in His forming and fashioning the earth to be a good place for mankind to live. The condition of the earth in Genesis 1:2 is 'formless and void'. These two words describe the earth as uninhabitable for human beings. The word 'formless' (*tōhû*) is used in Deuteronomy 32:10 in parallel with 'desert' (*midbār*), which is an uninhabitable place (described in verse 10 as a 'howling waste of the wilderness'). The word 'void' (*bōhû*) can also mean 'empty' and it is used in Isaiah 45:18 in parallel with 'inhabited'. God's purpose in creating the heavens and the earth was not that they would be empty but that they would be inhabited. In fact, the phrase 'formless and void' is used in Jeremiah 4:23 to describe the land of Palestine as uninhabitable because of the judgment of God through the exile of His people. The fruitful land became a desert. In Genesis 1 God forms and fashions what was 'formless and void' and makes it inhabitable for humanity.

The character of God's creation is declared good. This declaration is made throughout Genesis 1 at distinct stages of the work of creation and is made in a summary statement in Genesis 1:31. The word 'good' can mean that something is beautiful (Exod. 2:2) or that something is useful in fulfilling a purpose.[2] The latter meaning fits Genesis 1 as various aspects of creation are declared good. The things which God creates fulfill their purpose in making the earth a place for human habitation. The fact that God's creation is good affirms the benefit of the material world for human beings (1 Tim. 4:4) and argues against the view that matter is evil.

---

2.   A. Bowling, "טוֹב (*tôb*)," in *TWOT* (eds. R. Laird Harris, Gleason Archer, and Bruce Waltke; 2 vols; Chicago: Moody Bible Institute, 1980), 1:345-46.

The Creation and Role of Mankind

It is clear that the creation of 'man' (*'ādām*) is special and that it represents the crown of God's work.[3] 'The majestic march of the days'[4] climaxes with the creation of human beings. The special place of human beings within God's creation is demonstrated in several ways in Genesis 1.

First, when God creates 'man' He uses terminology which was not used in reference to any other creation in Genesis 1. He does not say 'let the earth bring forth living creatures' as in verse 24, but rather states 'Let us make man.'

There is much discussion concerning the meaning of 'let us'. Some argue that the 'us' refers to the heavenly court that surrounds God's throne, a reference to angelic beings who act as messengers for God (1 Kings 22:19, Job 1-2).[5] However, God goes on to say that 'man' would be made in 'our image' and it is hard to conceive of human beings created in the image of the angels or of God and the angels.[6] Plus, there is no evidence for the existence of a heavenly court in Genesis 1.

When God takes counsel it is clearly stated with whom He takes counsel. God is the sole actor throughout Genesis 1. Isaiah 40:14 denies that God consults with anyone, whether human or heavenly, in the creation or administration of the world.[7] Cassuto argues that 'let us' is a plural of exhortation as when a person exhorts himself to do a certain task. He appeals to 2 Samuel 24:14 where the plural 'let us fall' is used, followed by the singular 'let me not fall'.[8]

This view is closely associated with the view that 'let us' is expressing self-deliberation. In this view God deliberates with Himself in the creation of 'mankind'.[9] Gerhard Hasel argues that the plural 'let us' is a plural of fullness which

3.   Matthews, *Genesis 1–11:26*, p. 160.
4.   This phrase comes from Derek Kidner, *Genesis* (Inter-Varsity Press, 1967), p. 54.
5.   Waltke, *Old Testament Theology*, pp. 212-14 makes the best case for this view.
6.   Keil and Delitzsch, *Genesis*, p. 61.
7.   John N. Oswalt, *The Book of Isaiah: Chapters 40–66* (Grand Rapids: Eerdmans, 1998), pp. 59-60.
8.   Cassuto, *Genesis Part 1*, p. 55.
9.   *Gesenius Hebrew Grammar* (ed. E. Kautzsch; rev. by A. E. Cowley; Oxford: Clarendon Press, 1910), sec. 124.g, n. 2 mentions this view but does not explain it. Gesenius' grammar will be abbreviated *GKC* throughout the rest of the commentary.

supposes that there is within the divine being a distinction of personalities so that there is an intra-divine deliberation among the 'persons' within the divine being. He goes on to say that 'in the creation of man a deliberating counseling between "persons" and a mutual summons within the deity or divine Being took place'.[10] In the context of Genesis 1:2, where the Spirit of God is mentioned as participating in creation, it makes sense that God here speaks to the Spirit as a co-participant in creation.[11]

However the phrase is understood, it highlights the importance of God's creation of 'man' because it is a unique phrase in Genesis 1. The ongoing march of creation in the pattern of 'God said' and then 'God created or made' is interrupted with 'let us make' to highlight the importance of the creation of human beings.

Second, the importance of the creation of 'mankind' is seen in the fact that only human beings are said to be created in the image of God. The plants and the animals are not created in His image. There is much discussion concerning the meaning of the image of God. The image of God is not specifically defined in Genesis 1 but the emphasis is on how those who are made in the image of God should function within God's creation. Of course, this has led to various reflections on what the image of God entails. Some argue that because human beings are a reflection of God the image includes both spiritual and material aspects. Although God does not have a physical body, some would argue, based on the unity of the human person, that the human physical form reflects God in some way. This view would stress that humans represent God on earth.[12] Others would stress that we are like God and unlike the animals in that humans are personal beings who are self-conscious and have the ability to be self-reflective. The ability of human beings to think and speak sets them apart from

---

10.   Gerhard F. Hasel, 'The Meaning of "Let Us" in Gen 1:26,' *AUSS* 13.1 (1975): pp. 58-66.

11.   Matthews, *Genesis 1–11:26*, pp. 162-63 and Hamilton, *Genesis Chapters 1-17*, p. 134. Others who argue for some kind of deliberation on the part of God include John Calvin, *Commentaries on the First Book of Moses called Genesis* (Grand Rapids: Baker, 1996), pp. 91-92 and John Currid, *Genesis 1:1–25:18* (Darlington, Evangelical Press, 2003), p. 85.

12.   David Atkinson, *The Message of Genesis 1–11* (BST; Downers Grove, IL: Inter-Varsity Press, 1990), p. 40, mentions the representational view.

the animals. Some would also bring in the New Testament perspective of what is restored to a person when they are regenerated, which includes knowledge, righteousness, and holiness (Col. 3:10; Eph. 4:24; WCF 4.2).[13]

The text emphasizes the role of those made in God's image within God's creation. In order to fulfill that role God created 'mankind' as male and female. This differentiation was necessary if 'mankind' was to fulfill God's purposes of being fruitful, multiplying, filling the earth, and subduing it (Gen. 1:28). The aspect of dominion over the animals also demonstrates the special place of human beings in God's creation. The fact that human beings rule over God's creation is based on their special place in God's creation.[14] However, this view is under attack today from many who do not want to give human beings a special place in God's creation, partly because they adamantly oppose the concept of dominion.[15] Many also misunderstand the concept. Dominion does not mean that human beings are free to exploit creation in a negative way without regard for the beauty and glory of God's creation; rather, in exercising dominion human beings mirror God's actions in Genesis 1. God's power and authority in bringing this world into existence is emphasized in Genesis 1 and the role of human beings reflects that aspect of God in ruling over creation (for the role of caring for creation, see the discussion on Genesis 2). Of course, human beings

---

13.   Keil and Delitzsch (*Genesis*, pp. 63-64) stresses the image as the spiritual and mental aspects of human beings with an emphasis on what is lost in the fall and restored in Christ.

14.   Matthews (*Genesis 1-11:26*, p. 169) argues that the language of 1:26 reflects the idea of a royal figure representing God as his appointed ruler (see also Psalm 8).

15.   Blaming the ecological crisis on the Christian view of dominion goes back to a seminal article by Lynn White, Jr., 'The Historical Roots of Our Ecological Crisis,' in an Appendix to the book by Francis A. Schaeffer, *Pollution and the Death of Man* (Wheaton: Tyndale House Publishers, 1970), pp. 97-116 (it originally appeared in *Science* 155 [1967], 1203-07). It is interesting that James Barr, who is no friend to evangelicals, writes the following: 'As far as one must speak of responsibility and guilt, I would say that the great modern exploitation of nature has taken place under the reign of liberal humanism in which man no longer conceives of himself as being under a creator, and in which therefore his place of dominance in the universe and his right to dispose of nature for his own ends is, unlike the situation of the Bible, unlimited' (Barr, *Ecology and Religion in History*, 1974, quoted in Joseph Blenkinsopp, *Treasures Old and New: Essays in the Theology of the Pentateuch* [Grand Rapids: Eerdmans, 2004]), p. 38.

rule creation under God's authority. Practically, this means that it is appropriate for human beings to use creation for their benefit. Dominion is a Biblical concept and any view that would deny the unique role of human beings within God's creation and place humans and animals on the same level is to be vehemently rejected.[16]

It is clear that human beings have a royal calling in their rule over creation. All human beings participate in this rule over creation by virtue of their being created in the image of God. In some views in the ancient Near East only the king partakes of the divine image. For example, a statement to King Esarhaddon of Assyria asserts, 'A (free) man is as a shadow of the god, the slave is as the shadow of a (free) man, but the king, he is like unto the (very) image of God.'[17] However, in the Scriptural account every human being is made in the image of God and thus takes on a royal, kingly function within creation.

Dominion, however, is made very difficult by the fall, but God sets out to restore man's dominion in redemptive history, beginning with the promise that one would come to crush the head of the serpent (Gen. 3:15). The covenant with Abraham includes the promise of kings and the possibility of restoring dominion in the land of Canaan (Gen. 17:7-8; 15:18-21). Israel and her kings do not exercise proper dominion because they fail to live in obedience to God and thus lose the land. The promises in the Old Testament of one who would come to rule righteously and establish a kingdom of peace (Gen. 49:10-11; Num. 24:17; Isa. 9:6-7; 11:1-16) are fulfilled in Jesus Christ. Jesus Himself exercises dominion by casting out demons (Mark 5), by restoring order in creation through healing (Mark 3:1-6), and by exercising power over creation (Mark 4:35-41). Hebrews 2 presents Christ as the man who fulfills the original role of dominion given to human beings and makes it possible for humans to share in that dominion restored to them in Christ. Thus, the kingdom is given to His disciples who will inherit the earth and participate in the reign of Christ by crushing Satan under their feet (Rom. 16:20). Full restoration will be

---

16.   For the implications of affirming that humans are no different from animals, see Peter Singer, *Animal Liberation* (New York: Harper Collins, 2002) and *Rethinking Life and Death* (New York: St. Martin's Press, 1996).

17.   Bruce Waltke, *Genesis* (Grand Rapids: Zondervan, 2001), p. 66, n. 47.

established when Christ comes again and we will reign with Him in the new heavens and the new earth (Rev. 22:5).[18]

The account of creation ends with God resting on the seventh day from the work of creation. This rest has implications for human beings because God also blesses the seventh day and makes it holy. The blessing of the day means that the day will be fruitful with respect to the purposes of that day, which parallels the blessing of male and female for the purpose of multiplying and filling the earth. The fact that the seventh day is holy sets it apart not only for God but also for human beings who will benefit from the 'rest' of that day. How human beings participate in the rest of the seventh day is not spelled out explicitly, but the blessing of the seventh day must have implications for human beings. It will include imitating God in stopping the activity of work in order to rest, which must include not just a physical rest but also a spiritual rest. God does not get tired and yet He rested on the seventh day, and it will become clear that human beings are also to enter into that rest. The fall into sin will highlight the necessity of rest from the weariness of work and also the necessity of spiritual rest which can only be found in God. Thus a pattern of work and rest is established that human beings will imitate in honor of God.

The concept of rest is lost in the fall as Adam and Eve are expelled from the garden of Eden. God seeks to restore that rest through the restoration of fellowship with mankind and in establishing places of rest which exemplify His presence, such as the tabernacle and the land of Canaan. Such rest is forfeited by the sin of Israel so that they lose the place of rest in the destruction of the temple and the loss of their land. Jesus comes to restore God's rest by establishing fellowship with God through His death on the cross. He is the temple and He comes to establish His dwelling in a new temple, the church. Thus He offers rest to the weary (Matt. 11:28) and makes it possible for God's people to enter into His rest (Heb. 4), both now through faith in Christ but also in the future when full rest will be restored in the presence of God in the new heavens and the new earth. There will be no temple in that

18.   See Dan G. McCartney, 'Ecce Homo: The Coming of the Kingdom as the Restoration of Human Vicegerency,' *WTJ* 56 (1994): 1-21.

place of rest because God Himself will be with His people, which will lead to the vanquishing of tears, pain, sorrow, and death (Rev. 21:3-4).

STUDY QUESTIONS

1. How does the fact that God spoke and the world came into existence affect our understanding of His providential care of and power over creation?

2. How does the fact that human beings are created in the image of God affect your view of the relationship between human beings and animals, your view of other human beings, and your view of your role in God's creation?

3. What is the Biblical concept of rest? How is it ignored in modern society?

2

God Provides Everything for Adam and Eve
(Genesis 2)

The first section of Genesis to be introduced by the word 'toledot' is 2:4–4:26 (The Account [Toledot] of the Heavens and the Earth). This section of Genesis is part of the larger unit of Genesis 2:4-11:9, which describes the fall and its results. In Genesis 2:4 the word 'toledot' is followed by a narrative account of what happened to the heavens and the earth. After the broad, sweeping, majestic view of creation in Genesis 1 and its emphasis on the sovereignty of God, Genesis 2 takes a closer look at God's preparation of a place for Adam and Eve to live, the creation of Adam and Eve, and the role they have in the garden.

Genesis 2 no longer describes God in His majesty as the creator but it gives a much more personal account of His care for and interaction with His creation. This explains why Elohim alone is not used for God in Genesis 2 but Lord God (Yahweh Elohim) is used. At this point in the narrative the name Yahweh (Lord) is not fully understood, but this name becomes significant as the covenant name of God in the Exodus from Egypt. Yahweh remembers His covenant with Abraham and fights to deliver His people from the bondage of Egypt. In Genesis 2 Yahweh demonstrates His close relationship with Adam and Eve in the way they are created and in His concern for their welfare by providing for them all that they need.

Everything in Genesis 2 is geared toward the benefit of human beings, who are God's highest creation. God provides life to Adam by breathing into him the breath of life so that he becomes a living being. God Himself fashions the first man from the dust of the ground. This act of God demonstrates His close involvement with the creation of man in that He gives personal attention to the formation of both Adam and Eve. Also, the word play between 'man' (*'ādām*) and 'ground' (*'ădāmāh*) shows that mankind is related to the ground by his very constitution so that when sin enters the world mankind will return to the ground in death. But on the positive side, mankind will also be perfectly suited to work the ground in the fulfillment of his divinely given task of caring for the garden.[1]

God not only provides life for man but He also provides work. The man is placed in the garden 'to work it and to keep it' (Gen. 2:15). It is significant that work is part of man's original vocation given to him by God. Work is something that is beneficial to human beings in fulfilling the calling God has given to them. The two words used for the work in the garden are *'ābad* ('to work') and *šāmar* ('to keep'). The former word can have the meaning 'to serve' and the latter the meaning 'to guard'. These terms stress that work is not just something that is beneficial to the one doing the work but that work also includes various responsibilities. Thus work includes service to others and the obligation to use appropriately whatever property God has entrusted to us (Gen. 30:31).[2] Work also includes responsibility to God. The two terms used in Genesis 2:15 for human work are also used to describe the work of the priests and Levites at the tabernacle (Num. 3:7-8). There is a spiritual dimension to human work because it is done as service to God and has the purpose of faithfully keeping the instructions of God (Lev. 8:35). The implication is that the purpose of work is more than an activity that allows a person to provide for his needs but that work is a vocation which enables a person to fulfill a calling of service to others and to God.[3]

---

1. Matthews, *Genesis 1–11:26*, p. 196.
2. Matthews, *Genesis 1–11:26*, p. 210.
3. See Gene Edward Veith, *God at Work: Your Christian Vocation in All of*

The aspect of work as service to God is enhanced by the presentation of the garden as a special place of God's presence. The fact that it is a garden stresses that it is a special place, an enclosed protected area associated with the blessings of God. Those blessings include fellowship with God and the abundant provision of Adam's every need. The fact that there is a river that flows out of the garden (Gen. 2:10) is significant not only because water is an important source of physical life, but also because water flowing from the place of God's presence becomes a picture in later Scripture of the abundant blessing of God that flows from the place of God's dwelling. This picture is found in Psalm 46, Ezekiel 47, and Revelation 22. In John 7, rivers of living water flow from the Holy Spirit in the one who believes (v. 38). Thus spiritual blessings flow abundantly from the presence of God. The tree of life also shows up in Revelation 22 in the new heavens and the new earth. It is also interesting that there are cherubim that guard the garden when Adam and Eve are expelled from the garden. Thus, there is clear evidence that the garden is a special place of God's presence, that it foreshadows the later tabernacle and temple,[4] and that what is lost through the fall is ultimately restored in the new heavens and the new earth.

In Genesis 2, Adam's special role in the garden is not only seen in the description of his work in the garden (Gen. 2:15), but also in the exercise of dominion in naming the animals (Gen. 2:18-20). The naming of the animals fulfills the God-ordained role given to mankind in Genesis 1:26-28 and demonstrates Adam's authority over the animals. It is also clear, however, that the purpose for naming the animals includes a search for a companion for Adam. For the first time something has been declared 'not good' by God; it is not good that Adam is alone (Gen. 2:18). It becomes evident that the right match was not found for Adam in the animal world. Thus God forms 'a woman' not from the ground but from Adam himself. The woman that God forms for Adam is

---

Life (Wheaton: Crossway Books, 2002) and Stephen J. Nichols, What is Vocation? (Phillipsburg, NJ: P & R, 2010).

    4.   See G. K. Beale, The Temple and the Church's Mission: A Biblical Theology of the Dwelling Place of God (Downers Grove, IL: Inter-Varsity Press, 2004), pp. 66-80.

the right 'helper fit for him' (Gen. 2:20). This is demonstrated in Adam's response when the woman is brought to him (Gen. 2:23). Adam, in essence, declares 'finally' ('this at last') because there is someone of his own kind who is of his own flesh. He then names her 'Woman' (*'iššāh*) because she was taken out of 'Man' (*'iš*). There follows a statement in Genesis 2:24 that is a commentary on the creation of woman, which is the foundational statement for marriage in Scripture. The marriage relationship entails a leaving behind of all other loyalties, including family loyalties, the establishment of a new relationship by the couple's sole commitment to each other, and the demonstration of the union of that relationship by becoming one flesh. The beauty and transparency of marriage are demonstrated in the final statement of verse 25: 'the man and his wife were both naked and were not ashamed.' The man and his wife live together in complete harmony.

It is appropriate to draw some conclusions based on what has been presented so far concerning the role of mankind in his various relationships. First of all, human beings imitate God in carrying out their proper role in creation. In Genesis 1 God is presented as the majestic, sovereign creator of the heavens and the earth who rules over His creation by forming and fashioning it. The role of mankind in Genesis 1:26-28 in having dominion over creation parallels the presentation of God as mankind imitates God's rule over creation under His authority. In Genesis 2 God is presented as more intimately involved with His creation as He cares for mankind by providing all that is needed to live a fruitful life. The role of mankind in Genesis 2 imitates God with the emphasis on caring for and keeping the garden. Thus Genesis 1–2 presents a complete picture and a proper balance of the role of human beings within God's creation. Both dominion over creation and care for creation are important for understanding mankind's role in creation.[5] Dominion apart from care for creation can lead to exploitation and the abuse of creation. Care for creation

---

5.   For a view that seeks to treat the environment properly but also rejects global alarmist views and views that focus on major government intervention, see 'The Cornwell Declaration' in *Environmental Stewardship in the Judeo-Christian tradition: Jewish, Catholic, and Protestant Wisdom on the Environment*, ed. Michael B. Barkey (Grand Rapids: Acton Institute, 2000).

separated from dominion can lead to a distorted view of the proper relationship of human beings to creation and to the animal world. Dominion means that human beings are able to use creation for their benefit but they are to do so within the proper limits of caring for creation. There may be differences of opinion among Christians on specific issues related to the proper use of the environment, but it is important to keep both dominion and care for creation as the proper framework for discussing these issues.

A second issue that arises from Genesis 2 is the relationship between the man and the woman in marriage. It is important to keep a proper balance between the leadership role of the man and the equality of the woman in the relationship. It is clear that the man is created first and that the woman has her origin from the man. The authority of the man in the relationship is seen in the fact that Adam has a representative role in Genesis. The name 'ādām not only refers to a particular individual named Adam but it also has the generic sense of 'mankind'. The actions of Adam affect those he represents so that when he fails it affects his descendants. In Genesis 3, God holds Adam responsible for the sin of eating from the tree by addressing him first, even though it was Eve who first partook of the fruit. This coincides with Paul's understanding of the representative role of Adam in Romans 5:12-21 and 1 Corinthians 15:21-22. The authority of Adam is also seen in his naming of the one brought to him as 'Woman' (Gen. 2:23) and in giving her the name 'Eve' (Gen. 3:20). On the other hand, Eve's full equality with Adam is also demonstrated in that she is also created in the image of God. One implication of this is that she will have full access to a relationship with God, which is demonstrated in the fact that she is held responsible for her actions in the sin of eating from the tree. Also, Eve is given to Adam to assist him in his work in the garden. The word 'helper' ('ēzer), used for Eve in Genesis 2:20, is a very strong word used for the help that God gives to people, which demonstrates the woman's essential role in aiding the man to fulfill his calling.[6] One way in which the woman will help in the fulfillment of the divine mandate to be fruitful and multiply is to be the one who will

---

6.   Waltke, Genesis, p. 88.

bear children. The importance of this role is seen when God specifically mentions it in giving the consequences of the curse of sin (Gen. 3:16). Thus, the woman does not occupy an inferior position in the marriage relationship but she fully assists her husband in fulfilling the divine mandate.

Third, the fact that the first couple is male and female and that the marriage relationship is highlighted has important implications for issues the church is facing today. There are segments of the church that argue for the legitimacy of monogamous homosexuality as a proper expression of love between two men or two women.[7] This is a very difficult position to argue on the basis of Scripture. The fact that the first couple are male and female and that this is necessary to carry out the divine mandate to be fruitful and multiply automatically sets homosexual relationships outside the bounds of what is normative for marriage, partly because such a relationship is not able to produce children in a natural way. Plus, all the references to homosexual relationships in Scripture are negative, which makes it difficult to argue from Scripture the legitimacy or the positive benefits of that relationship.[8] Many who argue for homosexuality have abandoned Scripture as their ultimate authority and have substituted something else, such as human experience and/or their definition of human love, as their highest authority.

The importance of marriage in fulfilling the divine mandate also raises questions concerning the subject of singleness. In the cultural context of the Old Testament there was a high expectation that a person would marry and have children because marriage and children were so important for the ongoing legacy of the name of the family and for inheritance issues. However, as with other practices in the Old Testament, there is an important redemptive historical shift that takes place at the coming of Christ. Jesus Himself affirms God's original design of marriage in Matthew 19:4-6 and affirms the importance of that relationship by stating that a divorce

---

7.   Letha Scanzoni with Virginia Mollenkott, *Is the Homosexual My Neighbor?* (New York; Harper, 1994) and Rollan McCleary, *A Special Illumination: Authority, Inspiration, and Heresy in Gay Spirituality* (London: Equinox Publishing, 2004). See also Guenther Haas, 'Perspectives on Homosexuality,' *JETS* 45.3 (2002): 497-512.

8.   Robert Gagnon, *The Bible and Homosexual Practice: Texts and Hermeneutics* (Nashville: Abingdon Press, 2001).

should not be granted except for sexual immorality (19:9). The disciples are surprised by the strictness of Jesus' words and assert that if that is the case it is better not to marry (19:10). Jesus uses their response to teach further on the fact that 'not marrying' may now be an option for those who do not marry for the sake of the kingdom of heaven (19:11-12). In other words, there may be situations where singleness is better because it enables a person to focus all his or her energy on serving Christ without worrying about the responsibilities that come with marriage (see 1 Cor. 7:32-35).[9] Jesus Himself never married. Although marriage is still important, singleness is an option and those who are single should not be made to feel like second-class citizens in the kingdom of God.

Genesis 2 lays out all the wonderful provisions that God grants to Adam in the garden. In addition to the ones listed above, there is also the provision of limits in the command that God gave to Adam. The command has a positive aspect to it in that God grants to Adam the freedom to eat from every tree of the garden; however, there is also a prohibition with a penalty attached to it. The prohibition is that Adam is not to eat from the tree of the knowledge of good and evil (for further discussion of this tree, see Genesis 3). The penalty for disobeying this command is death: 'in the day that you eat of it you shall surely die' (2:17). The purpose of this prohibition is not explicitly stated but it becomes clear from the events of Genesis 3 that this tree is a test of Adam and Eve's loyalty to God through obedience to His command. The result from eating this tree is death, first spiritual and then physical. The fact that God prohibits Adam and Eve from eating from the tree of life after they have disobeyed God's command implies that if they had obeyed the command of God they would have been allowed to eat from the tree of life. Thus it is appropriate to see the command in Genesis 2:16-17 as a probationary test for Adam. He failed the test and so Adam himself and his descendants became subject to death. The implication is that if Adam had passed this test, not only would he have been

---

9.   See Christine A. Colón and Bonnie E. Field, *Singled Out: Why Celibacy Must be Reinvented in Today's Church* (Grand Rapids: Brazos Press, 2009) which seeks to develop a positive view of singleness in the context of the concept of celibacy.

able to enjoy life in all its fullness, his descendants would have enjoyed such life as well. This fullness of life which was lost can be compared to the life that will be restored in the new heavens and the new earth. Although the two may not be completely identical, the life that Adam would have received would have been on a glorified level of existence as a permanent possession.[10]

Although the term 'covenant' is not used in Genesis 1–3, the relationship between God and Adam is best understood as a covenant relationship. The term 'covenant' is not used in 2 Samuel 7 for the relationship that God established with David, but Psalm 89 does refer to it as a covenant. The same is true for Genesis 1–3. The term 'covenant' is not used, yet Hosea 6:7 refers to God's relationship with Adam as a covenant.[11] Plus, elements of a covenant relationship are present in Genesis 1–3. As with all covenants, God takes the initiative as the authoritative member of the relationship. There are stipulations to the relationship between God and Adam as laid out in the prohibition that God gives to Adam, which also has the penalty of death attached to it. If disobedience to God's command brings the curse of death, it is implied that obedience to the command will bring the blessings of life.[12]

Covenants operate on the representative principle and include descendants, which is true of Adam's role in Genesis. He is a representative for his descendants and what he does impacts his descendants. Adam's sin is charged against his descendants, that is, it is imputed to them, a point Paul makes in Romans 5. Certainly the effects of Adam's sin on his descendants are evident in Genesis 4 with the triumph of sin.

The type of covenant relationship between God and Adam best fits what comes to be known as a treaty covenant where the blessings of the covenant are given in response to obedience and the curses of the covenant fall on the covenant-breaker. This is the same type of covenant as the Mosaic covenant, where in some sense there is a works principle

---

10. Kline, *Kingdom Prologue* (Overland Park, KS: Two Age Press, 2000), p. 21, and L. Berkhof, *Systematic Theology* (Grand Rapids: Eerdmans, 1941), pp. 211-18.

11. For different views on Hosea 6:7, see Byron Curtis, 'Hosea 6:7 and Covenant Breaking like/at Adam,' in *The Law is Not of Faith*, eds. Bryan D. Estelle, J. V. Fesko, and David VanDrunen (Phillipsburg, NJ: P & R, 2009), pp. 170-209.

12. Berkhof, *Systematic Theology*, pp. 211-218.

operative in relationship to whether Israel keeps the land (Lev. 18:5, Deut. 26–27). The Mosaic covenant is a part of the covenant of grace so that the law is given in the context of redemption and is a guide for how Israel is to live in a way that is pleasing to God (third use of the law). However, Paul also recognizes in Romans 10:5 a principle of righteousness based on the law that a person who does the commandments shall live by them.[13] Thus the law also functions to condemn us of our sin and show us our need of a Savior (the second use of the law). Paul also speaks of a righteousness based on faith that trusts in the finished work of Christ (Rom. 10:6-13). This righteousness based on faith is at the heart of the covenant of grace.

The covenant arrangement with Adam has traditionally been called the covenant of works (WCF 7.2) and it is absolutely necessary for a proper view of justification by faith because imputation is at the heart of the covenant of works. Just as Adam's sin was imputed to his descendants, so the righteousness of Christ is imputed to those who believe in Him. Many who have denied the covenant of works have also denied the imputation of Christ's active obedience in fulfilling the demands of the law.[14] Such a denial can affect how one understands justification by faith, which can affect how one understands the gospel itself.

STUDY QUESTIONS

1. Consider your view of work in light of Genesis 2. Do you see it as an act of service to God? Do you see it as a blessing given to you by God? How can you fulfill God's calling of service to others and to God in your workplace?

---

13. Guy Waters, 'Romans 10:5 and the Covenant of Works,' in *The Law is Not of Faith*, pp. 210-39.

14. N. T. Wright, *What Saint Paul Really Said: Was Paul of Tarsus the Real Founder of Christianity?* (Grand Rapids: Eerdmans, 1996), p. 110; Norman Shepherd, *The Call of Grace* (Phillipsburg, NJ: P & R, 2000); and Rich Lusk, 'A Response to the Biblical Plan of Salvation,' in *The Auburn Avenue Theology, Pros and Cons: Debating the Federal Vision*, ed. Calvin Beisner (Fort Lauderdale, FL: Knox Theological Seminary, 2004), p. 120.

2. In light of human dominion over creation and the responsibility to care for creation, is it appropriate to cut down trees for the wood to make baseball bats and to build houses? How can humans use creation for their benefit but also be good stewards?

Reflections on marriage and other relationships based on Genesis 2:

3. How do you view your role and the role of your spouse in your marriage? How are those roles practically lived out in your marriage? How can you encourage your spouse in their role?

4. Why is Genesis 2 so important in the discussions of homosexuality?

5. How are discussions of singleness different from discussions of homosexuality? How should the church view singleness in light of Genesis 2 and New Testament teaching?

3

The Destructive Power of Sin
(Genesis 3–4)

Genesis 3–4 completes the first toledot of Genesis (2:4–4:26). God has provided everything that Adam and Eve need in the garden and now a test of their loyalty to God arises. Their decision to disobey God has momentous consequences for all their relationships, but especially their relationship with God. The destructive power of sin is manifested in God's creation. Adam and Eve lose their place in the garden because of their disobedience, and the triumph of sin becomes evident in Genesis 4, which describes a division between the godly and the ungodly lines.

Genesis 3: The Fall and Its Results
In Genesis 3:1 a new character is introduced – 'the serpent', who is described as 'more crafty than any beast of the field which the Lord God had made' (NASB). A first-impression reading of this verse is that the serpent is part of the animal kingdom but is set apart from the other animals by the characteristic of being 'crafty' (*'ārûm*). This word is used in a positive sense in other parts of the Bible where it means 'prudent' (Prov. 12:16, 23; 14:8, 15); but it is also used in a negative sense with the meaning 'crafty' (Job 5:12; 15:5).[1] It will become clear in Genesis 3 that the negative meaning 'crafty' fits the serpent. Yet this serpent is different from the other animals not only because he is crafty

---

1. Ronald B. Allen, עָרוּם (*'ārûm*), *TWOT*, 2:697-98.

but also because he speaks. This raises the question whether the serpent is being used by someone else as an instrument to accomplish his purposes. Later Scriptures will support the view that behind the serpent is Satan himself, who is seeking to bring about the fall of Adam and Eve (Rev. 12:9; John 8:43-45).[2] Nevertheless, from Adam and Eve's perspective the serpent is an animal over whom they should exercise dominion.

The craftiness of the serpent is seen in the way he approaches Eve and questions her concerning the prohibition that God had given to them: 'Did God actually say, "You shall not eat of any tree in the garden?"' (Gen. 3:1). The serpent questions what God has said, and the question itself is meant to raise doubts or plant seeds of dissatisfaction concerning whether God really has the best interests of Adam and Eve in view. The question emphasizes God's prohibition and overlooks the abundant provision of trees God had given to Adam and Eve. Eve's response corrects the serpent's question by emphasizing that there is only one tree that they are prohibited from eating (3:2), but she then embellishes God's prohibition by adding 'neither shall you touch it' (compare 2:17 with 3:3). Perhaps this addition seems minor, but it is important how human beings handle the Word of God. The fact that Eve makes the command stricter by the addition of not touching it gives evidence of the growing suspicion in her mind.

The big lie from the serpent comes in verse 4 where he directly contradicts God's command by emphatically stating, 'You will not surely die.' The reason given for this bold statement raises the question of whether God is holding back Adam and Eve from greater fulfillment. The serpent holds out the hope that by eating of the tree they can be 'like God knowing good and evil' (3:5).[3] The serpent states

2. Walter Kaiser argues that the term 'serpent' is a title and not a reference to a particular shape that Satan assumed or an instrument he used to manifest himself in the garden (*The Messiah in the Old Testament* [Grand Rapids: Zondervan, 1995], pp. 38-39). Although this is possible, the comparison to the other animals supports the view that the serpent is a part of the animal kingdom.

3. The King James Version has 'gods' for Elohim instead of God, which makes the reference to divine beings. Although the following participle ('know') is plural, which would support the translation 'gods', it is also possible that the plural participle 'knows' refers back to the second-person plural verb 'you will be', which would support the translation 'God'. This is the view of Hamilton, who argues that the phrase could be translated 'you shall be as God, *that is*, you shall know good and evil' (*Genesis 1–17*, p. 189).

that God wants to keep Adam and Eve from becoming like Him in reference to 'knowing good and evil', a phrase that is best understood as referring to the ability to discern for oneself what is good and evil.[4] The issue concerns the source of knowledge and whether God is the ultimate source of knowledge or whether human beings take upon themselves the role of determining what is good and evil. By disobeying the command of God, Adam and Eve clearly assert their own moral autonomy to determine for themselves what is right and wrong (Gen. 3:6). Instead of submitting to the authority of God's Word to make them wise (Ps. 19:7-8), they want to decide this issue for themselves. To act autonomously is to act like God.[5]

The results of disobeying God are devastating because every relationship is affected. When Adam and Eve partake of the fruit, something immediately happens within them so that they no longer see themselves and the world in the same way. Genesis 3:7 states, 'Then the eyes of both were opened, and they knew that they were naked.' At the end of Genesis 2 they were naked and not ashamed, but since they now are ashamed to stand naked before each other, they sew fig leaves together to cover their shame. Sin leads to guilt, shame, and the loss of transparency. Their relationship with God is also broken. Instead of enjoying fellowship with God, they now hide from God when He comes into the garden. Genesis 3:8 implies that God's coming to the garden for fellowship with Adam and Eve was a regular occurrence, but the emphasis in verse 8 is on the coming of God in judgment.[6]

---

4. See Claus Westermann, *Genesis 1–11* (Minneapolis: Fortress Press, 1994), pp. 240-45, for a discussion of the various ways 'knowing good and evil' has been understood.

5. Hamilton (*Genesis 1–17*, p. 190) uses the term autonomy, Matthews (*Genesis 1–11:26*, p. 238) uses the phrase 'the acquisition of wisdom independently of God', and Waltke (*Genesis*, p. 92) understands the idea as a hunger for power that comes from knowledge that has the potential for evil as well as for good. Matthews (*Genesis 1–11:26*, p. 238) also comments that Eve usurps God's role in determining what is good.

6. Genesis 3:8 uses the *hitpael* verb form for the word 'walking' which can imply that God's coming to the garden was a regular occurrence. Hamilton (*Genesis 1–17*, p. 192) notes that the *hitpael* stresses habitual aspects of an action. God came to have regular fellowship with Adam and Eve. However, it is clear in the context of Genesis 3 that God is coming for judgment. Within that context the *hitpael* form of the verb could be connected to its use with agents of the divine counsel when on missions of surveillance and judgment (Job 1:7; Zech. 1:10). The word *qôl*, translated

Sin also affects the relationship between Adam and Eve. It is interesting that although Eve was the first to partake of the fruit, God first spoke to Adam as the covenant representative who is ultimately responsible for the act of sin. Although it is not absolutely clear that, when Genesis 3:6 states that Eve gave the fruit 'to her husband who was with her', the text means Adam was with Eve during the whole conversation, it seems likely that Adam was present for the discussion between Eve and the serpent. The serpent addresses Eve with plural verb forms as if he is addressing both the man and the woman.[7] Cassuto points out that the use of the preposition 'with' plus a suffix occurs when a person associates himself in a given action with someone who leads him (Gen. 6:18; 13:1).[8] Thus, Adam is being led by Eve and acquiesces to her initiative, instead of taking responsibility at that moment to obey God and not partake of the fruit.[9]

Although it is possible that, as covenant head, Adam's obedience would have covered for Eve's transgression, he nevertheless followed Eve down the path of sin and the results are seen not only in their hiding from God but in their blaming someone else for the sin. When God confronts Adam concerning whether he has eaten from the fruit of the tree, Adam blames Eve who was given to him by God (3:12). When God addresses Eve, she blames the serpent for deceiving her (3:13). Sin establishes patterns of behavior that affect the marriage relationship. Men either have a tendency to be passive and not accept their God-given role of covenant leadership in their families, or else they dominate their wives in inappropriate and abusive ways. Women have the tendency to blame the husband for the problems of the marriage and seek to control what happens in the family. Many times this happens because of the leadership void left by a passive husband. When God speaks to the woman and lays out the results of sin, he states, 'Your

---

'voice' or 'sound' is also used of the shattering thunder of God's coming for judgment (Isa. 30:31; Jer. 25:30; Joel 3:16) and the phrase 'cool of the day' could be referring to the 'spirit (rûaḥ) of the day', which would be a reference to the spirit of judgment on the day of the Lord (see Meredith Kline, *Images of the Spirit* [Eugene, Oregon: Wipf and Stock, 1999], pp. 97-114).

7. Currid, *Genesis*, 1:120 and Matthews, *Genesis 1–11:26*, p. 238.

8. Cassuto, *Genesis Part 1*, p. 148.

9. Hamilton (*Genesis 1–17*, p. 191) calls the sin of Eve a sin of initiative and the sin of Adam a sin of acquiescence.

desire shall be for your husband, and he shall rule over you'
(Gen. 3:16). God makes a similar statement to Cain in Genesis
4:7: 'sin is crouching at the door. Its desire is for you, but you
must rule over it.' The structure and terms used in both verses
are almost identical. In Genesis 4:7 sin's desire is to conquer
Cain, but he must in turn rule over it. The issue is whether sin
will control the life of Cain. Genesis 3:16 speaks about a similar
conflict of control in the marriage relationship. Eve's desire is
for her husband, which in the context of the consequences of the
curse of judgment has a negative meaning. Her desire will be
to usurp her husband's authority, which parallels Genesis 4:7
where sin's desire is to conquer Cain. In response, the husband
will seek to assert his rule over his wife so that the original,
harmonious relationship of the man and wife before sin is now
distorted. Marriage becomes a battlefield over who will control
the relationship.[10]

The judgment of sin also affects mankind's relationship to
creation, which is directly related to the work that God had
given to mankind. The mandate to be fruitful and multiply is
now difficult because childbearing and birth become a hard
and painful process (3:16). The task of dominion over creation
is now a hard task because the ground itself is cursed with the
result that working the ground for food becomes an arduous
task (3:17). The ground no longer cooperates but brings
forth thorns and thistles. In this context death is also defined
as a returning of the body to the dust of the ground (3:19).
Physical death becomes apparent in the following chapters
of Genesis, but spiritual death is what has been described
in the change that takes place within Adam and Eve and in
their broken fellowship with God. In fact, because of their
disobedience Adam and Eve lose the Garden of Eden as the
special place of God's presence so that they are driven out of
the garden by God (3:24). In asserting their moral autonomy
instead of obeying God's command, they lose everything.

God's response in the context of the judgment of sin is
extremely significant because it gives hope not only in the
immediate situation that Adam and Eve face, but also for the

---

10. Commentators who argue this view include Matthews (*Genesis 1-11:26*,
p. 251), Hamilton (*Genesis 1–17*, p. 202), Currid (*Genesis*, 1:133), and Waltke
(*Genesis*, p. 94).

future of their descendants. The covering that Adam and Eve make for themselves out of fig leaves is not adequate so God Himself covers them with 'garments of skins' (3:20). Human beings are not able to cover their own guilt and shame but must rely on God to provide an appropriate covering. It is significant that God uses animal skins to cover them, which foreshadows the importance of substitutionary sacrifice in the sacrifices of animals later in the Old Testament. Although God drives the couple out of the garden, this is a gracious act because it keeps them from partaking of the tree of life and living forever (3:22). If they would have partaken of the tree of life in their state of sin, the future hope of restoration would not have been possible because they would have been established in their own moral autonomy without hope of change.[11] In this way, physical death is not final because there is the hope of restoration in this life and the hope of life after death. This aspect of God's grace is so important that God sets up cherubim to guard the way to the tree of life (3:24).

God's grace is also seen in the fact that although the work that God had given to Adam and Eve would now be very difficult, it was not impossible. God sends them out of the garden but He sends them out 'to work the ground' (3:23), a phrase which uses one of the words from Genesis 2:7. Also, Adam names his wife 'Eve', which means the mother of all living (3:20). Even after the effects of the curse are announced concerning childbearing, the mandate to be fruitful and multiply will be carried out.

Finally, the hope of restoration for the future descendants of the human race is seen in that God commits Himself to deal with the serpent. The serpent is cursed more than the other animals because of its role in tempting Adam and Eve. The curse on the serpent is stated as 'on your belly you shall go, and dust you shall eat, all the days of your life' (3:14). This curse is not speaking about a change of locomotion for the serpent, just as eating dust does not refer to the literal diet of the serpent. These phrases are a metaphorical way of stressing the humiliation and subjugation of the serpent.[12]

---

11. Matthews, *Genesis 1–11:26*, p. 256, and Collins, *Genesis 1–4*, p. 175.

12. Cassuto (*Genesis Part 1*, p. 160) points to other places in Scripture where eating dust is used metaphorically for humiliation and defeat, such as Isaiah 49:23

The text is also clear that God will put enmity not only between the serpent and the woman, but between the seed of the serpent and the seed of the woman. The serpent will have a seed or descendants who will follow in his way, but the woman will also have descendants. In the immediate context, the descendants of the serpent are the Cainites who allow sin to dominate their lives. Jesus Himself speaks to certain Jewish people of His day as those who are of their father the devil (John 8:44) because they are not willing to believe His testimony. In Genesis 4 there will be a division of the human race between those who are separated from God (4:14) and those who worship Him (4:26). There will be hostility or warfare between these two groups.

God also promises, however, to send one from the seed of the woman who will do battle with the serpent and conquer him. Although the term 'seed' (*zeraʿ*) is a collective singular and can refer to descendants (plural), it is clear that a single individual is in view in the statement, 'he shall bruise your head, and you shall bruise his heel' (3:15). Although the collective singular noun 'seed' can be used with either singular or plural verbs, the pronouns used with 'seed' determine whether 'seed' has in view one descendant or many descendants. If the pronouns are plural, then 'seed' refers to a plurality of descendants, but if the pronouns are singular, then 'seed' refers to a single individual.[13] In Genesis 3:15 the pronouns are singular so that 'seed' is referring to an individual who will come to do battle with the seed of the serpent. The result of the battle is described by the verb *šûp̄*, which is translated 'bruise' (ESV, NASB) or 'strike' (NIV). The victory of the seed of the woman over the seed of the serpent is seen in the location of the verbal action. The seed of the woman is bruised on the heel, which is not ultimately fatal, but the seed of the serpent is bruised on the head, which is a fatal blow. The enmity between the two seeds begins in Genesis 4. Already in Genesis 5:29 people are looking for the one who will come to deliver them from the curse of sin. The identity of this one is further developed in Genesis, where the seed of the woman is

---

and Micah 7:17.

   13. C. John Collins, 'A Syntactical Note on Genesis 3:15: Is the Woman's Seed Singular or Plural?' *TynBul* 48.1 (1997): 141-148.

narrowed to the seed of Abraham, and then further narrowed
to the tribe of Judah. The royal nature of the coming one also
becomes clear (Gen. 49:10-12). The New Testament clearly
identifies Jesus as the seed of the woman, the son of Adam
(Luke 3:38), who is also the son of Abraham (Matt. 1:1), the
one from the tribe of Judah who has come to do battle with the
serpent (Matt. 8:28-34; 12:22-32) in order to defeat Satan, sin,
and death (Luke 10:17-20; Col. 1:13; Rev. 12:7-12).

Genesis 4: The Character of Two Communities

Genesis 4 shows the immediate results of sin in the family of
Adam, the division of humanity into two communities because
of sin, and the triumph of sin in the ungodly community. The
enmity between the two seeds becomes evident in the story of
Cain and Abel. Genesis 4 begins with Eve giving birth to two
sons whose names may reflect aspects of the story. The name
Cain (*qayin*) sounds very much like the verb *qānāh*, which
can mean 'acquire' or 'get', and the relationship between the
two may be based on the fact that they sound very similar
(assonance). The meaning of Eve's statement in 4:1 has been
debated based on the translation of the preposition *'eṭ*. Some
have taken it as the direct object marker, which leads to the
idea that Eve thought that this child was the divinely promised
seed of Genesis 3:15.[14] Others take it as the preposition 'with',
which some understand as an expression of arrogance on
Eve's part (as Yahweh created the first man, so she created the
second man).[15] The best way to understand the phrase is as an
expression of faith on the part of Eve which recognizes that
the birth of Cain is ultimately from the Lord.[16] The name Abel,
on the other hand, is the Hebrew *heḅel*, which can signify
fleeting, vain, or meaningless. This name expresses the impact
of sin on human life, and foreshadows what will tragically
happen to Abel in that his life will be cut short.

---

14. Kaiser, *The Messiah in the Old Testament*, p. 42.
15. Cassuto (*Genesis Part 1*, p. 201) comments that Eve boasts of her generative powers which approximate in her estimation the creative powers of God (see also Sailhamer, *The Pentateuch as Narrative*, pp. 111-12).
16. Matthews, *Genesis 1–11:26*, p. 265; Keil and Delitzsch, 'Genesis,' 1:109; and Kidner, *Genesis*, p. 74. Hamilton (*Genesis 1-17*, p. 221) gives evidence for understanding the preposition to mean 'from' instead of 'with'.

The two brothers developed different interests, with Abel becoming a keeper of sheep and Cain a worker of the ground. At an appropriate time[17] each brought an offering to Yahweh (the LORD). Cain brought 'an offering of the fruit of the ground' and Abel brought 'of the firstborn of his flock and of their fat portions'. Abel's offering was accepted by God but Cain's offering was rejected.

Of course, the question arises concerning why Abel's offering was accepted and Cain's offering was not. Some argue that Cain's offering was rejected because it was not a blood sacrifice. Although animal sacrifice is central to how one approaches God, it is not the best explanation of the rejection of Cain's sacrifice in this text. Offerings taken from the fruit of the ground were acceptable to God; in fact, the term *minḥāh* is used in this passage for both Cain and Abel's offering. It is a term that can refer to any offering, but it is also specifically used in Leviticus 2 of the grain offering. Thus, the problem is not that Cain brings an offering from the fruit of the ground.

Others differentiate the two offerings by the fact that Abel's offering is from the firstborn of his flock and that 'fat portions' are mentioned, which indicates he is bringing the best of what he has to God. Although the text does not say that Cain brings from the firstfruits of his crop, not all grain offerings would be firstfruits, which could only be brought right after harvest time.

The best explanation of why Cain's offering is rejected and Abel's offering is accepted is the heart condition of the one bringing the offering. This fact is demonstrated in the way the text reads in verses 4-5, where the person is mentioned before the offering is mentioned: 'the Lord had regard for Abel and his offering, but for Cain and his offering he had no regard.' The person is highlighted more than the offering itself. Hebrews 11:4 puts the emphasis on faith as the reason

---

17. The translation 'in the course of time' literally reads, in the Hebrew, 'at the end of days'. The phrase is ambiguous and is translated differently by different commentators. Hamilton (*Genesis 1–17*, p. 218) translates the phrase as 'some time later'. Cassuto (*Genesis Part 1*, p. 205) notes that the phrase either means at the end of a year or at the end of some time and he prefers 'at the end of some time'. Wenham (*Genesis 1–15*, p. 103), on the other hand, argues for 'after a year' as the best translation based on the fact that the word 'after' is normally followed by a precise period of time (Exod. 12:41) and that it seems natural to suppose that sacrifices would be brought at the end of an agricultural year.

for the difference between the two offerings: 'by faith Abel offered a better sacrifice than Cain.'

The condition of Cain's heart becomes clear in his response to God's rejection of his offering. He became angry and sad, which demonstrates the effects of sin in his life. However, Cain has the opportunity in this situation to respond appropriately so that he can be accepted by God (v. 7). But it is also clear that sin is seeking to dominate Cain, and that if he does not bring sin under control, it will rule him. Sin wins this battle and triumphs when Cain murders Abel.

The results of sin become evident not only for Cain but also for his family. There are similarities with Genesis 3, but in some ways there is also an intensification of the curse of sin in Genesis 4. When God asks Cain, 'Where is Abel your brother?', he rejects knowledge of and responsibility for his brother: 'I do not know; am I my brother's keeper?' Like Adam and Eve in Genesis 3, he avoids taking responsibility for his actions, but it is impossible to hide what he has done from God, who has heard Abel's blood crying for justice from the ground. The very ground that received Abel's blood will have a role in the effects of this sin as the ground itself will no longer be productive for Cain, which means he will be a fugitive and a wanderer on the earth. Cain understands the implications of this wandering when he says that he will be driven from the face of the ground and that he will be hidden from God's face (v. 14). Cain and his family will be alienated from God, which means they will also be alienated from the godly community. Thus he separates himself and his family from 'the presence of the Lord' and settles in Nod, east of Eden. The location of Nod is unknown, but there is a play on words as Nod is related to the term *năd*, which means 'wanderer'. Not only is this an accurate description of Cain, but also his separation from the presence of the Lord is emphasized in the relation of Nod to the garden of Eden.[18]

God extends common grace to Cain and his family in many ways. Common grace can be defined as grace that extends to all people in distinction to the special grace which is limited to God's people.[19] The latter grace is redemptive and results

---

18. Matthews, *Genesis 1–11:26*, p. 278.
19. See Berkhof, *Systematic Theology*, pp. 434-46, for further discussion of the

in salvation, whereas common grace is God's benevolence received by human beings by virtue of the fact that they live in God's world and experience common and general blessings. When Cain hears of the consequences of his sin in being driven away to become a fugitive on the earth, he is concerned that 'whoever finds me will kill me' (Gen. 4:14). Cain fears that someone will retaliate and seek to execute retributive justice for his murder of Abel. God responds to Cain's concern by assuring him of protection through a declaration and a 'mark on Cain'. The declaration is that if anyone kills Cain, vengeance shall be taken on him sevenfold. It is not clear how this vengeance will be administered, but at this point God is the one offering protection to Cain, so one assumes that this refers to divine vengeance.

The 'mark on Cain' is more difficult to explain. A variety of explanations have been given to explain this mark, including an oath, a city as a refuge, the name of Cain itself, or even a tattoo or special hairstyle.[20] However, the word 'mark' (*aot*) can also mean 'sign' and the verb translated 'set' (*c'm*), followed by the *lamed* preposition, can be translated 'give to' as in Numbers 6:26 and Daniel 1:7. This would yield the translation, 'Yahweh gave to Cain a sign.' Instead of the Lord putting a mark on Cain it may be better to understand that he gave to Cain a sign that assured him that no one finding him would kill him.[21] We are not told what the sign is, which would explain why there is no agreement concerning the identification of the mark or sign. Later on, capital punishment will be required for murder (Gen. 9:6), so the question is why does God spare the life of this murderer? It may be that God is trying to prevent an escalation of bloodshed which would be very harmful to the family of Adam and Eve at this stage of their history. God treats Cain with mercy to preserve the future of his descendants.

---

distinctions within common grace.

   20. Kline argues for the oath (*Kingdom Prologue*, p. 165), Sailhamer for the city (*Pentateuch as Narrative*, p. 114), and Wenham mentions the tattoo or hairstyle but then argues for the name Cain itself (Wenham, *Genesis 1–15*, p. 109).

   21. This view is similar to Kline's view that God gave to Cain an oath assuring him that no one would kill him, but he tries to make sense of the Hebrew word for 'sign'.

The development of the line of Cain is described in Genesis 4:17-24. Even though Cain represents the ungodly community separated from the presence of Yahweh (the Lord), God's common grace is demonstrated in their ability to carry out the mandate God had given to 'mankind' in Genesis 1:26-28. Their descendants multiply as children are born and they rule over creation in the development of civilization and culture. Cain built a city (Gen. 4:17), Jabal developed husbandry (4:20), Jubal developed music (4:21), and Tubal-cain developed the work of craftsmen (workers in bronze and iron, 4:22). These developments come from the ungodly line, which shows that unbelievers are able to understand the way the world works as established by God even while not necessarily acknowledging God as the ultimate source of these blessings. Thus, believers can learn things from unbelievers while recognizing that their faulty presuppositions will keep them from understanding many basic things about the world because they do not acknowledge God. The appropriate response is not rejection of these developments but instead we should seek to use them within the framework of believing God and giving Him the glory.

Yet while the ungodly line moves forward in the development of culture, it also advances in the progression of sin. The line of Cain shows technical ability but moral failure. The arrogant boast of Lamech demonstrates the progression of sin. Lamech is the seventh name in the genealogy of Cain. The number seven represents completeness which is exemplified in the fact that Lamech is the epitome of Cain's corrupt family. The progression of moral corruption includes bigamy, pride in boasting to his wives, and a revenge murder. He shows disdain for life by killing a young man for striking him, a response that goes beyond the proper bounds of retaliation. He is worse than Cain because he boasts, 'If Cain's revenge is sevenfold, then Lamech's is seventy-sevenfold' (v. 24). God's promise to avenge Cain's life seven times (v. 15), which is a merciful provision by God for a shameful criminal, is taken by Lamech as a badge of honor so that his boastful actions merit much more.[22] What God intended for mercy Lamech distorts for his own prideful use. Moral wickedness dominates the ungodly line.

---

22. Matthews, *Genesis 1–11:26*, pp. 282 and 289.

The godly line of Adam through Seth presents a very different picture. The name Seth means 'appointed' and he is so named because 'God has appointed for me another offspring instead of Abel' (v. 25). It is noteworthy that interest in the seed becomes prominent in the godly line of Adam with the birth of Seth. In Genesis 4:1 the word 'man' is used for Cain, but in verse 25 the word 'seed', translated 'offspring' in the esv, is used for Seth. Seth also has a son named Enosh, a term that means 'weakness' and emphasizes the frail condition of humanity.[23] Then at the end of Genesis 4, in the context of the godly line, the worship of the Lord is mentioned. True worship occurs as a part of the godly line. God faithfully preserves His people.

Study Questions

1. List the consequences of sin from Genesis 3. How do you see those consequences manifested in your life and/or in the world?

2. How would you define the seed of the serpent? Who does it refer to?

3. What are some examples today where unbelievers understand in a limited way how God's world works even if they do not believe in God? What are the implications of this for believers? What are some modern-day examples of technical advancement but moral failure?

4. How is the godly line described at the end of Genesis 4? How should those things manifest themselves in the life of God's people today?

---

23. Waltke, *Genesis*, p. 101.

4

The Preservation of the Godly Line
(Genesis 5–6a)

The Generations (Toledot) of Adam (Gen. 5:1–6:8) covers a long period of time. The genealogy of Adam begins with Adam and ends with Noah and his sons (Gen. 5:1-32). At the end of Genesis 4 the godly line is resumed after the author gives an account of the development of sin in Cain's family – the genealogy of Adam carries forward the godly line through Noah. There is then a description of the increasing wickedness of human beings on the earth which is contrasted with the lifestyle of Noah (Gen. 6:1-8). The intensity of the wickedness on earth will lead to the judgment of the flood in the next section (6:9–9:29).

The Genealogy of Adam (Gen. 5:1-32)
The beginning of Genesis 5 connects back to the creation account by reminding the reader of certain things concerning mankind (vv. 1-2). Mankind had been created in the likeness of God, which is a reference to the image of God (Gen. 1:27). God also created mankind male and female and blessed them, which is a reference to His mandate that they should be fruitful and multiply (Gen. 1:28). These important aspects of Genesis 1 are now fulfilled in this genealogy, not only in the emphasis on 'other sons and daughters', but also in how the way the relationship between Adam and his son Seth is described. Adam fathers a son 'in his own likeness, after his image' (v. 3).

There is a movement in verses 1-2 from the statement about mankind (*'āḏām* in a generic sense), who was made in the image and likeness of God, to a specific statement concerning Adam (also *'āḏām*) passing down that image and likeness to his son Seth. Thus each child born partakes of the likeness of his father, but even more each partakes of the image and likeness of God.

The genealogy progresses according to a standard formula, which can be presented as follows (PN means 'personal name'): when PN (1) had lived x years, he fathered PN (2). PN (1) lived after he fathered PN (2) y number of years and he had other sons and daughters. Thus all the days of PN (1) were x + y years, and he died.[1] The result of reading in succession this formula is to emphasize the phrases 'sons and daughters' and 'he died'. The former phrase emphasizes God's promise of preservation through procreation[2] and the latter phrase shows the effect of the curse in the physical death of human beings. Although people lived a long time, death reigned even in the line of the godly community. With this pattern established, the reader comes to expect the refrain 'and he died'; therefore when that pattern is broken it stands out. The pattern is broken twice in Genesis 5:1-32; and each is significant. The first time the pattern is broken is with Enoch (vv. 21-24) where the phrase 'and he died' does not occur. Instead, verse 24 states that 'Enoch walked with God, and he was not, for God took him.' The idea is that Enoch escaped physical death by being taken away by God. Before then, Enoch walked with God, which is the way to life (Gen. 6:9;

---

1. These formulas are adapted from Matthews, *Genesis 1–11:26*, p. 298. Many argue that there are gaps in the genealogy of Genesis 5, which means that it cannot be used to determine the age of the earth (William Henry Green, 'Primeval Chronology,' *BibSac* 47 [April 1890]: 285-303, along with many modern authors such as Gleason Archer, *A Survey of Old Testament Introduction* [Chicago: Moody Press], pp. 209-12; K. A. Kitchen, *Ancient Orient and Old Testament* [Chicago: InterVarsity Press, 1966], pp. 35-39; and Gordon Wenham, *Genesis 1–15*, pp. 123-34). For an alternative view that distinguishes genealogies that have gaps from those that do not, and argues that Genesis 5 should not be understood as having gaps because a father's age given at the birth of the son is meant to convey chronological information, see Travis R. Freeman, 'Do the Genesis 5 and 11 Genealogies Contain Gaps?' in *Coming to Grips with Genesis*, pp. 283-313. Even if the genealogy in Genesis 5 has gaps, it would not support the age of the earth that is argued in an old-age view of the universe (billions of years).

2. Matthews, *Genesis 1–11:26*, p. 296.

17:1-2; Deut. 30:15-16). This does not mean that everyone who walks with God will avoid physical death, but it does mean that everyone who walks with God will experience the same kind of life that Enoch experienced, both in this life and in the next life. The implication is that there is spiritual life which extends beyond this life after death. Death does not have the final word.

The second time the pattern is broken is with the birth of Noah when his father Lamech (not the Lamech of Genesis 4) offers the hope that his newborn son will bring relief from the painful toil of work (vv. 28-31). The name Noah (*nôaḥ*) is related to the Hebrew word for rest (*nûaḥ*), and there is a wordplay in verse 29 between the name Noah and the word translated 'relief' (*nāḥam*). What is significant about this statement from Noah's father is that people are looking for someone to be born from the seed of the woman who will deliver them from the curse of the fall. Although Noah is used by God to bring relief, he is not the one promised in Genesis 3:15 who will defeat the serpent.

The Increase of Wickedness: A Precursor to the Flood (Gen. 6:1-8)

The genealogy of Adam ends with a narrative conclusion (6:1-8) which demonstrates the increase of wickedness on the earth as a justification for the judgment of the flood. Genesis 6:1 is a summary statement showing the multiplication of humanity on the earth through procreation in fulfillment of the creation mandate to be fruitful; however, the way the multiplication is described raises possible problems, which are confirmed in verses 5-7 with the description of the wickedness that had become great on the earth. Several important questions arise concerning Genesis 6:1-4 which need to be addressed to better understand exactly what is happening in these verses and how it relates to the wickedness of verses 5-7.

The key participants in the multiplication of mankind on the earth are identified as the sons of God and the daughters of men. There are three main views concerning the identification of the sons of God.[3] The first view is that the sons of God are

---

3. See Matthews, *Genesis 1–11:26*, pp. 323-32 for an excellent discussion of these issues.

angelic beings who take for themselves human wives and through this union produce the mighty Nephilim. The sin then is the disregard for the ordinance of marriage which God established for human beings.[4] This view wins the linguistic argument in that the exact phrase 'sons of God' is used of angelic beings in Job 1:6 and 2:1. This view also stresses that the two phrases, 'the sons of God' and 'the daughters of men', seem to be in contrast with one another, so that 'the daughters of men' are human and 'the sons of God' are not human. Appeal is also made to the fact that the angelic view goes back to the Jews of the second century B.C. (1 Enoch 1-6) and that 1 Peter 3:19 and Jude 6 seem to confirm it. Nevertheless there are problems with this view. The rationale given for such a union is that this was man's attempt to circumvent God's plan by being enticed into intermarriage with demons in order to prolong life;[5] yet the initiative for these marriages is taken by the angels (the sons of God) and not by the daughters of men. Further, the emphasis in the passage is on 'flesh' (6:3); after all, the result of the marriages is individuals called 'men of renown' (6:4) and not angels or some kind of semi-divine beings. It is also significant that the punishment of the flood only affects human beings and not the angels. In addition, there is no evidence that angels have the power to procreate; they are spiritual beings and not corporal beings (Matt. 22:30; Mark 12:25). Finally, there are better explanations for 1 Peter 3:19 and Jude 6 than the argument that they are referring to angels in Genesis 6.[6]

Another view of the sons of God is that they are earthly kings or dynastic rulers, who continue the progress of sin by producing a state of tyranny, violence, and corruption. The

4. It is interesting that three authors of the Reformed persuasion each argue for one of the different views presented here. Willem VanGemeren, 'The Sons of God in Genesis 6:1-4,' WTJ 43 (1981):320-48, argues for the view that the sons of God are angelic beings.

5. VanGemeren, 'The Sons of God,' p. 347.

6. Matthews (Genesis 1–11:26, p. 327) presents the alternative view that 1 Peter 3:19 is referring to Christ 'in spirit' who preached repentance through Noah to the human generation of the flood during the building of the ark. This human audience was alive then but now is confined to prison awaiting judgment (see also 2 Pet. 2:5). Keil and Delitzsch ('Genesis,' 1:132-35) note that Peter only speaks of sinning angels in general and that the book of Enoch, to which Jude is supposed to refer, has several different, even contradictory, accounts of the sin of angels. Thus, it is not sure that Peter and Jude are referring to the specific sin of angels intermarrying with humans.

sin is the sin of polygamy and the development of harems. The offspring of these marriages are mighty tyrants who continue the violence and tyranny of their fathers.[7] Yet there are questions that arise with this view as well. Although the term God/gods (Elohim) can refer to rulers or judges (Ps. 82:1; Exod 22:8-9), and the phrase 'the sons of God' can refer to individual kings, the term 'sons' is not ever used for a group of kings. Plus, the larger context of Genesis does not speak of kingship, and the phrase 'any they chose' (v. 2) does not explicitly speak of choosing many wives.[8]

The third view argues that the sons of God represent the godly line of Seth who married women from the ungodly line of the Cainites. Therefore, the phrase 'any they chose' refers to a lack of discrimination by the sons of God when choosing appropriate marriage partners. The sin relates to the unholy marriages that led to the blurring of the godly and ungodly lines.[9] This view fits the context of Genesis where previously there has been a clear separation of the godly and ungodly lines.[10] One might question whether such marriages would be enough to bring about the wickedness described in Genesis 6, but intermarriage with unbelievers has a tremendous effect on the ability to raise godly offspring, which impacts the next generation. The result can lead to a decrease in godly influence and thus an increase in corruption and violence. Intermarriage with unbelievers is a serious problem that Israel faced as they went into the land of Canaan (Deut. 7:3-4) and as they returned to the land from the exile in Babylon (Ezra 9:1-6; Neh. 13:23-27).

The children born to these marriages are called 'mighty men' and 'men of renown' (literally 'men of the name', 6:4). In light of the description of wickedness that follows, these men are best described as warriors who were known for their violence and who sought to develop a reputation, or a name

---

7. Meredith Kline, 'Divine Kingship and Genesis 6:1-4,' *WTJ* 24 (1962), pp. 187-204.

8. Matthews, *Genesis 1–11:26*, p. 329.

9. John Murray, 'The Sons of God and the Daughters of Men,' in *Principles of Conduct* (Grand Rapids: Eerdmans, 1957), pp. 243-249.

10. Matthews (*Genesis 1–11:26*, p. 330) points out that the phrase 'daughters of men' in Genesis 6:2 should not be limited to Cainite women because 6:1 speaks of procreation among people in general, but the phrase 'daughters of men' does include Cainite women.

for themselves, by their wicked exploits.[11] The relationship of these warriors to the Nephilim is debated. Some argue that the Nephilim are also the offspring of the marriages,[12] but the way they are described, as being 'on the earth in those days, and also afterward' (6:4), leads to the conclusion that they were contemporaries of the mighty warriors and thus were already on the scene. The mention of the Nephilim adds to the atmosphere of violence described in the chapter as they too were known for their fierceness.

The other major question in Genesis 6:1-4 is the meaning of verse 3 where the debate centers on several issues of interpretation. Does the word 'spirit' (*rûaḥ*) refer to God's Spirit in terms of personal presence or to the life-giving spirit or breath of Genesis 2:7? Does the verb *dôn* mean 'to contend' or 'to abide'? What does '120 years' mean? However one answers the first two questions, the meaning is very similar. If 'spirit' refers to God's Spirit who no longer contends with the human family, then His long-suffering is about to come to an end and he will no longer suspend judgment. If 'spirit' refers to the human spirit which is necessary for survival, and that spirit is no longer going to abide or remain with human beings, then their lives are going to come to an end. The reference to flesh emphasizes human frailty and could even refer to mortality.[13] In such a context, the 120 years is best understood to refer to the shortening of life rather than to the length of time God gave mankind before the coming of the flood. God's judgment will include a shortening of life spans for human beings which will become evident after the flood.

The negative results of the intermarriages and the reason for the coming judgment of the flood is made clear in Genesis 6:5 where the nature of the wickedness that permeates the earth is described. The wickedness is very intense ('great on the earth'). It is inward; it flows from the heart ('thoughts of the heart'). It is also pervasive ('only') and constant ('continually'). God's response to this wickedness is given in verses 6 and 7. The effect of the wickedness on God Himself is stated in two

---

11. Matthews, *Genesis 1–11:26*, pp. 338-39.
12. Cassuto, *Genesis Part 1*, p. 298; Waltke, *Genesis*, p. 118; and Westermann, *Genesis 1–11*, p. 378.
13. Matthews, *Genesis 1–11:26*, pp. 332, 334.

ways. First, 'it grieved him to his heart'. The wickedness of humanity brings distress and pain to Yahweh (the Lord). He is not pleased with human wickedness and the consequences of such wickedness on His good creation. And then twice it states that God was 'sorry that he had made man on the earth'. The word translated 'sorry' is *nāḥam*, which has a variety of meanings depending on the context in which it is used. It is used twice in 1 Samuel 15 with different meanings. Early in the chapter it is used in a way that is similar to Genesis 6 where God tells Samuel that he regrets (*nāḥam*) that he has made Saul king (1 Sam. 15:11). Then, later in the chapter (1 Sam. 15:29) Samuel states that God is not like man that he should have 'regret', perhaps better translated 'relent', because the context stresses that the kingdom is going to be taken away from Saul. God does not lie (1 Sam 15:29) and the decision to take the kingdom from Saul will not be changed. So there are some situations where God does not relent from a decision, but there may be other situations where God does decide to change direction based on the response of human beings. The former situations are in line with God's sovereign decree and the latter situations describe how a sovereign God, who transcends time, interacts meaningfully within time with His creatures.[14] Both in Genesis 6 and in 1 Samuel 15 the word *nāḥam* is used when God is ready to make a momentous decision that will change things, either for His creation in Genesis 6 or for God's people in 1 Samuel 15. The momentous change in Genesis 6 is stated in the second response of God to man's wickedness where He declares that He will blot out human beings along with animals, creeping things, and birds (Gen. 6:7). The way in which God is going to accomplish this will become clear in the next section, which tells of the flood. Although things look bleak for the future of God's creation, there is hope stated in relationship to Noah, who 'found favor in the eyes of the Lord' (v. 8). Noah is not like the rest of mankind. Noah and his family are the instruments that God will use to save both humans and animals from complete destruction.

---

14. See the excellent discussion of God's relationship to time in John Frame, *No Other God: A Response to Open Theism* (Phillipsburg, NJ: P & R, 2000).

STUDY QUESTIONS

1   What evidence is there in the genealogy of Genesis 5 that death will not have the final word? What hope does that give to people today?

2   Describe sin and its consequences in Genesis 6:1-8. What evidence is there in today's culture of the same pervasive nature of sin and its consequences?

3   What does it mean in Genesis 6 when the author says that God 'was sorry' (*nāḥam*) that he had made man? How does the use of this word in 1 Samuel 15 help clarify the meaning in Genesis 6?

5

The Judgment of the Flood and the Salvation of a Remnant
(Genesis 6b–9)

The Account (Toledot) of Noah (6:9–9:29) is the story of the flood, which reveals that although God judged the world because of sin He also delivered a remnant through Noah and his family in order to give mankind a new start. The judgment of God destroyed the seed of the serpent (the ungodly line) but the righteous seed of the woman was spared.[1] The story of the flood and its aftermath covers several chapters, which can generally be divided into Preparations for the Flood (6:9-22), the Preservation of Noah's Family through the Flood (7:1–8:19), God's Covenant with Noah (8:20–9:17), and the Continuing Problem of Sin after the Flood (9:18-29).

Preparations for the Flood (Gen. 6:9-22)
The beginning of the account of the flood, like each toledot section, restates important information from the previous account to help move the story forward. Noah himself is described in verse 9 as 'a righteous man, blameless in his generation'. His conduct demonstrates a practical righteousness which can be characterized as 'blameless'. The word 'blameless' (*tām*) refers to what is complete and whole. This description of Noah does not suggest that he is sinless; rather it indicates that his life

---

1. Waltke, *Genesis*, p. 121.

reflects a wholeness of character in which what he professes to believe is actually how he lives his life. He is not a hypocrite. The reason that Noah is able to live such a life is that he 'walked with God'. This phrase describes a close relationship with God and was also used of Enoch, who escaped death itself (Gen. 5:24). Noah is clearly part of the lineage of Seth by both physical descent and moral conduct.[2] The contrast between Noah's life and those of his generation is brought out in verses 11-12 where the term 'corrupt' is used three times to describe 'the earth' and 'all flesh'. The earth is also described as 'filled with violence' and the perversion of all flesh is described as 'their way was corrupted'. These expressions reinforce the descriptions of violence in 6:5-7 and the use of 'way' emphasizes that the corruption is so extensive it entails the regular conduct, or way of life, of all flesh.

Part of God's response reiterates Genesis 6:7 where he confirms to Noah His plan to destroy all flesh because they have filled the earth with violence. This also means that the earth itself will be destroyed (6:12-13). The way God is going to carry out this destruction is through 'a flood of waters upon the earth to destroy all flesh in which is the breath of life under heaven' (v. 17). Everything on the earth will perish. However, Noah and his family, which includes Noah's sons and their wives, will be delivered, along with a representative group from the animals, two of every kind of animal, male and female. God also tells Noah how he will be delivered from the flood by instructing him to build an ark. The ark described in the Genesis account has been called a 'seaworthy' vessel, especially as compared to the ark in the Babylonian account of the flood where it is a perfect cube of 120 cubits in dimension; the cubical construction would cause it to sink.[3] The ark in Genesis can be described as a large floating barge that is approximately 450 feet long, 75 feet wide, and 45 feet high (6:14-15), sealed watertight inside and out with pitch.[4] Noah lives up to his character in being obedient to

---

2. Matthews, *Genesis 1–11:26*, p. 358.

3. Matthews, *Genesis 1–11:26*, p. 363.

4. Matthews, *Genesis 1–11:26*, p. 364. He describes the measurement of a cubit as from the length of the elbow to the tip of the fingers. He also shows how to convert a cubit into a modern measurement (halving the number of cubits and multiplying by three to get the number of feet).

all that God had commanded him to do in preparing for the flood (6:22). Although the text is silent concerning Noah's interaction with the ungodly world of his day, 2 Peter 2:5 can call Noah a 'herald of righteousness' because his righteous and blameless life and his obedience to God in building the ark would speak to his generation concerning the importance of righteousness. Just as the judgment of God fell suddenly and unexpectedly on the world of that day, so we should be ready for the coming day of the Lord which will come in the same way (2 Pet. 3:1-13).

Preservation of Noah's Family through the Flood (Gen. 7:1–8:19)
The first part of chapter 7 emphasizes that Noah's righteousness was demonstrated in his obedience to all that God had commanded him to do. He was obedient in making all the preparations for the flood (6:22), so that when the flood came Noah was ready for the destruction that was unleashed on the earth. There is a clear reversal of Genesis 1 in the flood. In Genesis 1, God takes what is formless and void (uninhabitable) and makes it into a cosmos, but in the flood God destroys the cosmos so that it reverts to the chaotic condition of being uninhabitable for humans and animals. Thus it is not surprising to see allusions to Genesis 1 in these chapters of Genesis. It is stated in 6:5 that the LORD saw the wickedness, which alludes to the earlier statement that the Lord saw that the creation was good (1:10; 1:31). Also, the Spirit appears in 6:3, not in a positive, supervisory role, but in a context that mentions the judgment of shorter life spans.

The violent nature of the total destruction of life on earth is emphasized in the flood account. Several times God declares that every living thing outside the ark will be destroyed (7:4, 21-23). The way the flood is unleashed upon the earth also emphasizes complete destruction, not only because everything is covered with water, including the mountains (7:19), but also because powerful forces are brought to bear on the earth. The fountains of the great deep are mentioned in 7:11, which refer to subterranean waters[5] that 'burst forth', a verb which refers to the violent splitting apart of something (Exod. 14:16, 21;

---

5. Matthews, *Genesis 1–11:26*, p. 376.

Ps. 78:13; Isa. 63:12). This would have produced tremendous changes for the earth's surface, especially if earthquakes and tsunamis were the result of the unleashing of this great power from the great deep. The windows of heaven are also opened up and rain falls upon the earth. The result is the death of those outside the ark who have the breath of life (7:22). The way the flood is described gives the impression of a global catastrophe. Several times it is stated that 'all flesh' (6:13, 17; 7:21), or 'every living thing I have made' (7:4, literally, 'all existence'; 7:22-23) will be destroyed in the flood, including the birds. It also states that 'all the fountains of the great deep burst forth' (7:11) and that 'all the high mountains under the whole heaven were covered' (7:19-20).[6] The length of the flood also emphasizes total destruction – it lasted almost a year. It started on the seventeenth day of the second month when Noah was 600 years old (7:11) and the waters were dried up on the first day of the first month when Noah was 601 years old (8:13).

The preservation of human and animal life through the flood also alludes to Genesis 1. Noah is to bring two of every kind of birds, animals, and creeping things of the ground (6:20; 7:14), which is a reminder of Genesis 1:21, 24-25. They are to be male and female (7:16; 8:17), so that after the flood they can multiply on the earth in fulfillment of the original creation mandate. God also uses a wind (*rûaḥ*), perhaps an allusion to Genesis 1:2, to cause the waters to recede from the earth in order for the dry land to appear again (Gen. 1:9; 8:13).

Although the obedience of Noah is important in the flood account, the salvation of Noah, his family, and the animals comes from God, who 'remembered Noah' and those with him in the ark (8:1). Not only did God protect Noah by shutting him in the ark (7:16), God also remembered Noah by causing the flood waters to recede. God was faithful to His promise to preserve Noah and those with him from destruction. Peter uses the flood account as a type of baptism. Just as Noah and his family passed through death into salvation by being brought

---

6. For arguments in favor of a universal flood, see John Whitcomb and Henry Morris, *The Genesis Flood* (Phillipsburg, NJ: P & R Publishing, 1961) and William D. Barrick, 'Noah's Flood and its Geological Implications,' in *Coming to Grips with Genesis*, eds. Terry Mortenson and Thane Ury (Green Forest, AR: Master Books, 2008), pp. 251-82. For arguments for a limited flood, see Davis A. Young, *The Biblical Flood* (Grand Rapids: Eerdmans, 1995).

safely through water, so the Christian passes through death into salvation represented by the waters of baptism, which is not just an external cleansing but is an internal transformation which affects the conscience (1 Pet. 3:20-21).

God's Covenant with Noah (Gen. 8:20–9:17)

When Noah comes out of the ark he worships Yahweh by building an altar and offering as sacrifices some of the clean animals he had taken with him on the ark. Noah's worship is a 'pleasing aroma' to God, which means that his worship is acceptable to the Lord. God responds by making a promise never again to destroy the world and 'every living creature' as He did with the flood, so that the regular seasons would continue as long as the earth remains (8:20-22).

God ensures the fulfillment of these promises by entering into a covenant with Noah, his offspring, and with all the living creatures. The particular type of covenant that God establishes with Noah is called a royal grant covenant where a superior grants to a servant certain benefits and secures those benefits with an oath.[7] The master usually grants such a covenant to a servant who has demonstrated faithfulness and loyalty to him; the master takes the oath and guarantees that the benefits of the covenant will be given. In His covenant with Noah, God as the superior party promises to Noah certain benefits on the basis of his loyalty to God, which was demonstrated in Noah's obedience to all that God had commanded him to do (Gen. 6:22; 7:5). God promises that He will 'never again' destroy the earth through a flood and He offers a sign that will be a reminder of His covenant promise. The sign is a rainbow, which stands as a living reminder to God and to all of creation that He has made this covenant promise. The term for 'rainbow' is *qešet*, which also refers to the bow used as a weapon. Instead of a symbol of combat it is now a symbol of peace.[8]

---

7. See M. Weinfeld, 'The Covenant of Grant in the Old Testament and in the Ancient Near East,' *JAOS* 90 (1970): 184-203. He applies the grant covenant to Abraham and David, but it also fits the arrangement of the Noahic covenant. The Mosaic covenant fits more the structure of a treaty covenant.

8. Hamilton, *Genesis 1–17*, p. 317.

In the Noahic covenant there is a commitment to creation. The world was destroyed by the flood and God makes a promise that the regular functioning of creation will continue (8:22). The covenant is thus not just made with Noah and his descendants but is also made with all living creatures, including the animals (9:10-11). God's commitment to His purposes in creation is also demonstrated in what He tells Noah at the beginning of Genesis 9. The benefits of a covenant usually center around land and offspring, and both of these are prominent in the covenant with Noah in a very broad sense. God promises never again to curse the earth, and the promises of this covenant include future generations of the descendants of Noah (9:9-12). God's commitment to creation is necessary if He is going to continue to work out His redemptive purposes for mankind. Thus in the Noahic covenant there are elements that relate to both God's common grace to humanity and to God's redemptive purposes for His people. The common grace aspects include the preservation of the created order, the institutions of the family and state, and the continuation of dominion (9:1-7). The redemptive aspects include the evidence in Noah's life of divine grace, the fact that God works through the family of Noah as the godly line, the worship of God through the offering of sacrifices, and the separation of the godly line from the ungodly line after the flood (Gen. 9:18–11:9). Thus God's covenant with Noah was a necessary step for working out God's purposes in history for the restoration of His creation. It is appropriate to view the Noahic covenant as an outworking of God's covenant of grace established in Genesis 3:15.

God's commitment to His original purposes at creation is demonstrated in the re-establishment of those purposes after the flood. Noah can be seen as a second Adam who is given the original mandate that was given to Adam but with the recognition that it must now be carried out in a fallen world. Just as God blessed mankind in Genesis 1:28, so God blesses Noah and exhorts him to be fruitful, to multiply, and to fill the earth. This assumes that the institution of marriage is still relevant (Gen. 2:24). Human dominion over God's creation is also reaffirmed but with the recognition that animals will fear human beings. This fear is a reflection of the fact that the harmonious relationships between humans and animals have been destroyed by sin, but there is also the fact that God now allows human beings to eat meat for food instead of only plants (9:3-4). The only stipulation is that the meat be drained properly of the blood because 'you shall not eat meat with its life, that is, its blood' (Gen. 9:4). This stipulation demonstrates reverence for life. Also, the lives of human beings made in the image of God are more important than animal life (Gen. 1:26-28). This makes human life so significant that the taking of a human life by one person requires that their life be taken in return, 'for God made man in his own image' (Gen. 9:6). It is appropriate to see here the foundation of government and that capital punishment is an appropriate response to murder.

The Continuing Problem of Sin after the Flood (Gen. 9:18-29)
The judgment of the flood did not eradicate sin from mankind; this even becomes evident within the family of Noah after the flood. Another division of the human race between the godly and the ungodly will be one of the results of this incident. The sons of Noah are presented again (Shem, Ham, and Japheth), with the note that Ham was the father of Canaan, a connection which will be important for the negative results of this story of sin. It is also noted that from the three sons of Noah 'the people of the whole earth were dispersed' (v. 19). The three sons of Noah are the fountain from which all the peoples of the earth originate, which becomes evident in the family of nations in Genesis 10, but it also means that the sin within Noah's immediate family is going to have ramifications for his descendants.

After the flood Noah planted a vineyard and drank from the fruit of his labor; in fact, he drank too much wine, became drunk and lay uncovered in his tent. The sin of Ham is recounted in verse 22: he 'saw the nakedness of his father and told his brothers outside'. The other two brothers take a garment and walk backwards into the tent so that they do not see 'their father's nakedness'; instead, they cover it (v. 23). The major question is what does the text mean when it says that Ham 'saw the nakedness of his father'? Some argue that this phrase refers to some kind of homosexual contact between Ham and his father Noah. In other words, Ham took advantage of his father's condition to have sex with him.[9] This view is based on the use of the word 'see' in Leviticus 20:17 where a man sees the nakedness of his sister, which seems to be more than merely seeing her nakedness because later in the verse it says he 'uncovered his sister's nakedness'. In Leviticus 20 the term 'uncover' refers to a sexual relationship. However, such terms are used of heterosexual relationships in Leviticus. Further, the use of the phrase 'see their father's nakedness' is also used of Shem and Japheth when they walk backwards into the tent so as *not* to see or observe their father's nakedness. The phrase in relationship to them does not refer to a homosexual relationship but to the physical act of seeing their father's nakedness.[10] In light of the way the phrase is used in the context of the story the best understanding is that 'to see their father's nakedness' refers to the physical act of seeing Noah uncovered and naked in the tent. The sin primarily involves the disrespect that Ham has for his father because instead of quietly taking care of the situation by covering his father he makes his condition known to his brothers.[11] It is easy today to overlook the seriousness in that culture of disrespecting the father.

Noah woke up from the effect of the wine, and verse 24 states that he 'knew what his youngest son had done to him'. The text does not specify how Noah knew what Ham had done but it is likely he came to such knowledge because it was told to him by his two other sons. Noah's response is to offer a curse and a blessing, which have implications for the future relationship among the descendants of the three brothers. The curse itself does not fall on Ham; it falls on Canaan, the descendant of Ham. The curse specifically states that 'a servant of servants shall he be to his brothers' (v. 25). Some wonder why Ham himself is not cursed, but it would

---

9. Robert Gagnon, *The Bible and Homosexual Practice* (Nashville: Abingdon, 2001), pp. 63-70, and O. Palmer Robertson, 'Current Critical Questions with the "Curse of Ham",' *JETS* 41.2 (1998): 177-88.

10. Based on the idea that the father's nakedness is really the mother's nakedness (Lev. 18:7), some have argued that Ham had sex with his mother, which is called the maternal incest view (John S. Bergsma and Scott W. Hahn, 'Noah's Nakedness and the Curse on Canaan,' *JBL* 124.1 [2005]: 25-40).

11. Matthews, *Genesis 1–11*:26, p. 420; Hamilton, *Genesis 1–17*, p. 323; and Waltke, *Genesis*, p. 149.

not be unusual for original readers to read that the actions of Ham would have consequences for his descendants. A similar thing takes place in Genesis 49 where the actions of each of the sons of Jacob have implications for their descendants. The curse on Canaan, that he is to be a servant to his brothers, shows the continuing conflict between the seed of the woman and the seed of the serpent.[12] Although some connections can be made to the fulfillment of this curse with Canaanite cities and kings in Genesis 14,[13] it is hard not to see a connection with the Israelite conquest of the land of Canaan. This was the promise given to Abraham (Gen. 15:18-21) and the charge that God gave to Moses (Deut. 7:1-2), which is carried out by Joshua.[14] The descendants of Ham become like Ham in their disobedience and become subject to Israel when Joshua leads Israel into the land.[15]

The blessing of Shem and Japheth gives priority to Shem, who will be the son through whom the godly line will lead to Abram. The God of Shem, Yahweh, is blessed and the blessing of Japheth includes God enlarging Japheth so that he will dwell in the tents of Shem. This phrase refers to a peaceful harmony that will take place between the descendants of Shem and Japheth.[16] In the table of nations that follows in Genesis 10 the descendants of Japheth are those who dwell in the areas of Anatolia and Greece. Through the line of Shem, God promises to bless all the families of the earth (Gen. 12:1-3), which Isaiah also sees taking place at a future day (Isa. 19:23-25; 66:19-20). This peaceful coexistence is fulfilled in Jesus Christ and the mission He gives to His people to go into the world with the gospel (Matt. 28:19-20). In his missionary journeys, Paul takes the gospel to the Gentiles in the area of Greece, and many of the descendants of Japheth came to dwell peacefully in the

---

12. Currid, *Genesis 1:1–25:18*, p. 224.

13. See U. Cassuto, *A Commentary on the Book of Genesis: Part 2 From Noah to Abraham* (Jerusalem: Magnes Press, 1992), p. 168.

14. Matthews, *Genesis 1–11:26*, p. 423.

15. This text should not be used to argue that there is a curse on black people, which was a view previously used to support slavery (see L. Richard Bradley, 'The Curse of Canaan and the American Negro,' *CTM* 42/2 [1971]: 100-10 for how Genesis 9:25-27 has been used to support slavery).

16. Kaiser argues for a Messianic meaning of Genesis 9:27, which understands the verse to say that *God* will dwell in the tents of Shem instead of the view that Japheth will dwell in the tents of Shem (see *Messiah in the Old Testament*, pp. 44-45).

tents of Shem when they were united to Christ in His body, the church (Eph. 2:11-22). Gentiles become sons of Abraham through faith in Jesus Christ (Gal. 3:29).

Study Questions

1 How does the 'seed' theme continue in the account of the flood and its aftermath? What can the flood teach the church about judgment and blessing?

2 Why is God's covenant with Noah important? What does God promise in this covenant? How are the common grace elements and the redemptive elements of the covenant still relevant to people today?

3 What relevance does the curse upon Ham have for today? What hope does the blessing of Shem give to people today?

6

The Division of the Nations: Continuing Sin and the Line of Salvation
(Genesis 10–11)

The next section of Genesis, 'The Generations (Toledot) of Shem, Ham, and Japheth' (Gen. 10:1–11:9), gives an account of how the world was populated after the flood. Genesis 10 is a genealogy of the sons of Noah that describes the development and the dispersion of the nations on the earth after the flood (Gen. 10:32). All of the nations have their origin in the sons of Noah. The genealogy of Genesis 10 lays out the setting for the nations that Israel will interact with later in her history. These nations will ultimately be recipients of God's blessing through the nation of Israel. This section ends with an account of the Tower of Babel which demonstrates that humanity after the flood has not changed from humanity before the flood. Sin is still a problem which shows the need for God to make a new start with the family of Abram in order to accomplish His purposes for the restoration of creation (11:10-26).

The Genealogy of Shem, Ham, and Japheth (Gen. 10:1-32)
The purpose of Genesis 10 is stated in verse 32: '... from these the nations spread abroad on the earth after the flood.' The order in which the descendants of the three sons of Noah are given is significant. The order is Japheth, Ham, and

Shem. This order leaves the account of the promised line of Shem to the end so that it can be further developed in later chapters; it also starts with the nations farthest away from the land where the promised line of Shem will one day dwell. The genealogy of Genesis 10 is not a linear genealogy like Genesis 5, which covers a long period of time by lining up the descendants; rather, it is a segmented genealogy which shows the relationships among those listed in the genealogy (like a family tree). It is also significant that names are used in a variety of ways in Genesis 10. Some names are of persons (Japheth, Nimrod), some names are of people groups (Ludites, Caphtorites), and some names are of place names (Mizraim, Sidon). Thus the sons of Noah are divided by ethnicity, geography, and language.[1] The fact that there are seventy nations in the genealogy shows that the table of nations is representative of the totality of all peoples.[2]

Japheth's descendants spread to the more distant lands in relationship to the land of Canaan (10:2-5). The first tier of Japheth's descendants includes Gomer, Magog, Madai, Javan, Tubal, Meshech, and Tiras. Gomer may represent the Cimmerians who originally inhabited the area north of the Black Sea. Madai may refer to the Medes who inhabited the region northeast of the Tigris River. Javan refers to people who settled in southern Greece and western Asia Minor. Tubal and Meshech are also associated with Asia Minor. Magog may refer to regions far to the north, and in the book of Ezekiel Magog, along with Gog, represent fierce nations that gather together against God's people near the end of history. The sons of Gomer (Ashkenaz, Riphath, and Togarmah) may also represent nations to the far north, with Ashkenaz being identified with the Scythians. The sons of Javan represent Mediterranean peoples, with Kittim associated with Cyprus and Tarshish probably connected to southwest Spain.[3]

The descendants of Ham (10:6-20) are people who will interact more closely with the nation of Israel, either as influential neighbors or bitter enemies. The first tier of Ham's descendants includes Cush, Egypt, Put, and Canaan. Cush is

---

1. Waltke, *Genesis*, p. 165.
2. Matthews, *Genesis 1–11:26*, p. 437.
3. Matthews, *Genesis 1–11:26*, pp. 440-41.

identified as Africa's Nubia, which originally referred to the
region between the second and third cataracts of the Nile. The
location of the sons of Cush (v. 7) is associated with African
and Arabian locations. Nimrod is given several verses of
explanation (vv. 8-12) because he is the founder of several
important cities that impacted the history of Israel (Babylon
and Nineveh). He is also described as a 'mighty hunter before
the LORD' which became a proverb in Israel, 'Like Nimrod
a mighty hunter before the LORD.' It is hard to know how
to take the phrase 'before the LORD'. It could be understood
as expressing God's favor, or as expressing Nimrod's sinful
rebellion, or as a neutral expression merely noting that
Nimrod's activities especially stood out. The fact that he is
associated with the founding of Babel leads to a negative
understanding of Nimrod's exploits.[4] Thus it is possible that
Nimrod is highlighted because he founded cities by aggressive
force, which is different from the gradual dispersion of the
peoples in the rest of the account of the nations.[5]

The descendants of Egypt (Mizraim) are people groups,
many of whom are connected to the region of Egypt, but the
Caphtorites are associated with the island of Crete, which
had a long association with Egypt (Amos 9:7; Jer. 47:4). The
Philistines are specifically said to come from Casluhim.[6] Put
may be a reference to the Lybians, but there is no further
tracing of his descendants.[7]

The descendants of Canaan (10:15-20) occupy a major role
in the genealogy of Ham as eleven groups are descended
from Canaan. Sidon refers to the important city of Phoenicia.
Heth refers to the Hittites associated with the inhabitants of
Canaan who were in the land of Canaan before the patriarchs
(Gen. 15:20). Then there follows a list of peoples within the
land of Canaan. Some, like the Jebusites and the Amorites, will
be significant for Israel's conquest of the land. The description
of Canaan's territory also demonstrates the importance of the

4. Matthews (*Genesis 1–11:26*, p. 450) shows the lexical connections between
the Tower of Babel episode and the Nimrod narrative.
5. Matthews, *Genesis 1–11:26*, p. 448 and Waltke, *Genesis*, p. 169.
6. For a discussion of the problems of the relationship between the Philistines
and the Casluhites and the Caphtorites see Matthews, *Genesis 1–11:26*, pp. 452-54.
7. Matthews, *Genesis 1–11:26*, pp. 445, 455.

land of Canaan, with an emphasis on areas to the south that become significant for Abraham's travels in the land (v. 19).[8]

The genealogy of Shem (10:21-31) mentions Eber before the descendants are given because with Eber an important division takes place between the line of Joktan and the line of Peleg. The line of Joktan is given first because it is the non-elect line. The line of Peleg is picked up after the Tower of Babel to trace the descendants of Peleg to Abram. The descendants of Shem are part of the dispersion of the nations, but the line of Peleg will also be instrumental in bringing the blessing of God to the nations.[9]

The first tier of the sons of Shem (v. 21) includes Elam, Asshur, Arpachsad, Lud, and Aram. Although the locations of Arpachsad and Lud are not known for sure, Elam is located in the mountainous region east of the Tigris-Euphrates Valley, Asshur is located on the upper Tigris River in northern Mesopotamia (Assyria), and Aram includes the area of Syria. Only descendants of Aram (v. 23) and Arpachsad (v. 24) are given: Aram, because of its important connections with Israel, and Arpachsad, because of the importance of Eber. With Eber there is a division between Joktan and Peleg (v. 25).

The name Peleg means division and there is a wordplay between Peleg and the comment 'for in his days the earth was divided' (*plg*). This wordplay ties Peleg to a specific event known to the original readers but lost for us today, so that the meaning of 'the earth was divided' is not certain.[10] It could refer to irrigation canals dug at that time to water the earth (as the term is used in Psalm 1:3), or it could refer to the division just noted in the text in the line of Shem between Joktan and Peleg, or it could refer to the division that takes place in reference to the Tower of Babel episode where there is a scattering of the people; however, the term 'scattering' is not the same as the term 'division'. The context favors a connection to the Tower of Babel account which establishes the fact that the line of Shem is a part of the dispersion of the nations.[11] The line of Shem is still among the nations and has not yet been called

8. Matthews, *Genesis 1–11:26*, p. 458.
9. Matthews, *Genesis 1–11:26*, p. 439.
10. Matthews, *Genesis 1–11:26*, p. 463.
11. This view is favored by Waltke and Matthews.

out in a distinct way from the nations, which will occur after the Tower of Babel incident.

The Tower of Babel (Gen. 11:1-9)

The Tower of Babel demonstrates not only the problem of sin after the flood but also the powerful effect of what sin might accomplish if people come together in defiance against God to do what they want to do, instead of what God wants them to do. God's command had been to be fruitful, multiply, and fill the earth, but the people in Genesis 11 sought to come together to make a name for themselves so they would not be dispersed over the face of the earth. They attempted to build a city with a tower, 'with its top in the heavens' (v. 4). It is possible that the tower was an early ziggurat, a massive and lofty, solid brick staircase structure that served as a stairway to reach the gods. The staircase was painted blue at the top to blend in with the celestial home of the gods in the sky and it also had a shrine for the gods. Such a tower represented the place where the gods interacted with human beings, which is what the phrase 'with its top in the heavens' means. The emphasis should not be so much on the height of the tower, as if it is as tall as a skyscraper, but on what the tower represents. Others argue that the ziggurat did not develop until much later in history and that this tower may have been a fortified tower or fortress that could be used for defensive purposes in protecting a city.[12] Even if that is the case, the tower is still presented in the text as a way for the people to try to reach the sphere of the gods. Here we see the ungodly line of Cain transgressing the boundaries God set for humanity by disobeying the command to fill the earth and by seeking to reach the place of the gods in order to make a name for themselves.[13]

Although from a human standpoint the efforts at the Tower of Babel seem impressive, and even God acknowledges the ingenuity of human beings and the possibilities of the

---

12. Alfred J. Hoerth, *Archaeology and the Old Testament* (Grand Rapids: Baker, 1998), p. 197.

13. See Waltke, *Genesis*, p. 177, for a comparison between the line of Cain and the builders of the Tower of Babel to show that the builders of the tower are the spiritual heirs of the line of Cain.

power of human sin (v. 6), yet the futility of their actions is emphasized. God has to come down to see the tower, so that the tower is not really effective in trying to reach the dwelling place of the true God.

God easily disperses this gathering of human beings by 'confusing' their languages, so that they are not able to communicate with each other. The name of the city was called Babel, which some connect to the Hebrew verb which means 'confuse' (*bālal*), but there also may be a parody on the Akkadian name 'babilu' which means 'gate of the gods'. It also may be significant that in the Babylonian creation myth Babylon is founded at the time of creation, but in Genesis the area of Babylon is not prominent. Rather, it is associated with rebellion against God. The result of the confusion of their languages is that the people are dispersed throughout the world (v. 9).

There is an interesting relationship between the Table of Nations in Genesis 10 and the Tower of Babel account in Genesis 11:1-9. Part of the purpose of the Tower episode is to show how the earth went from speaking one language (11:1) to speaking different languages (11:9). However, already in Genesis 10 there is recognition that these nations 'each had their own language' (10:5, 20, 31). Thus, the Tower episode actually happened before the results of what Genesis 10 describes. This raises the question of the purpose of the order of these accounts. The dispersing of the nations after the flood can be seen from two perspectives. In Genesis 11 the nations are dispersed as a result of God's judgment (11:8), and if that account had come first the emphasis would have been on the theme of judgment. In Genesis 10 the dispersing of the nations can be read as a blessing in fulfillment of the divine command of Genesis 9:1. It is also not unusual for Hebrew narrative to move from the broader perspective to a narrower one, as in Genesis 1–2. And finally, ending this narrative account with the judgment of God highlights the need for God to act in a specific way to fulfill His promise to restore creation. Through the line of Abram someone will come to reverse the confusion of languages and bring healing to the nations. This is initially fulfilled at Pentecost with the outpouring of the Holy Spirit so that people with different languages understand each other

(Acts 2). It is finally fulfilled when peoples from every nation and language will gather around the throne to praise God and the Lamb (Rev. 4:9-11).

The Generations (Toledot) of Shem (Gen. 11:10-26): The Chosen Line of Peleg

Genesis 11:10 begins a major section of Genesis that covers Patriarchal History (11:10–37:1). The term 'patriarch' refers to Abram and his descendants, Isaac and Jacob, who laid the foundation for the nation of Israel through the twelve sons of Jacob. In Genesis 10:25 there are two sons born to Eber. The son, Joktan, and his descendants are given in 10:26-31, which is followed by the Tower of Babel narrative (11:1-9). The second son, Peleg, and his descendants are listed after the account of the Tower of Babel. The line of Peleg leads to Terah, who is the father of Abram, the one through whom God chooses to bring His blessing to the nations. In response to the wickedness of humanity, God chooses an individual and his family as the instrument of blessing for God's plan to restore human beings and creation. Abram and his family are the ancestors of the nation of Israel, God's chosen people.

Joktan was the father of Arabian tribes and Peleg's descendants end up in northwest Mesopotamia.[14] Some of the names, such as Reu, cannot be identified with a specific geographical location, but others, such as Serug and Nahor, are associated with Mesopotamian cities.[15] Terah, who was from the Ur of the Chaldeans (Gen. 11:31), is the important link in the line of Shem that leads to Abram. This short genealogy forms an important transition from the Primeval History of Genesis 1–11 to the Patriarchal History that begins in Genesis 11:10.

One of the purposes of this genealogy is to show that God's purposes cannot be hindered by the sinfulness of humanity or by the scattering of the nations at Babel. God preserves His promised seed.[16] The structured genealogy also establishes a sense of order after the confusion of the Babel incident.[17] The

---

14. Matthews, *Genesis 1–11:26*, p. 497.
15. Matthews, *Genesis 1–11:26*, p. 498.
16. Sailhamer, *The Pentateuch as Narrative*, p. 136.
17. Waltke, *Genesis*, p. 185.

structure of the genealogy in 11:10-26 parallels the genealogy of Genesis 5. There is a sense of stability and permanence because it shows coherence with the promised line that comes from Adam.[18] The blessing of procreation is emphasized with the repeated phrase 'had other sons and daughters', which is also found in Genesis 5. The emphasis of fruitfulness over death is stressed by the omission of the phrase 'and he died', unlike Genesis 5. Although death still exists, the line of Shem through Abram gives the hope of blessing that will one day overcome the power and curse of sin and death.

STUDY QUESTIONS

1   What is the purpose of the genealogy of Genesis 10? How does it relate to the history of Israel?

2   What does the Tower of Babel teach about the capability of human beings and the spiritual condition of human beings?

3   What clues does Genesis 11 give to provide hope in the midst of the judgment of God and the scattering of the peoples? How does the gospel reverse the scattering that takes place in connection with the Tower of Babel?

---

18. Matthews, *Genesis 1–11:26*, p. 487.

7

The Life of Abraham: God's Call and the Promise of Land

(Genesis 11:27–14:24)

The Account (Toledot) of Terah (11:27–25:11) is actually the story of the life of Abraham. This narrative can be divided into the following sections: The Call of Abram (11:27–12:9), Faith in God's Promise of the Land (12:10–14:24), God's covenant with Abram (15:1-21), Faith in God's Promise of the Seed (16:1–22:24), Receiving a Portion of the Inheritance (23:1-20), and Passing on the Covenant Promises (24:1–25:11). The first two sections will be covered in this chapter. The response of Abram to God's promises will be significant in the development of the story of Abram.

The Call of Abram (Gen. 11:27–12:9)

The call of Abram can be divided into the historical background of the call (11:27-32), the promises of God's call (12:1-3), and Abram's obedience to the call (12:4-9). Genesis 11:27-32 gives the historical background to Abram's call by describing the family of Abram and the geographical location of Abram's family. Terah fathered Abram, Nahor, and Haran. Haran is important because he fathered Lot, who goes to the land of Canaan with Abram and is involved in key events of Abram's life. Haran died in Mesopotamia. Abram and Nahor took wives for themselves: Nahor married Milcah – her family connections are given here because her granddaughter Rebekah, born to Milcah's son Bethuel, will later marry Isaac (Genesis 24); the one detail mentioned concerning Abram's wife Sarai is that she was barren (v 30), and her barrenness will become an important part of the story of Abram and the divine promise to him of a seed.

The geographical background to the family of Abram is Mesopotamia; they originated in the Ur of the Chaldeans. Later it will be stated that the family background of Abram was pagan because they worshipped the gods of Mesopotamia (Josh. 24:2). However, Terah initiated a move from Ur to the land of Canaan and took along Abram, Sarai, and Lot. They did not make it to Canaan but settled in Haran. The death of Terah is then given (v. 32). So at the end of Genesis 11 Abram is still living in Mesopotamia without any indication that he plans to keep moving toward the land of Canaan. In fact, the phrase 'they settled there' casts a negative light on the stay in Haran as it is the exact same phrase that is used in 11:2 of the decision of the residents of Shinar to disobey God's mandate to fill the earth.

The call itself and the promises of God in relation to the call are given in Genesis 12:1-3. With Terah dead, God told Abram to leave his country, his family, and the security of his 'father's house', the smallest family unit and the most important to the identity of the individual,[1] for a land that he had not yet seen. God also promised to bless Abram in a number of ways. Not only did God promise to give him a land, but he promised to make him into a great nation. For a nation to come from Abram he will need to produce at least one descendant. These two promises of a land and a seed will dominate the narrative account of Abram. God also promises to make the name of Abram great. This is in direct contrast to the Tower of Babel episode where people try to make a name for themselves (Gen. 11:4). Human attempts to become great will fail but God will make Abram's name great.

There is also an emphasis in 12:1-3 on the word 'blessing', which occurs five times in three verses. This matches the five times that the word 'curse' (*'ārar*) occurs in Genesis 1–11

---

1. Matthews, *Genesis 11:27–50:26*, p. 111.

(Gen. 3:14, 17; 4:11; 5:29; 9:25). God will use the blessing of Abram to counter the curse of sin which was prominent in the first eleven chapters of Genesis. God promises not only to bless Abram but also to bless all those who are a blessing to him, and also to curse ('*ārar*) anyone who seeks to dishonor or harm him. God's curse acts as a protection for Abram against any that would try to harm him. Thus God will protect Sarah even in spite of his deceit in Genesis 12:10-20 and 20:1-18 because the seed is in jeopardy. A long time later, God will bless the descendants of Abram in the land of Egypt with fruitfulness and will bring plagues on the Egyptians for their harsh treatment of Israel in order to deliver them. Laban will recognize that God has blessed him because of Jacob (Gen. 30:27) and God also will bless Potiphar because of Joseph (Gen. 39:5). The blessing of God will come to all the families of the earth through Abram.

Not everyone understands the sense of Genesis 12:3 as affirming that Abram is the instrument of blessing for the nations. Some argue that the meaning of 12:3 is that Abram is the model of blessing for the nations, indicating that others will bless themselves by Abram in the sense that they will appeal to the blessing Abram has received as an example of the way they can also be blessed. In this view, Abram becomes a type of the man who is blessed, with others seeking to be blessed similar to how he was blessed.[2] However, this view secularizes the promise and robs it of its predictive significance by denying that Abram is an instrument of blessing to the nations.[3] We should note that Peter cites Genesis 12:3 in Acts 3:25 in his reminder to Jewish people that they are first in line to receive this blessing of Abraham that flows from the work of Jesus Christ, the seed of Abraham. Paul quotes Genesis 12:3 to demonstrate that the blessing of Abraham

---

2. J. Skinner, *A Critical and Exegetical Commentary on Genesis* (2nd ed.; Edinburgh: T & T Clark, 1910) and Westermann, *Genesis 12–36*, pp. 151-52. This view is partly based on the fact that the word 'bless' is used in both the *Nifal* (Gen. 12:3) and the *Hitpael* (Gen. 22:18). The *Nifal* is typically passive and the *Hitpael* is typically reflexive. This view emphasizes the reflexive meaning of the *Hitpael*. However, O. T. Allis ('The Blessing of Abraham,' *PTR* 25 [1927], 263-298) shows that the *Hitpael* is also used with a passive meaning.

3. Allis, 'The Blessing of Abraham,' pp. 266-68; see also Matthews, *Genesis 11:27–50:26*, p. 117, and Hamilton, *Genesis 1–17*, pp. 374-75.

has come to Gentiles through faith. In fact, those who have faith are the sons of Abraham, are justified like Abraham, and have been blessed along with Abraham, the man of faith (Gal. 3:6-9). In this way the blessing of Abraham has come to the nations through Jesus Christ and is available to all who believe in Jesus.

The obedience of Abram to God's call is narrated in Genesis 12:4-9. The focus in these verses is on Abram's journey to the land that God had promised him. In fact, Genesis 12–15 emphasizes the promise of the land, which is seen not only in the content of these chapters but also in the fact that the idea of the land frames these chapters. In Genesis 12:1 God tells Abram to go to the land that 'I will show you'; and in Genesis 15:18 God tells Abram that 'to your descendants I will give this land'. The first step of obedience is for Abram to leave Haran and to go to the land of Canaan (12:4-5). Abram is seventy-five years old when he obeys God's call. He takes his wife, his brother's son Lot, all their possessions, and all the people they have acquired and they journey to Canaan.

When they arrive at Shechem, an important place later in Israel's history, God reaffirms the promise of giving the land to Abram's offspring. There is also the comment that the Canaanites were in the land, which means that Abram must receive the promise of the land by faith. He demonstrated his faith in the promise of God by building an altar to Yahweh (the LORD). Then he continued traveling south through the land, building altars, until he came to the dry, southern part of the land called the Negeb. The altars not only demonstrate his belief in the promise of God to give this land to his descendants; the altars are also a way for Abram to lay claim to the land as belonging to God even although Abram himself is only a sojourner in the land. Hebrews 11 reminds us that it was by faith that Abram obeyed God's call to leave his homeland and to come to the land God had promised to give to his descendants as his inheritance. More is at stake than just an earthly piece of property; Abram realized that the earthly inheritance was not his final destination, rather his sojourn would end in a glorious city built by God (Heb. 11:10). Instead of an alien living in tents, Abram would one day be a permanent resident in the city built by God. Only by faith can we see beyond the partial fulfillment of the promises of God in our lives to our final destiny in the new heavens and the new earth which God has planned for His people.

Faith in God's Promise of Land (Gen. 12:10–14:24)
God made certain promises to Abram in Genesis 12:1-3 and two of those promises become particularly significant to him because the fulfillment of those promises impacted his life. The promise of land is the focus of Genesis 12–14 and the promise of seed is the focus of Genesis 16–22, with the covenant God made with Abram in Genesis 15 emphasizing both promises. The challenge for Abram was how he was going to respond to God's promises when there was a delay in the fulfillment of the promise, as there was with the land, or when it did not seem possible for the promise to be fulfilled, as was the case with the promise of the seed. Abram's response to the promises of God was significant not only for his own life but also for his descendants.

Fearful in Egypt (Gen. 12:10-20)
Abram's faithful response of obedience in coming to the land and claiming the land according to God's promises is followed by an event in his life that raises questions concerning his actions. A severe famine that took place in the land of Canaan prompted Abram to go down to Egypt. So he left the land of promise and went to a foreign country. It is interesting that in Genesis 12:1 there is a clear command by God to go to the land of Canaan; yet in 12:10 there is no divine command or divine initiative telling Abram to leave the promised land. Further, Abram reacted in a way that demonstrated fear rather than faith. He was afraid that the Egyptians would see that Sarai was beautiful and then they would try to take her by killing him. So he instructed Sarai to say that she was his sister, which was a half-truth because they had the same father. Nevertheless, this was a lie because it communicated to the Egyptians that Abram and Sarai were not married. Abram here was not living by faith in the promise of Genesis 12:3 that God would bless those who bless him but curse the one who dishonors him. The lie had the intended effect of saving his life, but Sarai is taken into Pharaoh's house as his wife

(12:15, 19). Abram himself benefitted from this arrangement because Pharaoh treated him very well by increasing his riches (12:16).

Although Abram's plan seems to have worked, there was trouble brewing. For one thing, the future seed was in jeopardy because Sarai had been taken into Pharaoh's house. Also, God afflicted Pharaoh and his house 'with great plagues because of Sarai'. Abram was not acting as an instrument of blessing to the nations; instead he was the cause of their affliction. The text does not tell us how Pharaoh found out that Sarai was Abram's wife, but when he did find out he rebuked him, gave Sarai back to him, and sent him away with 'all that he had' (12:20). This episode shows that God was faithful to His promises to protect His servant and the seed, even when His servant lived by fear instead of by faith.

This incident in Abram's life shows that God works in typical ways, according to patterns, which can be a tremendous encouragement to God's people. The events of Abram's life foreshadowed what would take place among his descendants when they later came to Egypt. The difference is that Jacob and his sons went to Egypt at God's direction and with His blessing (Gen. 46:4), which is not evident in Genesis 12. However, even as the Egyptians added to Abram's wealth, so the Israelites would plunder the Egyptians on leaving Egypt. Just as the future seed was in jeopardy when Sarai was taken into Pharaoh's house, so the future of Israel would be in jeopardy when the Egyptians tried to stop the Israelites from multiplying by killing off their male children. Even as God afflicted Pharaoh and his house with plagues to protect Sarai, so God would afflict the Egyptians with plagues to deliver His people from the bondage of Egypt. And as Pharaoh sent Abram out from Egypt, so a later Pharaoh also sent Israel out of Egypt. God's power is demonstrated in the protection of His people, His ability to bless His people in the midst of hardship, and in the deliverance of His people from danger.

In Genesis 13 Abram returned to the land of Canaan. He traveled to Bethel where he had made an altar when he had first arrived in the land. There he called on the name of the LORD, which can be seen as a renewal of his faith in God after his failure to trust God in Egypt. His faith is evident in

Genesis 13, where he demonstrates trust in the promises of God.

Secure in God's Promise (Gen. 13)

Genesis 13 reminds the reader that Lot was with Abram and informs the reader that the possessions of Abram and Lot became so abundant that the land could not support both of them dwelling together (13:5-6). Their flocks were so large that their herdsmen experienced conflict and strife, perhaps related to which flocks would get the best grazing areas. The situation was so serious that a separation between Abram and Lot became necessary. Abram demonstrated security in the promise of God concerning the land by allowing Lot to choose the part of the land that he desired to possess. Abram was the senior partner in this relationship, and so he could have chosen the portion of the land that he wanted. By letting Lot choose, Abram showed that he was resting in God to fulfill His promise rather than trying to grab it for himself. Abram's faith in God's promise was rewarded after Lot separated – by a reaffirmation of God's promise that Abram's descendants would not only possess the land, but that they would also become as numerous as the dust of the earth (13:14-16). In response to God's command Abram again traveled throughout the length and breadth of the land. Then he settled at Hebron and worshipped the LORD by building an altar.

It is interesting to examine the basis of Lot's choice concerning which part of the land he wanted to possess. He made his choice based on what looked good and what could give him the best chance of prosperity. Lot 'saw that the Jordan Valley was well-watered' (13:10). Of course, water is extremely important for surviving in the land. Lot's choice seems on the surface to be a great choice because the Jordan Valley is described as being 'like the garden of the LORD', no doubt a reference to the Garden of Eden. It is also described as being 'like the land of Egypt in the direction of Zoar'. Egypt was considered the breadbasket of the ancient Near East, so this region must have been rich in resources.[4]

---

4. Matthews, *Genesis 11:27–50:26*, p. 136,

Yet there are hints of danger alongside the note of prosperity. The city of Zoar was at the edge of the land of Canaan, and Lot chose to live among the cities of the valley east of the Dead Sea, which were outside the promised land. He even moved his tent as far as Sodom (13:12). The men of Sodom are described as 'very wicked, great sinners against the LORD' (13:13). The coming destruction of Sodom and Gomorrah is even mentioned (13:10). Lot's choice of land was based on sight and self-interest (13:11, 'he chose for himself'). He not only separated from Abram but he began to live outside the promised land, in the vicinity of great wickedness. Lot made it hard for his family to succeed spiritually, and at this point in the narrative the reader can only wonder how Lot and his family would fare living among great sinners.

A King Defending the Land (Gen. 14)

In Genesis 14, trouble comes to the land in the form of military conflict. A coalition of four kings from the area of Mesopotamia, led by Chedorlaomer, sought to reassert their control over five cities east of the Dead Sea. These cities – which included Sodom, Gomorrah, and Zoar – rebelled against the coalition of kings after serving them for twelve years. The battle culminated in the Valley of Siddim, just south of the Dead Sea, with the kings of the cities east of the Dead Sea going to battle against the kings from Mesopotamia. The northern armies from Mesopotamia won the battle and took as plunder people and provisions from Sodom and Gomorrah; Lot and his family were captured and were in the process of being taken as spoils of war to Mesopotamia. Lot had actually moved into the city of Sodom by this time (14:12). His separation from Abram had many implications, some to be worked out in later chapters, but one implication prominent in this account is that Lot was no longer under Abram's protection after his separation from Abram. Lot settled in the particular city of Sodom and became caught up with the politics and the wickedness of the city (Genesis 19).

The word of Lot's capture came to Abram who was living safely by the oaks of Mamre near Hebron. Abram is identified as 'the Hebrew' (14:13), a term usually used by non-Israelites to identify the descendants of Abram, and later used to

identify the members of the nation of Israel.[5] In this context
it stresses his separate identity from the Amorites with whom
he had become allied. Abram lived peacefully in the land
even as he maintained his separate identity from the people
living in the land. When Abram heard of Lot's capture, he
led 318 men from his own household in pursuit of Lot. These
men 'born in his house' (14:14) demonstrate both the wealth
of Abram in having such a large household and the power of
Abram in having 'trained men'. The word 'trained' is used in
second-millennium texts to refer to 'armed retainers' used by
Canaanite chiefs.[6] Abram and his house were a major force,
which is demonstrated in his defeat of the Mesopotamian
coalition of kings. Thus, Abram rescued Lot with all his
possessions, including other people from Sodom who had
been captured (14:16). In this account Abram acted as a king
defending the land by intervening on behalf of its oppressed
subjects. There was blessing in being associated with Abram
and there was curse when one dishonored Abram or those
related to him (Gen. 12:3).

The story of the aftermath of the battle includes Abram's
interaction with two kings (14:17-24). His encounter with the
king of Sodom frames his dealings with Melchizedek, king
of Salem. The king of Sodom presented a business offer to
Abram – he can take the goods for himself but should give
the people he rescued back to the king of Sodom. The victory
was seen as a human victory, with the normal consequences
of dividing the spoil among the victors (14:21-24). Abram
rejected the offer because he did not want to be indebted to
the king of Sodom and because he wanted to honor God as the
true source of his wealth. He only accepted enough from the
spoils for the provisions already consumed and for payment
to the allies that accompanied him in the battle.

Abram's interaction with Melchizedek, king of Salem, was
very different because of its spiritual emphasis. Melchizedek
was not only king of Salem but he is identified as a priest of
God Most High. His abrupt appearance, his worship of the

---

5. Matthews (*Genesis 11:27–50:26*, p. 146) points out that the term 'Hebrew'
may have come from the ancestor Eber (Gen. 11:16), although some connect it to the
verb 'to cross over' (*ʿābar*).

6. Hamilton, *'ḥān'k*, *TWOT* 1:301.

true God, and his interaction with Abram as his superior has led to much debate and speculation concerning Melchizedek.[7] The best approach is to understand Melchizedek as a real historical person who functions as a type of Christ.[8] He was king of Salem, which is probably a reference to Jerusalem. Little is known concerning Jerusalem at this time.[9] He was priest of 'God Most High' ('ēl 'elyôn), identified as the 'Possessor' (qōnēh)[10] of the heaven and earth (14:19). Melchizedek emphasized God's sovereign lordship over creation and the nations. Abram identified God Most High with Yahweh (the LORD) in his speech to the king of Sodom (14:22). As a priest, Melchizedek blessed Abram by God Most High and blessed or praised God for delivering Abram's enemies into his hand. He also offered provisions to Abram in the form of bread and wine.[11] Melchizedek himself embodies these blessings: his name means 'king of righteousness', and he is king of Salem, which means king of peace. Melchizedek is presented as greater than Abram because he blessed him, and Abram responded by giving a tenth of everything to Melchizedek in honor of his position.

The author of Hebrews uses Melchizedek to argue for the superiority of the priesthood of Jesus Christ. Melchizedek

---

7. Qumran understands Melchizedek as an eschatological, heavenly being, but a common view among Jewish commentators is that Melchizedek was a man who was an anointed priest of God Most High. The latter view was also a common view of the church fathers, although there were exceptions (for review and analysis of the various views of Melchizedek see Matthews, *Genesis 11:27–50:26*, pp. 151-56, and Philip E. Hughes, *A Commentary on the Epistle to the Hebrews* [Grand Rapids: Eerdmans, 1977], pp. 237-45).

8. James Borland (*Old Testament Appearances of Christ in Human Form* [Ross-shire: Christian Focus, 1999], pp. 139-147) presents evidence against the view that Melchizedek is a pre-incarnate appearance of the second person of the Trinity, which includes the fact that it would be unusual to pose as a king of a Canaanite city, that the performance of a religious ceremony is unusual in other Christophanies, that there is no confirmation that the LORD appeared, and that the book of Hebrews states that he resembles the Son of God (7:3), not that he is the Son of God.

9. Matthews (*Genesis 11:27–50:26*, p. 149) notes that the earliest mention of Jerusalem outside the Bible occurs in the Egyptian Execration Texts (c. 1850) and the Amarna texts (fourteenth century).

10. This verb means 'to acquire' or 'to get' in the sense of obtaining something or someone (Gen. 25:19; 39:1). It is also used in parallel with 'Maker of heaven and earth' (Pss. 115:15; 121:2; 124:8) and so may mean here 'Creator'.

11. Bread and wine are best understood as luxurious refreshment for returning warriors (Judg. 8:5; 2 Sam. 16:1-2). There does not seem to be any overt cultic (worship) significance to these provisions (Matthews, *Genesis 11:27–50:26*, p. 149).

cannot be a pre-incarnate appearance of the Son of God because Hebrews 7:3 states that he resembles the Son of God in continuing as a priest forever. Jesus was from the tribe of Judah and not from the priestly tribe of Levi; but His priesthood is superior to the Levitical priesthood because of its eternal nature. Hebrews even makes the point that the descendants of Levi honoured Melchizedek by paying tithes through Abram to Melchizedek (Heb. 7:9). Melchizedek's priesthood is a higher order than the Levitical priesthood, and the priesthood of Jesus Christ partakes of the same order (Heb. 7:17; Ps. 110:4). Melchizedek also typifies Christ by the fact that he was both king and priest in one person. Jesus' reign and ministry will establish righteousness and peace.

STUDY QUESTIONS

1   What difference does it make concerning your relationship to Abram if Abram is seen as an instrument of God's blessing or as a model for how God blesses?

2   Compare and contrast Abram in Egypt in Genesis 12 with his relationship to Lot in Genesis 13. What is the main difference in Abram's actions in the two incidents?

3   Characterize the basis of Lot's choice of land. How is that a temptation in our culture and in your life?

4   Who was Melchizedek? How does he relate to Christ?

8

The Life of Abraham: God's Covenant and the Promise of a Seed
(Genesis 15–17)

The Account (Toledot) of Terah (11:27–25:12), which is an account of the life of Abram, continues in Genesis 15–22 with a focus on the promise of a child for Abram and Sarai. Genesis 12–14 has concentrated on the promise of land and Genesis 16–22 will center on the promise of a seed, and both promises of land and seed come together in Genesis 15, which culminates in God's covenant with Abram.

God's Covenant with Abram (Gen. 15:1-21)
God appears to Abram in a vision at the beginning of Genesis 15 after Abram honors God as the source of his wealth in Genesis 14. God tells Abram not to fear, which may be in response to the coming of the word of Yahweh (the LORD) to him in the vision, but it is also interesting that the exhortation not to fear is associated with the issue of descendants (Gen. 26:24; 35:17; 46:1-7). Abram should take courage because Yahweh proclaims to him, 'I am your shield,' a statement that emphasizes that God is the one who protects and gives security to Abram. God also affirms that Abram's 'reward will be very great'. Abram's response is to point out that God's promise of an offspring has not yet been fulfilled in his life, which means a servant may end up as heir of the household.

Abram suggests Eliezer of Damascus, who is outside the family. However, God affirms His promise to Abram of a child, 'your very own son' (v. 4), who will be the heir. God even promises that Abram's offspring will be as numerous as the stars of heaven. Abram's response is to believe in the promise of God that a son will be born to Sarah, and in return God 'counted it to him as righteousness' (v. 6). Abram's faith is what God accepts as the instrument of righteousness through which He is able to credit Abram with righteousness. Abram is not credited with righteousness on the basis of his actions but on the basis of his trust in God's promises. In Romans 4 Paul uses Abraham as an example of one who is not justified by his works but who is justified by his faith.

God also raises the issue of land in verse 7 by stating, 'I am the LORD who brought you out of the Ur of the Chaldeans to give you this land to possess.' This is an affirmation of the promise of land from Genesis 12:1-3; however, Abram responds with a question concerning how he is to know that he will possess it. God then confirms the promise of land with a covenant ceremony (15:9-21). God's covenant with Abram fits the royal-grant type of covenant where a master promises benefits to a servant and secures them by an oath.[1] This covenant is normally given to the servant in response to his loyalty to the master. In the case of Abram, God takes the initiative and calls Abram to leave his family and country and to go to a land that God will show him. Abram shows that he is a faithful servant by forsaking everything and coming to the land of Canaan. The benefits in a grant covenant focus on land and offspring, which God had promised to Abram when He called him in Genesis 12:1-3. It is also significant that the curse in this type of covenant is to protect the servant from the harm of others, which fits God's promise in Genesis 12:3 to curse the one who dishonors Abram. Thus it is not surprising that the covenant ceremony in Genesis 15, that ratifies these promises to Abram, stresses that God takes the oath to secure the promises He has made to Abram.

Abram is told to bring several animals, to cut them in half, and to lay the halves over against each other (vv. 9-10). As the

---

1. M. Weinfeld, 'Covenant Grant in the Old Testament and the Ancient Near East,' *JAOS* 90 (1970):184-203.

sun goes down, Abram falls into a deep sleep (*tardēmāh*), a term associated with divine revelations in dreams and visions (Job 4:13; 33:15; Isa. 29:10).[2] Also, 'a dreadful and great darkness fell upon him,' which provides an appropriate atmosphere for revealing what will happen to Abram's descendants. God reveals to Abram the history of his descendants. They will be afflicted for 400 years in a land that is not their own; eventually God will bring judgment on that nation and the descendants will come out of that land with great possessions. Abram's descendants will come back to the land of Canaan in the fourth generation, when the iniquity of the Amorites is complete. The ceremony itself included a statement of these promises to Abram (vv. 17-21), and contained a description of the boundaries of the land and its occupants. Abram himself, however, will live a long life and die in peace (vv. 12-16). Thus God confirms to Abram that he will have descendants and that those descendants will one day come back to the land God has promised to Abram.

God confirms the covenant promises to Abram of land and offspring by taking upon Himself the responsibility to fulfill the promises. The smoking firepot and the flaming torch symbolize the presence of God as they pass between the slain animals. God is the only party to pass between the animals; this means that He takes it upon Himself to ensure that the promises are fulfilled. God swears an oath to keep the promises of the covenant and places Himself under the possibility of covenant curse if He does not keep them. In other words, the curse would fall on God, and He would become like the slain animals if He is not faithful to the covenant.[3] On the one hand, it is difficult to conceive of God undergoing covenant curse, but He allows Himself to be bound by this covenant obligation to show that He is serious about keeping the covenant promises. On the other hand, we know that God did take upon Himself a covenant curse, not because He had failed to keep the covenant promises to Abram, but because the descendants of Abram failed to keep the covenant (Exod. 24:7; Deut. 27–28). Thus, God in the person of Jesus

---

2. Matthews, *Genesis 11:27–50:26*, p. 172.
3. Kline, *Kingdom Prologue*, pp. 297-98.

Christ took upon Himself the curse of the covenant that should have fallen on all who are covenant-breakers.

Producing an Heir through Human Means (Gen. 16:1-16)
The promise of a descendant is prominent in Genesis 16:1–22:24; in fact, the issue of seed frames these chapters as Genesis 16 begins with the fact that Sarai had not borne Abram any children and Genesis 22:17 affirms the promise that Abram's descendants will be as numerous as the stars of heaven. In these chapters we are told how God fulfilled His covenant promise of a seed.

At the beginning of Genesis 16 the statement that Sarai had not produced any children stands in sharp contrast to the covenant ceremony of Genesis 15 and the promise of an heir for Abram and Sarai. It does not seem that God's plan for a son will be fulfilled because they have been in the land for ten years already (v. 3). Thus Sarai comes up with her own plan for obtaining a son. Sarai recognizes that the LORD has prevented her from having children; so she offers to Abram her Egyptian servant Hagar so that 'it may be that I shall obtain children by her' (16:1-2). Although such a practice may have been common in the culture of that day, it stands sharply opposed to God's promises and the fact that He had committed Himself in a covenant to fulfill the promise of a seed for Abram and Sarai.

There are several details in Genesis 16 that emphasize that this plan was not a good idea. There are interesting parallels with Genesis 3 placing Sarai in the role of Eve and Abram in the role of Adam. Like Eve, Sarai took and gave to her husband (v. 3), except Sarai is not giving fruit from the tree but is giving Hagar as a wife to raise up a seed. Like Adam, Abram listened to the voice of his wife and walked on the path of disobedience. Hagar conceives a child and even before the child is born there is trouble in the household. When Hagar conceived, she 'looked with contempt' on Sarai. Although the servant wife who conceived did not replace the wife who was barren, Sarai perceives that Hagar is a threat to her place in the house. She blames Abram for the situation even though it was her idea for Abram to raise up a child through Hagar. It is evident that she now regrets the decision and is looking for vindication of her place in the household.[4] Abram confirms Sarai's place in the household but also abdicates himself of responsibility by giving Sarai the power to treat Hagar however she wanted (v. 6). Sarai 'dealt harshly' ('*ānāh*) with Hagar, a verb that means 'to afflict'. In some way Sarai mistreated Hagar, so Hagar decides that the best option for her is to flee. Trying to accomplish the promises of God through human means has disastrous consequences. In this case the whole household loses: Sarai loses respect, Hagar loses a home, and Abram is caught in the middle of this quarrel between two women.

We can see that there was a clear contrast between the way God promised that an heir would be produced and the way that Abram and Sarai try to bring about an heir. God's promise of an heir through Sarai required faith in God's power to bring life out of the dead womb of Sarai, who had not only been barren all her life but was now at an age that was past childbearing. The right response would have been to believe in God's promise. However, Sarai became impatient with the promise of God and devised a human plan to produce an heir. This plan did not require faith but was a natural, human response to the problem. In other words, Abram and Sarai tried to solve this problem through their own ability. Paul in Galatians 4 bases his argument for justification by faith on these principles inherent in the Genesis narrative. The response of belief in the promise of God to produce an heir corresponds to justification by faith and produces children of promise who are free. The plan to solve this problem through human means corresponds to justification by works where one seeks to obtain the promise through human effort. This leads to slavery and losing the inheritance (Gal. 4:21-31).[5]

---

4. Matthews, *Genesis 11:27–50:26*, p. 186.

5. Paul, in Galatians 4:24, uses the term *allēgoreō* to describe his approach. Certainly Paul's approach is not the allegorical approach of Philo and Origen who interpret Scripture allegorically through a philosophical system that is imposed on the text. Some use the term typological to describe Paul's approach (Timothy George, *Galatians* [Nashville: Broadman & Holman, 1994], p. 339, and Chrysostom in *A Select Library of the Nicene and Post-Nicene Fathers* [Grand Rapids: Eerdmans, 1989], 13:34). What is clear is that Paul's argument in Galatians 4 is rooted in the actual events of history that are narrated in Genesis 16. Allegory is usually not rooted in history. Paul then shows how the principles of faith in God's promise and trusting in one's own efforts relate to the groups of his own day.

The situation becomes so bad between Hagar and Sarai that Hagar flees from Sarai (16:7-14). The angel of the Lord finds Hagar by a spring of water in the wilderness, and tells her to return to Sarai and to submit to her. Then Hagar receives a promise concerning her son and her descendants. First, the promise is that her descendants will be very numerous, so numerous that they cannot be numbered (v. 10). Second, the name of the son is given (v. 11). He shall be called Ishmael 'because the Lord has listened to your affliction'. Ishmael means 'God hears', so his name will be a constant reminder that God had heard the anguish of Hagar in her affliction. Third, the character of Ishmael is presented as hostility toward everyone, even against his own kinsmen (v. 12). He is described as a 'wild donkey of a man', a phrase which indicates a lifestyle outside of accepted social conventions (Hosea 8:9). He will live an independent existence because 'his hand is against everyone and everyone's hand is against him'. Ishmael is presented as an antagonist who does not get along well with others, even with his own family.[6] This description fits well with the fact that Ishmael is not the promised seed. In fact, he and his descendants will act against those of the promised seed and will live out the hostility described between the two seeds in Genesis 3. The descendants of Ishmael settled in the area of Arabia (Gen. 25:12-18) and some Muslims today trace their lineage back to Abraham through Ishmael.[7]

Hagar responds by calling the name of the Lord who spoke to her, 'You are a God of seeing'.[8] She recognizes that God has seen her affliction, but her statement also recognizes that God has cared for her: 'Truly here I have seen him who looks after me.' Thus the well is called Beer-lahai-roi, which means 'the well of the living one who sees me'. God's promises to Hagar must have been accepted by her because the chapter ends with the fact that Hagar bore Abram a son whom Abram called Ishmael. Hagar had returned to her mistress in obedience to the angel of the Lord. Although Ishmael is not the promised

---

6. Matthews, *Genesis 11:27–50:26*, pp. 190-91

7. See Bassam M. Chedid, *Islam: What Every Christian Should Know* (Darlington, England: The Evangelical Press, 2004), pp. 40-49.

8. Waltke (*Genesis*, p. 255) comments that the name for God literally reads 'God of my seeing', which can either mean 'the God who sees me' (which fits the context) or 'the God I see' (which fits her explanation).

child, he is for the time being a part of Abram's household and so will experience protection and blessing because of that association.

The Covenant of Circumcision (Gen. 17:1-27)

Genesis 16 ends with a statement of the age of Abram at the time of the birth of Ishmael. He was eighty-six years old. Genesis 17 begins with the statement that Abram was ninety-nine years old when Yahweh (the LORD) appeared to him. There is an astonishing thirteen years of silence between Ishmael's birth and God's appearance to Abram. One can only wonder at Abram's struggle of faith and conversations that might have taken place between Abram and Sarai during this time (we get a glimpse of Sarah's attitude in Genesis 18:12). Abram's failure to bring about the promised child through human, natural means does not destroy God's covenant promise. In fact, the appearance to Abram by God stresses His power as He identifies Himself as 'God Almighty'. He exhorts Abram with two imperatives, 'walk before me and be blameless,' which emphasize Abram's faithfulness and obedience. The importance of walking with God has already been seen in Genesis with Enoch, whose relationship with God led to escape from physical death (Gen. 5:24), and with Noah, who was delivered from immediate death in the waters of the flood (Gen. 6:9). In other words, walking with God leads to salvation. The second imperative, 'blameless,' does not mean sinless. God's salvation is not based on our perfection but on His grace; however, once called by God, He expects a life from His people that reflects His character and values. The word 'blameless' stresses that a person's life has wholeness to it in the sense that a person is not a hypocrite who says one thing and does another.

The two obligations given to Abram are followed by two actions that God Himself takes. The sequence of two imperatives ('walk ... and be blameless') followed by two cohortatives ('I may make my covenant ... and may multiply you greatly') indicates purpose or result.[9] Abram's obedience will result in the two actions taken by God. The terminology

---

9. Matthews, *Genesis 11:27-50:26*, p. 201.

used here matches terminology used in royal-grant covenants where a superior party grants blessings to an inferior party who shows integrity and fidelity in service (see the discussion of Genesis 12).[10] The promises that God gave to Abram in Genesis 12, and were ratified in a covenant ceremony in Genesis 15, are confirmed by God in Genesis 17 in the covenant sign of circumcision. Genesis 17 is not a separate covenant but is the confirmation of the existing covenant with Abram by means of a sign. The phrase, 'that I may make my covenant,' uses the verb *nātan*, which is not used for the making of a covenant but is used for the appointment of covenant signs of confirmation, as in the rainbow which was a sign of the Noahic covenant (Gen. 9:12-13).[11] The phrase, 'I will establish my covenant,' in 17:7 (*qûm* in the hifil) supports the view that Genesis 17 is the confirmation of a covenant. The normal terminology for making a covenant is 'to cut' (*kārat*) a covenant.[12] Thus, God confirms that He will bring about what He has already promised to Abraham. Circumcision in Genesis 17 will testify to the reality of the relationship already established.

The first part of Genesis 17 can be divided into three sections based on the responsibilities that each party has to the covenant. Thus 17:4-8 is introduced with 'I' (*'ănî*), which some versions translate by the phrase 'as for me' (KJV, NASB, NIV). These verses deal with what God promises to accomplish through this covenant confirmation. Then 17:9-14 begins with 'You' (*'attāh*), translated 'as for you' (ESV, NASB, NIV), where God lays out Abram's responsibilities in keeping God's covenant. Finally, in 17:15-21 God focuses on Sarai ('As for Sarai' in verse 15) and her responsibilities in keeping God's covenant. The end of the chapter gives an account of Abraham's obedience by relating that he circumcised himself and his whole household (17:22-27).

In Genesis 17:4-8 God confirms His promises to Abram of seed and land. There are two statements of covenant confirmation followed by statements of what God is going to accomplish. The first statement of covenant confirmation comes in 17:4, 'my covenant is with you,' which is followed

---

10. Kline, *Kingdom Prologue*, pp. 310–11.
11. Kline, *Kingdom Prologue*, p. 314.
12. Leonard J. Coppes, קום (*qûm*), *TWOT*, 2:793.

by the promise that Abram will be the father of a multitude of nations. God promises to make Abram 'exceedingly fruitful', and the evidence of this fruitfulness will be that nations and kings will come from him (v. 6). To reinforce this promise God changes Abram's name to Abraham; from Abram (meaning 'exalted father') to Abraham (meaning 'the father of a multitude'). Every time Abraham hears his new name he will be reminded of this promise of God. The second statement of covenant confirmation comes in verse 7 where it is pointed out that the covenant which is established between God and Abraham is also between God and the descendants of Abraham 'throughout their generations for an everlasting covenant'. This covenant commitment includes the promise that God will be God to Abraham and his descendants, and that the descendants of Abraham will possess the land of Canaan.

In the next section, Genesis 17:9-14, God lays out for Abraham ('As for you') his responsibility to keep the covenant. God's covenant is not only made with Abraham but includes his descendants, and so the covenant sign emphasizes that the covenant is 'between me and you and your offspring after you' (17:10). The covenant sign is circumcision performed on an eight-day-old infant. Circumcision was practiced by other nations, but they associated it more with puberty or the passage into manhood.[13] In the covenant with Abraham it was performed on the male infants to show that the covenant includes the children. The fact that the covenant sign of circumcision was performed only upon males does not mean that females were not part of the covenant, but it stresses the representative nature of the covenant relationship. This principle is even important when it comes to which males should be circumcised, because not only males born into one's house are circumcised but also any males bought with money are to be circumcised (vv. 12-13). These latter males would not be natural-born citizens of Israel; yet they should still be circumcised because they become a part of the household and are under the authority of that household, and so are also under the authority of God. The covenant sign of circumcision

---

13. Waltke, *Genesis*, p. 261.

is so important that it is virtually identified with the covenant itself ('this is my covenant' in verse 10); this means that not to circumcise a child is to break the covenant. If someone fails to keep the covenant the consequences are serious: 'any uncircumcised male ... shall be cut off from his people' (v. 14). In fact, the phrase 'uncircumcised' becomes a derogatory term used for other nations, like the Philistines (Judg. 14:3).

God then turns to Sarai in verse 15 ('As for Sarai'); she is also given a new name to reflect the covenant promise of a child to be born through her who will be the commencement of a multitude of descendants. Sarai is given the name Sarah. The exact meaning of this name change is not as clear as the change of Abram's name to Abraham. Both Sarai and Sarah may be dialectical variants which mean 'princess'. Waltke comments that the birth name 'Sarai' looks back on her noble descent and the new name 'Sarah' looks forward to her noble descendants.[14] This explanation fits with God's promise not only to give to her a son, but also that her descendants will become nations, with kings of peoples coming from her (v. 16).

Abraham's reaction covers a range of human emotions as he falls on his face in reverence, then laughs at the prospect of a child being born to a couple as old as they are, and then pleads that God would accept Ishmael as the promised child (vv. 17-18). God promises to bless Ishmael by making him into a great nation, but God's covenant will be established with Isaac, who will be born to Sarah. The chapter ends by showing Abraham's obedience to the covenant, which demonstrates his faith in the covenant promise. He is circumcised, Ishmael is circumcised, and all the men of his household are circumcised.

Circumcision is the sign of the covenant; each person who is circumcised becomes a member of the covenant community, and now has the privileges and responsibilities that come with being a member of it. Circumcision is an external rite that symbolizes internal cleansing. The removal of the foreskin symbolizes the purification necessary for a relationship with a holy God (Deut. 10:16).[15] The responsibilities that come with membership in the covenant are also symbolized in

---

14. Waltke, *Genesis*, p. 262.
15. O. Palmer Robertson, *Christ of the Covenants* (Phillipsburg, NJ: P & R, 1980) p. 150.

circumcision. The cutting rite of circumcision symbolizes the cutting off of those who fail to keep the covenant (Gen. 17:14).[16] The fact that God swears the oath of this covenant and commits Himself to the fulfillment of the covenant (Gen. 15:12-15) is demonstrated in the coming of Christ who takes upon Himself the curse of the covenant by being 'cut off' on the cross.

The significance of circumcision and its relationship to the new covenant is a debated topic which has implications for believer's baptism and infant baptism. The issues are complex, so only the basic positions related to Genesis 17 will be set forth.[17] Those who argue for believer's baptism do not see a parallel between physical circumcision and baptism. They argue that Paul in Colossians 2:11 sets forth a parallel between spiritual circumcision (regeneration) and baptism. Physical circumcision did not ensure that one was regenerate because there was still the need for a circumcision of the heart. Baptism, the sign of the new covenant, is for those who have already been spiritually circumcised. Thus the typological antecedent to baptism is not physical circumcision but spiritual circumcision.[18] In contrast, those who argue for infant baptism see a parallel between circumcision and baptism. Circumcision is identified with the covenant (Gen. 17:10), and so symbolizes the essence of the covenant, which is a relationship with God. This aspect is emphasized in several ways in the New Testament. Circumcision and baptism point to the same inner reality because Paul states that 'you were circumcised ... having been buried with him in baptism' (Col. 2:11-12). Also, Paul states in Romans 4:11 that Abraham 'received the sign of circumcision as a seal of the righteousness that he had by faith while he was still uncircumcised'. Circumcision is a seal

---

16. Kline, *Kingdom Prologue*, p. 314-15.

17. For a book that seeks to set forth the various views of baptism, see David Wright, ed., *Baptism: Three Views* (Downers Grove, IL: Inter-Varsity Press, 2009). For a book that seeks to set forth the basics of both views in a story format, see Richard P. Belcher, Sr., *A Journey in Baptism* (Columbia, SC: Richbarry Press, 2003).

18. Thomas R. Schreiner, 'Baptism in the Epistles,' in *Believer's Baptism: Sign of the New Covenant in Christ* (Thomas R. Schreiner and Shawn D. Wright, eds.; Nashville: Broadman & Holman, 2006), p. 76. Other works that argue for believer's baptism include David Kingdon, *The Children of Abraham* (Cambridge: Carey Publications, 1973) and Fred Malone, *The Baptism of Disciples Alone: A Covenantal Argument for Credobaptism versus Paedobaptism* (Cape Coral, FL: Founders Press, 2003).

of the righteousness that comes by faith. As a sign applied to infants, it points to the reality of righteousness which will be granted when the child comes to faith.[19]

Another area of dispute is how the principle of Genesis 17:7 should be understood: 'I will establish my covenant between me and you and your offspring after you throughout their generations for an everlasting covenant.' Those who support believer's baptism argue that in the covenants of the Old Testament this principle referred to a natural, physical seed that included all those who were physically descended from Abraham, which resulted in a mixed community of Israel that was composed of believers and unbelievers. However, with the coming of Christ the seed is now spiritual and only includes those who believe in Jesus Christ, both Jews and Gentiles (Gal. 3:29).[20] This principle is seen in the Book of Acts and in Paul's epistles where the emphasis is on faith and repentance, which leads to baptism. The fact that households were baptized in the Book of Acts does not prove anything because the emphasis is on hearing the word and believing (Acts 10:44-48; 11:15-17; 16:32-34).[21]

Those who argue for infant baptism understand the principle of Genesis 17:7 to be the basis for infant baptism because the covenant sign is given to infants. In fact, by definition covenants always include descendants. Thus Moses is able to say to the second generation of Israelites who are waiting to go into the promised land that the covenant at Sinai was made with them, even though most of them were not even alive at the time of the original covenant (Deut. 5:2-5). The covenant was made with them because covenants include descendants. Thus we should not be surprised if the new covenant operates according to this principle because this principle is at the heart of how covenants work. In Acts 2:39

19. Robertson, *Christ of the Covenants*, pp. 160, 165-66. Works that argue for infant baptism include John P. Sartelle, *Infant Baptism: What Christian Parents Should Know* (Phillipsburg NJ: P & R Publishing, 1985), Bryan Chapell, *Why Do We Baptize Infants?* (Phillipsburg, NJ: P & R Publishing, 2006), and Gregg Strawbridge, ed., *The Case for Covenantal Infant Baptism* (Phillipsburg, NJ: P & R Publishing, 2003).

20. Stephen J. Wellum, 'Baptism and the Relationship between the Covenants,' *Believer's Baptism*, pp. 133-35.

21. Robert H. Stein, 'Baptism in Luke-Acts,' *Believer's Baptism*, pp. 61-63.

the promise mentioned by Peter includes 'your children'.[22] As the gospel moves out into Gentile territory whole households are baptized. In a missionary setting, such as the Book of Acts, it is appropriate that the emphasis was on faith in Jesus Christ and on repentance, which are necessary for a personal relationship with God. However, the fact that households were baptized demonstrates that certain characteristics of covenants in the Old Testament continue in the new covenant, such as the representative nature of the covenant and that covenants always include descendants. Thus the parallel between Abraham circumcising his whole house and baptism being applied to the one who believed and their household is very important (Acts 16:15, 32-33; 18:8; 1 Cor. 1:16).[23]

It is also significant that there are legal aspects to covenant administration that continue to operate in the new covenant. In Romans 11:16-24, Paul mentions a holiness that comes from being connected to the tree that is *not* the inward holiness that is a result of the Spirit's work in the life of a believer. This holiness is shared by the branches that are connected to the root of the tree. Since the new covenant church is depicted in Romans 11 with the same imagery as that of Israel, this principle of covenant administration continues in the new covenant because Gentiles who are grafted in can also be cut off (Rom. 11:21-22).[24] Household baptisms in Acts operate according to this principle. Also, Paul can apply the covenantal blessing of the fifth commandment to children of the covenant community, even placing upon them the blessings and curses of the covenant, which demonstrates that they are part of the covenant community (Eph. 6:1-3). Thus the church should not be defined only in terms of election (believers), but it also includes believers and their children.

---

22. For an analysis of the principle of seed in relationship to Acts 2, see Joel R. Beeke and Ray B. Lanning, 'Unto You, and to Your Children,' in *Covenantal Infant Baptism*, pp. 49-69. Although the principle of the seed is clear in Acts 2, some would argue that the promised seed here is the elect seed and that the principle of baptizing infants should not be based on this promise because election is narrower than the administration of the covenant (see Kline, *Kingdom Prologue*, pp. 364-65).

23. Jonathan M. Watt, 'The *Oikos* Formula,' in *Covenantal Infant Baptism*, pp. 70-84.

24. For further discussion of covenant administration, see Meredith Kline, *Kingdom Prologue*, pp. 362-64, and Berkhof, *Systematic Theology*, pp. 284-89.

Those who argue for believer's baptism have the goal of a pure community with everyone expressing faith in Christ as a basis for membership in the community. This is a worthy but an impossible goal to achieve this side of the new heavens and new earth. Almost every believer knows of someone who expresses faith in Christ, gives evidence of being converted, and so is baptized and joins the church. But the commitment does not last and the person falls away from Christ (Matt. 13:1-9, 18-23), which taints the purity of the community. Faith before baptism does not guarantee a pure community. On the other hand, those who practice infant baptism recognize that infants and children are a part of the covenant community.[25] They are taught the Word of God and are encouraged to believe in Jesus Christ as their Savior. It is possible that covenant children can grow up in the church and then reject Jesus. This does not mean that there are believers and unbelievers permanently existing in the church; rather it is a reminder that if someone rejects their covenant responsibilities then the possibility of the covenant curse of church discipline comes into play. The goal of church discipline is restoration, but it can also lead to separation from the community (1 Cor. 5). Thus, both those who believe in believer's baptism and those who believe in infant baptism have the same goal, which is a church community that honors Christ. Both views need church discipline to accomplish that goal.

STUDY QUESTIONS

1   How does God take upon Himself the responsibility to fulfill the covenant promises to Abram in Genesis 15? What comfort should that give to God's people today?

2   How does Sarah's plan to obtain a child illustrate the principle of justification by works? Read Galatians 4:21-31 and list the characteristics of the two

---

25. See Richard L. Pratt, Jr., 'Infant Baptism in the New Covenant,' in *Covenantal Infant Baptism*, pp. 170-73, for the evidence in the New Testament that the church is a mixed community based on the fact that judgment comes to those who have been part of the church.

groups that Paul discusses. Which group describes your life?

3   What is the purpose of the covenant in Genesis 17? Make a list of what circumcision means as a sign of the covenant.

4   Compare and contrast the views of believer's baptism and infant baptism concerning circumcision and the principle of seed. Which view do you think explains the Biblical evidence better?

5   What is meant by the legal administration of the covenant? What evidence is there that the legal administration of the covenant continues in the New Testament? Relate this question to your view of baptism.

6   What is the basis for the idea that neither believer's baptism nor infant baptism can avoid the concept of a mixed church of believers and unbelievers? What is needed to keep a church as pure as humanly possible?

9

The Life of Abraham: A Man of Intercession
(Genesis 18–20)

In this chapter we will focus on Abraham's role as one who intercedes for others. The story falls under the general heading of Faith in God's Promise of a Seed (16:1–22:24). The topic of seed is significant because the account of Lot in Sodom and Gomorrah has consequences for his descendants, and in the account of Abraham and Abimelech the seed is in jeopardy again.

Abraham's Intercession for Sodom (Gen. 18:1-33)

This chapter begins abruptly with 'And the LORD appeared to him', a statement which immediately alerts the reader to the importance of the three men who visited Abraham. Although they are called men in verse 2, one is Yahweh (the LORD) and the other two are identified as angels in 19:1. It becomes clear in chapters 18–19 that the LORD and the angels take the appearance of men for the sake of the mission that they are carrying out. The LORD Himself is prominent in chapter 18, but only the angels go to Sodom in chapter 19. It is significant that on their way to visit Sodom the three visitors call to see Abraham in order to confirm the promise of a seed to him and to draw him into their mission concerning Sodom. In this way Abraham participates in the outworking of God's purposes for this wicked city.

When the men appear suddenly before him Abraham senses that they are not unimportant visitors. Not only does he offer them hospitality, which was important for that culture, but he gives honour to them. He addresses one of the visitors as 'Lord' (Adonai), which could be a term of respect, but it is also the form used for God. He refers to himself as a 'servant' in relationship to the three visitors. He offers to them water, a morsel of bread, refreshment and rest, and then prepares for them the fatted calf. Abraham is liberal in his hospitality and while they eat he stands by them, perhaps to attend to their needs.

In the course of their conversation they ask Abraham about Sarah. The LORD reaffirms the covenant promise of an heir that will be born to Abraham and Sarah: 'I will surely return to you about this time next year, and Sarah your wife shall have a son.' This promise of God seems incomprehensible because Abraham and Sarah are old, and Sarah is described as being past the ability to conceive: 'the way of women had ceased to be with Sarah' (v. 11). In other words, the menstrual cycle had ceased for Sarah so that, humanly speaking, it was impossible for her to conceive a child. Sarah's response to this announcement also demonstrates the impossibility (v. 12): She does not believe the promise; instead, she laughs to herself and comments, probably also to herself, that her body is worn out and that she is too old to have pleasure in this regard. Abraham and Sarah have accepted barrenness as normal for them, which was sensible at this stage in their life.

Although the reader knows that it is the LORD who has appeared to Abraham, the knowledge that this visitor had concerning Sarah's inner thoughts should have confirmed his divine identity to Abraham and Sarah. The LORD asks Abraham why Sarah laughed. Initially she denies that she laughed because she was afraid. Yet her unbelief has been exposed. Nevertheless, the LORD takes the opportunity to remind them that His promise to them of a son will be accomplished 'this time next year' (v. 14). He confronts them with a question, 'Is anything too hard for the LORD?' This question forces them to face whether or not they have faith in the power of God to accomplish His promises.

In one sense, the LORD's decision to reveal to Abraham what He is about to do is based on the fact that God's promises will be fulfilled through Abraham. His position of being chosen by God so that he will teach his children the way of the LORD (v. 19), and the fact that all the nations of the earth will be blessed in him (v. 18), show that Abraham has been granted this privileged position by God. He is the instrument through which God's blessings will come to the nations (Gen. 12:3). In this account, Abraham has the opportunity to be an instrument of blessing by pleading with God for a particular city.

When God reveals to Abraham the mission to Sodom and Gomorrah to see how grave their sin is, Abraham is concerned that the righteous in the city will be swept away with the wicked. He appeals to the justice of the Judge of the earth to spare the righteous so that they will not be destroyed along with the wicked (v. 23). Abraham begins the process of pleading for the city by mentioning the possibility of fifty righteous inhabitants, and God agrees not to destroy the city if fifty live there. Abraham probably knows something about the sin of Sodom, and so in several steps he intercedes for the city and is able to get the LORD to agree that if ten righteous can be found in Sodom then God will not destroy the city (v. 32).

Several things are important in this process of intercession. Abraham recognizes his inferior position before God. He acknowledges his own position of weakness that someone who is 'but dust and ashes' should speak to the Judge of all the earth (v. 27). He realizes that he might be testing the patience of God when he pleads that the LORD not be angry with him as he continues to intercede (vv. 30, 32). It is apparent that although he pleads with God at the beginning on the basis of justice (v. 25), he ends by appealing to the grace of God. God agrees to Abraham's terms of ten righteous. There is a glimpse here of God's willingness to show compassion to unworthy sinners, which is more fully developed in relationship to His own people in Exodus 32–34 (see the statement of God's character in Exodus 34:6-7). This account also shows the importance of intercession by the servants of God, which will later be associated with the work of the prophet (Gen. 20:7; Jer. 7:15-16). Abraham here can be contrasted with Jonah who does not plead for God's mercy for Nineveh but instead requests its destruction. The descendants of Abraham, who were supposed to be a blessing to the nations, failed in their mission. How different was the son of Abraham who not only pleaded for sinners (Luke 23:34), but also gave His life for the sake of their salvation.

The Rescue of Lot from the Destruction of Sodom (Gen. 19:1-38)

When Lot separated from Abraham in Genesis 13 he chose for himself the portion of land in the Jordan Valley, which was well-watered everywhere, like the garden of the LORD (13:10). He settled among the cities of the valley and moved his tent as far as Sodom (13:12). In Genesis 19, Lot is not just living near the wicked city of Sodom (13:13), but he is living in it and is a participant in its affairs. Lot is sitting in the gateway of the city when the 'men' arrive (19:1), which suggests that he is an integral member of the city, if not a leader in some capacity.[1] He calls the men of the city 'my brothers' (19:7), and his daughters are pledged to be married to inhabitants of the city (19:14). Clearly Lot has settled down in the wicked city of Sodom. The alluring nature of that wickedness is seen shortly in how difficult it was to get his family to leave Sodom.

When the two angels arrive at Sodom, Lot is a gracious host. He shows proper respect to the two guests by bowing in humility (v. 1) and by addressing them as 'my lords' (v. 2). He offers hospitality to them by requesting that they spend the night at his house where he can take care of their needs (v. 2). It is a bit strange that the two visitors would rather spend the night in the town square instead of in the house of Lot. It is not absolutely clear if this is a test for Lot[2] or if this is showing disapproval of Lot.[3] Lot prevails in his invitation and the visitors spend the night at his house (v. 3). Although Lot does the right thing in offering hospitality, some think his hospitality does not quite measure up to Abraham's hospitality in Genesis 18 in the way Abraham greeted the visitors ('he ran to greet them', Gen. 18:2), in the offer of the invitation itself ('if

---

1. Matthews, *Genesis 11:27–50:26*, p. 232.
2. Currid, *Genesis 1:1–25:18*, p. 340.
3. Matthews, *Genesis 11:27–50:26*, p. 234.

I have found favor in your eyes', Gen. 18:3), and in the food that is prepared.[4] However, the hospitality that Lot offers is one of the positive aspects of the story that demonstrates that he is not like the Sodomites in important ways.

The wickedness of the city of Sodom is demonstrated in their actions toward the visitors. The extent of their wickedness is seen in the participation of both young and old men, even 'all the people to the last man' (v. 4).This group is not just a small contingent of evil people that the rest of the city can organize against; rather this group represents the population of the whole city, which shows that evil and corruption have permeated every aspect of it.[5] Their request is to bring the men out to them 'that we may know them' (v. 5). It is clear that this is not an attempt to become acquainted with the visitors but that the men of Sodom want to know the visitors in a sexual way. Their plan is to sexually assault and rape the visitors.

Lot finds himself in a precarious situation. He is a part of the city of Sodom and he calls these men 'brothers' (v. 7), but he also feels obligated to protect the visitors because they are under his roof (v. 8). He calls their request wicked, which shows that he has not completely lost his sense of what is right and wrong, but his response to their request also shows how much Lot has been tainted by the thinking of the wickedness of Sodom. He offers to them his two virgin daughters and grants that the men can 'do to them as you please' (v. 8).[6] Perhaps Lot feels that his back is against the wall and that he must choose between the lesser of two evils. It seems that the protection of these two visitors is more important, because of hospitality, than the protection of his family. Although this may be an impossible situation, it would have been better to go down fighting than to give in to

---

4. Although English translations give the impression that Lot prepared a feast, Matthews (*Genesis 11:27–50:26*, p. 234) argues that the meal prepared by Lot falls short because of the ingredients described and because the use of unleavened bread shows it was made in haste.

5. In other words, it would be fruitless to call the police because the police are either a part of this group or they too are corrupt.

6. John H. Walton, *Genesis* (Grand Rapids: Zondervan), p. 477, suggests that Lot's response may be a sarcastic remark which is meant to prick the conscience of the mob, but the context and the following statement by Lot do not fit such a reading ('Only do nothing to these men, for they have come under the shelter of my roof'). It is more likely that Lot is trying to trap the Sodomites in a legal quandary because his two daughters are betrothed to Sodomite men (Currid, *Genesis 1:1–25:18*, p. 342).

the demands of the men or to offer your own daughters in their place. In the final analysis, Lot finds himself in this situation because he has chosen to live in a sinful city. Sooner or later such a choice was inevitable because one cannot compromise with wickedness and not be affected by it. And yet Lot has not fully given in to wickedness. His perception is different from the men of Sodom. Thus, 2 Peter 2:6-10 describes the torment of Lot as he lived day after day among the lawless wickedness of Sodom. He is also described as 'righteous', which refers to his hospitality toward the visitors and his statement to the men of Sodom that what they wanted to do was wicked. But even the righteous can be influenced by evil, which can begin to affect their outlook on life.

Lot's offer does not stop the men of Sodom from their wicked design; in fact, they become upset with his judgment of them and seek to break down the door of his house. The supernatural character of the visitors becomes apparent when they rescue Lot by striking the men of Sodom with blindness. They also reveal to Lot their plan to destroy Sodom and ask him if he has any relations in the city whom he can warn about the coming destruction. Lot warns his sons-in-law but they see him as 'jesting' (v. 14). The thought of the judgment of God is only a joke to them. One can understand that these men of Sodom might have a hard time accepting the seriousness of this situation, but Lot and his family also have a hard time leaving the city. In the morning the angels urged Lot to leave the city, 'but he lingered' (v. 16). The angels had to force Lot and his family to leave the city. Even though destruction is coming, the lure of the sin of Sodom is strong upon Lot and his family. They have become comfortable with the sin of Sodom. Once outside the city of Sodom, the angels tell Lot to escape to the hills and not to look back or stop anywhere in the valley lest they be swept away in the destruction of the city. Lot does not want to escape to the hills; rather, he wants to go to a nearby, smaller city, called Zoar. His excuse for this request to avoid the hills is 'lest the disaster overtake me and I die' (v. 19). His concern may be that he cannot make it to the hills before the disaster strikes,[7] but one wonders if Lot is

7. Matthews, *Genesis 11:27–50:26*, p. 240.

having a hard time fully leaving Sodom.[8] The same reluctance to leave Sodom is seen when Lot's wife disobeys the angels' instruction not to look back (v. 17) and she becomes a pillar of salt (v. 26).

The role of Abraham's intercession is not forgotten as the story shows Abraham's concern for what would happen to the city of Sodom. Abraham is able to see from afar the smoke from the destruction of the city (v. 28). His intercession had a role in the deliverance of Lot because it states that when God destroyed the cities of the valley he 'remembered Abraham' (v. 29). The extent of the wickedness of this area becomes apparent when it is realized that there were not ten righteous individuals living in the cities of the valley that would have prevented their destruction. Also, Abraham's concern for the deliverance of the righteous is contrasted with Lot's concern for holding on to his comfortable life in Sodom. His plea for the city of Zoar, as a place for him to live apart from the righteousness of the place, contrasts with Abraham's plea for Sodom on the basis of the righteous.[9] The lure of sin is strong and is hard to break in a person's life.

The influence of sin from living in Sodom for so long is demonstrated in Lot's family following the destruction of Sodom (19:30-38). It is a bit surprising that Lot did not stay in Zoar very long but moved to the hills and lived in a cave with his two daughters. The reason given is that Lot was afraid to live in Zoar (v. 30). The text does not say why Lot was afraid. Some have suggested he feared Zoar would be destroyed like Sodom, a fear that could have been increased if there were tremors in the land after the destruction of Sodom.[10] The result of his fear is that Lot and his two daughters end up living in a cave, isolated from the rest of society. This raises the problem of how the two daughters will find husbands in order to produce offspring so that their lines will be preserved (v. 31). The plan that the firstborn daughter presents is a plan that would be right at home in Sodom. In two successive

---

8. Currid, *Genesis 1:1–25:18*, p. 348. Waltke (*Genesis*, p. 278) comments that Lot's argument demonstrates a lack of faith, a jaded spiritual evaluation of justice, and a decadent taste for depraved urbanity.

9. Waltke, *Genesis*, p. 278.

10. Waltke, *Genesis*, p. 279. This assumes that earthquakes were used in the destruction of Sodom.

nights they make their father drunk with wine and each becomes pregnant by their father. Lot does not realize what has happened (v. 33), which may be a sign of his spiritual dullness. One can only speculate why Lot did not consider the effect of the isolation of his daughters from any community. Lot could even have returned to Abraham, the source of great blessing, but that might have exposed his failure. The result of the incest is the birth of two sons, one who becomes the father of the Moabites and the other the father of the Ammonites, two nations that at times will be antagonistic toward the descendants of Abraham. It is very difficult to break free from the embedded ways of sin once such thinking becomes a part of a person's general outlook. Lot and his daughters may have left Sodom, but Sodom did not completely leave Lot and his daughters.

Abraham Prays for Abimelech's Household (Gen. 20:1-18)
In Genesis 20 the narrative returns to Abraham and begins immediately with 'From there Abraham journeyed toward the territory of the Negeb.' The LORD had appeared to Abraham by the oaks of Mamre and now Abraham is on the move again toward the southern edge of the promised land. He ends up at the Philistine city of Gerar and puts forth the same plan of wife-sister deception that he had used in Genesis 12:9-20 with reference to Egypt. This seems to suggest that wife-stealing was a common threat.[11] However, there are significant differences between the account in Genesis 12 and this account. The earlier account focused more on the land promise because it was famine in the promised land that was the reason that Abraham went down to Egypt. No reason is given in Genesis 20 as to why Abraham is at Gerar and the emphasis seems to be more on the seed. The birth narrative of Isaac follows this episode and it is clear that Abimelech, king of Gerar, does not touch Sarah (20:6). There is also no mention of Sarah's beauty in Genesis 20, perhaps because she is now ninety years old instead of sixty-five! Further, there is an emphasis on Abraham's role of intercessor as he prays for the household of Abimelech.

---

11. Matthews, *Genesis 11:27–50:26*, p. 251.

For whatever reason, Abraham is in the Philistine city and the seed is in jeopardy again. Abimelech thinks Sarah is Abraham's sister, so he takes her into his house; but God acts to protect Sarah and to preserve the promise of a child to be born from Abraham and Sarah. God appears to Abimelech in a dream and tells him he is 'a dead man' because he has another man's wife (v. 3). Abimelech had not yet approached Sarah, which means he had not yet had a sexual relationship with her, and he pleads his innocence because he did not know that she was Abraham's wife. God acknowledges that Abimelech is innocent concerning the married state of Sarah and then explicitly says that He was the one who protected her. God did not allow Abimelech to touch her, which kept him from sinning against God (v. 6). Abimelech is told to return Sarah to Abraham or he would pay the consequences: 'you shall surely die, you, and all who are yours' (v. 7).

Abraham is presented both positively and negatively in Genesis 20. On the negative side, he again shows a lack of faith in the power of God to protect the seed that God had promised him. Instead he relies on a pattern of behavior which he had developed from the day that he left his father's house (v. 13), which shows that in this area of his life he has not grown in faith. Certain sinful ways of thinking and patterns of behavior can become comfortable, so that it is easy to revert to them instead of trusting in God. Abraham feared the power of the king of Gerar more than he trusted in the promise of God (v. 11). Abimelech rebukes Abraham for his unfounded fear (v. 10).

On the positive side, Abraham is presented as a mediator between God and Abimelech. The household of Abimelech had been struck with barrenness by God 'because of Sarah' (v. 18). Abraham prays for Abimelech's household and God heals them 'so that they bore children' (v. 17). In the role of intercessor, Abraham now brings blessing to this Gentile king. It is interesting that Abraham is called a prophet and that he fulfills that function through prayer. The official role of the prophet in relationship to the nation of Israel will be defined in Deuteronomy 18:15-22, but the prophetic role is not limited to that period of Israel's history. In fact, Abraham in one sense fulfills the role of priest (in the building of altars in

Genesis 12), the role of a king (in rescuing Lot in Genesis 14), and the role of prophet in praying for Abimelech's household. The irony of the situation is that Abraham prays for God to open the wombs of the household of Abimelech when the womb of Sarah, his own wife, is closed. But this is a reminder to Abraham as to who is in charge of these things and gives him hope that God will be faithful to His promise of an heir to be born to him through Sarah.

STUDY QUESTIONS

1   Does Abraham's ministry of intercession have any relevance to the church today?

2   Evaluate the character of Lot from 2 Peter 2:6-10 on the basis of the story of Genesis 19. How was Lot different from the people in Sodom? How had the thinking of Sodom affected Lot and his family? What danger signs are there in this story for God's people today?

3   What does the familiar story of Genesis 20 teach about the patterns of sin in a person's life? Can you identify such patterns in your life? Is there a particular sin that you struggle with?

4   What key activity is connected to Abraham's role as a prophet? What significance does this activity have for leaders in the church today? Can you think of New Testament texts that emphasize that role?

10

The Fulfillment of God's Promise in the Preservation of the Godly Line

(Genesis 21–22:19)

The promise of God to Abraham and Sarah that they would have a son of their own is fulfilled in Genesis 21 in the birth of Isaac. Although the promised child is born, there still remain challenges and obstacles in preserving the future of the one who represents the promises of God. These challenges include Isaac's relationship to Ishmael (21:8-21), future prospects in the land (21:22-34), and the testing of faith in God's promise in relationship to the seed (22:1-19).

The Birth of the Promised Child (Gen. 21:1-21)
The birth of Isaac is told in a rather matter-of-fact way, emphasizing that this is exactly what God had promised. The power to conceive comes from Yahweh (the LORD): verse 1 reminds the reader that the 'LORD visited Sarah' as He had promised; in fact, twice in verse 1 it is stated that the LORD did as He had said He would do. Thus Sarah gave birth to a son even though she and her husband were old and past the age of giving birth (v. 2). In fact, Abraham was a hundred years old (v. 5). He named the son Isaac and circumcised him when he was eight days old in obedience to God's covenant (Genesis 17). The marvel of the birth of this child is expressed by Sarah in the name of the child. The name Isaac comes from

the verb meaning 'to laugh' (ṣāḥaq). Instead of the laughter of unbelief, which Sarah expressed in Genesis 18:12, this is the laughter of joy in the fulfillment of God's promise. It is unbelievable that she should bear a child in her old age, but God has granted to her this 'laughter' and others will also 'laugh' with her because of the birth of this child.

It becomes clear, however, that not everyone 'laughs' with joy at the birth of Isaac. There is a rival heir who also 'laughs' (ṣāḥaq), but his laughing is not the laughter of joy but is the laughter of mocking (v. 9).[1] When Isaac was weaned Abraham threw a great feast. It is unclear at what age a child was weaned, but it could have been as old as two or three years of age (1 Sam. 1:22-24).[2] During the feast Sarah witnesses Ishmael treating Isaac in a way that disturbs her. Thus she requests that Abraham send away the slave woman and her son because she is concerned about the issue of who will be the true heir (v. 10). Abraham is displeased with Sarah's request because of his love for his firstborn son (v. 11), but God affirms that Sarah's request is appropriate because Isaac is the true heir. Sarah's request is in accord with the divine word of Genesis 15:4.[3]

Although Isaac is the true heir, Ishmael will be blessed because of his relationship to Abraham. God promises Abraham that he will make a nation from 'the son of the slave woman also because he is your offspring' (v. 13). God demonstrates mercy to Hagar and Ishmael in the wilderness when their water runs out. Hagar despairs of life and so separates herself from Ishmael so that she will not see him die. Although the only mention in the text is the weeping of Hagar, when the angel of God calls to Hagar he states that God has heard the voice of the boy. She is told to go and get the boy with the promise that God will make him into a great nation. God opened her eyes to see a well of water so that

---

1. The verb used in verse 9 is also ṣāḥaq. Although it might have a variety of connotations, such as entertainment and celebration (Matthews, *Genesis 11:27–50:26*, p. 268), a negative view is supported not only by Sarah's reaction but also by God's approval of her request to send Ishmael away.

2. Victor Hamilton (*The Book of Genesis: Chapters 18–50* [Grand Rapids: Eerdmans, 1995], p. 77), suggests the age of weaning could be a little older than two or three years of age.

3. Gordon J. Wenham, *Genesis 16–50* (Dallas: Word Books, 1994), p. 82.

they would not die. The rest of the verses summarize the early life of Ishmael: God was with him, he lived in the wilderness of Paran, he became an expert with the bow, and his mother took a wife for him from Egypt (vv. 20-21). The fulfillment of God's promise to make a nation from him is given in Genesis 25:12-18.

Abraham's Treaty with Abimelech (Gen. 21:22-34)

This episode emphasizes several things about Abraham which have already become clear in earlier accounts. Abraham is a powerful individual whose wealth and possessions make him a formidable force. It is interesting that the commander of the army of Abimelech, a man named Phicol, is involved in the negotiations with Abraham (vv. 22-24).[4] One is reminded of Genesis 14 and Abraham's role as king in rescuing Lot.

The importance of land rights are also emphasized in relation to a well of water that is the heart of a dispute between Abraham and the servants of Abimelech. This leads to a covenant between Abraham and Abimelech to ensure Abraham's right to the well in the future.[5] This incident reminds us of the promise of God to Abraham concerning the land.

The importance of seed is also significant in this passage, which can be seen in several ways. First, the interactions with Abimelech in Genesis 20:1-18 and 21:22-34 act as an envelope around the birth of Isaac, the promised seed who is born in Genesis 21:1-21. This passage also occurs right before the test of Abraham concerning his beloved son in Genesis 22. Thus the placement of the text speaks to the importance of the seed. Second, when Abimelech approaches Abraham to enter into a covenant not to deal falsely with him, this covenant includes not only the present generation but also future generations. Covenants always include future descendants, so that the

---

4. Waltke (*Genesis*, p. 298) sees two covenants in Genesis 21:22-34. The first one in verses 22-24 he calls a non-aggression pact which would establish peace between Abraham and Abimelech and their descendants.

5. This passage is a good example of a covenant between two parties where the two parties are virtually equal partners (a bilateral covenant). Many of the elements of a covenant are present, such as the terminology used to make a covenant (literally 'to cut' a covenant), the use of animals in the covenant ceremony, and the swearing of oaths.

agreement that Abraham enters into binds not only himself but also his posterity. This is a normal feature of covenants. This aspect of covenant is explicitly mentioned in verses 22-24 and is implicitly affirmed in verses 27-34 in the use of the name the Everlasting God (v. 33). The name Everlasting God emphasizes that God's promises extend beyond the present circumstances because He is not a deity limited either by place or time. He is able to ensure that covenant promises will extend to Abraham's posterity.[6]

The name of the well, Beersheba, also speaks of the certainty of this covenant. There seems to be a play on words, for Beersheba can either mean 'well of oath' or 'well of seven', a possible pun on a key word used in this text. The Hebrew root *šbʿ* can either mean 'to swear' (used three times in this passage) or 'seven' (used nine times). For someone to swear an oath means they are committed to the terms of the covenant in a legal sense. The ceremony of the animals also demonstrates the commitment of the parties to the covenant as the animals act as a witness to the agreement (v. 30). The fact that seven animals are used may signify a complete commitment as the number seven many times expresses completion.[7]

This passage is a good place to reflect on the significance of covenant and blessing. First, to be in a covenant relationship with God is to be the recipient of great blessing. Abimelech acknowledges this when he states that 'God is with you in all that you do' (21:22). The promises that God made to Abraham, and that were confirmed in the covenant of Genesis 15, are being fulfilled in the life of Abraham. These blessings promised to Abraham are ultimately fulfilled in Jesus Christ and the new covenant, so that even Gentiles who believe in Jesus are children of Abraham (Gal. 3:29) and receive the blessings of the covenant. Although now we have received only a down payment of all the blessings God has in store for us – which includes all the spiritual blessings that come from union with Christ – we are assured that the fullness of covenant blessing will be ours when Jesus returns. This fullness of blessing

---

6. Waltke, *Genesis*, p. 300.

7. Matthews (*Genesis 11:27–50:26*, p. 281) makes the comment that the offer of seven lambs is exceptional, which is indicated by Abimelech's puzzlement over their significance.

will include a complete restoration of creation, including our physical and spiritual lives in the new heavens and the new earth.

Second, great blessing even comes to those who are only in the covenant relationship in a legal sense. Ishmael is an example of this. Even though he is not the true heir and is a product of human effort (natural procreation), to bring about the promise of God, he is circumcised and thus comes under the blessing of being in a covenant relationship with God. This blessing in the Old Testament focuses on material blessings. Ishmael becomes a great nation and is blessed materially because of his relationship to Abraham. This shows that one can be part of the covenant in a legal sense but not be part of the elect, and that there are blessings that come to the one who is in the covenant only in a legal sense. Paul can state that to Israel belong the blessings of the covenant (Rom. 9:4) even though not all Israel are Israel. Blessings flow from being in a covenant relationship with God, even if that relationship is only legal and external (see Chapter 8 for further discussion of the legal administration of the covenant).

Third, if covenants always include descendants, then this key element of the covenant relationship would be assumed by the Jewish people in the first century when they hear of the new covenant in Christ and would be part of the justification of including infants in the new covenant through baptism. This principle is reflected in the household baptisms of Acts and the fact that Paul addresses the children in his letters as part of the church (Eph. 6:1-3). Thus there are benefits and great privileges of growing up in a godly home. The prayer is that such blessing will lead to faith in Jesus Christ and an acceptance of covenant responsibilities by each child.

Fourth, even those who are not in a covenant relationship with God are promised to be blessed depending on how they treat those who are in a covenant relationship with God. This principle is stated in Genesis 12:3 and is illustrated several times in patriarchal history and in the history of God's people, Israel. Abimelech is blessed because of his relationship with Abraham (as Laban is later blessed because of his relationship with Jacob in Genesis 30:27). The curse side is also demonstrated in Egypt's mistreatment of Israel leading to the plagues, the defeat of Sihon when he would not allow the Israelites to pass through his land (Num. 21:31-35), and the prohibition against Moabites entering the assembly of the LORD because the king of Moab hired Balaam to curse Israel (Deut. 23:3). Since those who believe in Jesus Christ are children of Abraham (Gal. 3:29), this principle has meaning for the church today and can be seen in God's commitment to avenge His people (Rev. 6:9-11). Those who mistreat God's people will not go unpunished, even if such punishment is not carried out until the day of judgment.

The Sacrifice of Isaac (22:1-19)
The events of Genesis 22 take place 'after these things' (22:1). Although this is a general time indicator which includes what has taken place in the previous chapter, in reference to Isaac it is a reminder that he has already been weaned. It is hard to know exactly how old Isaac is in this chapter. He is called a *na'ar* in verses 5 and 12, which has a broad range of age possibilities from an infant (Exod. 2:6) to a thirty-year-old (Gen. 41:12).[8] It is clear he is old enough to have the wood of the burnt offering laid on him so that he could carry it (v. 6). The translation 'boy' gives the sense that Isaac is still young and submissive to whatever his father tells him to do.

Now that the promised child has been born to Abraham, God puts Abraham to the test in reference to his son Isaac. No doubt Isaac is a cherished child. This is reflected in how he is described in verse 2: 'your son, your only son Isaac, whom you love'. This child was born after years of patient waiting; this child is the son of their old age who will bring them comfort and joy in their later years. But even more, this child represents the promises of God to Abraham and his hope for the future. All the promises of God hinged on Isaac, so when God tells Abraham to offer his son as a burnt offering God is asking Abraham to put to death his hope for the future. The test asks Abraham to choose God over his own son and to trust God to fulfill the promises He has made, even when it appears he is putting to death the hope for those promises.

---

8. Victor Hamilton, נַעַר (*na'ar*), *NIDOTTE*, 3:125.

Abraham passes the test, which is demonstrated in his actions in response to God's request. He acts in a decisive way in rising early and making all the preparations necessary for the sacrifice (v. 3). He affirms that God will provide all that is needed for the sacrifice (v. 8). He also comments to his young men that he and his son will go and will worship and will return. All these verbs are first-person plurals which can be translated 'we will go and we will worship and we will return'. Abraham demonstrates faith in the promise of God to provide whatever is needed for the fulfillment of His promises. So he builds the altar, lays the wood on the altar, binds Isaac and places him on the wood of the altar, and is ready to plunge the knife into his son when he is stopped from completing the sacrifice by the angel of the Lord. A ram caught in a thicket will be the sacrifice. There is no doubt that Abraham fears God (v. 12) and trusts in Him to fulfill His promises.

It is almost unimaginable that God would ask Abraham to sacrifice His son as a burnt offering. Is the God that Abraham worships no different than the pagan gods of the nations who require child sacrifice? The answer is obvious in light of the way God is presented in the Book of Genesis. In fact, even the way Abraham responds to this request demonstrates that God is not like other gods. Abraham is convinced that no matter what God has asked him to do in relationship to Isaac, God's promises for a future seed will be fulfilled. Hebrews 11:19 understands Abraham's response of 'we will go, we will worship, and we will return' (v. 5) as Abraham's faith that God could even raise Isaac from the dead. Thus Abraham's faith in the character of God shines forth. God is testing Abraham and in His sovereignty He plans for the ram to be available for the substitute sacrifice.[9] The faith of Abraham in God is borne out

---

9. It sounds a bit strange to hear the angel of the Lord, who is always closely associated with God, say to Abraham, 'now I know that you fear God' (21:12), as if God did not really know this before these events. Unless one is willing to deny the fact that God knows everything, this statement must refer to the fact that the evidence for Abraham's fear of God has now become manifested in history in light of the events surrounding the sacrifice of Isaac. Waltke (*Genesis*, p. 308) comments that God does not experience the quality of Abraham's faith until played out on the stage of history, Matthews (*Genesis 11:27–50:26*, p. 296) calls it a discovery of the depth of Abraham's loyalty, and Wenham (*Genesis 16–50*, p. 110) says that the knowledge of God is confirmed. For a discussion of God's relationship to time, and how difficult it is for those who are finite to speak of one who is not limited by time, see John Frame, *No Other God: A Response to Open Theism* (Phillipsburg, NJ: P & R Publishing, 2000).

by the name that is given to this place: 'the LORD will provide' (v. 14). In fact, this very place seems to be the spot that God will choose as the location where the sacrifices of Israel will be brought, as Moriah will be identified as the later Jerusalem (2 Chron. 3:1).[10] It is also significant that God does not ask Abraham to do what He Himself is not willing to do for the salvation of His people: give up His only Son as a substitute sacrifice for their salvation. Abraham's faith in God's power to raise the dead is displayed in the resurrection of God's Son on the third day.

Following Abraham's obedience to the command of God to sacrifice his son, God declares that He has sworn by oath that He will bless Abraham and fulfill the promises He has made to him. These promises include the multiplication of Abraham's offspring to become as numerous as the stars of heaven and the sand on the seashore, the triumph of Abraham's offspring over their enemies, and the blessing of the nations through Abraham's offspring. These promises begin to be fulfilled in the Old Testament, which may be the purpose of the concluding section of Genesis 22:20-24 (see next chapter). However, these promises to Abraham are now being fulfilled through the work of Christ who will produce an innumerable host of those who worship God (Gal. 3:29; Heb. 11:12), who will defeat all the enemies of God's people (Rom. 16:20; Rev. 19:11-21), and who will bring about God's blessing for all the nations of the earth (Acts 1:8; Rev. 21:24-26).

Genesis 22 is a good passage to discuss how to interpret a narrative because there are different ways that this text has been understood. Some argue that it is inappropriate to identify with the character of Abraham because his test is so unique that no one else really faces the same test. Instead, the original readers of the account would identify with Isaac because, if Isaac had been put to death, Israel would not have existed as a nation. If one identifies with Isaac, the point of the account is not the faith of Abraham but that God provides a substitute sacrifice for Isaac. Thus, the theme of the passage

---

10. Although Matthews (*Genesis 11:27–50:26*, pp. 290-91) is more skeptical of the specific identification of Moriah with the later temple mount, arguing that Genesis only refers to a mountain range, Waltke (*Genesis*, pp. 305-06) is more positive on the identification between the two and answers some of the objections.

is that the LORD provides a lamb for a burnt offering so that Isaac (Israel) will live.[11]

This approach is against any kind of exemplary exegesis where the character (Abraham) becomes an example for someone to follow. For example, it would be inappropriate to argue that just as Abraham was tested to give up something valuable so we may be called to give up something valuable as we respond in faith. There are dangers in exemplary exegesis, such as the error of making something which is particular to be universal, the error of making something that is descriptive to be prescriptive, and the errors of moralism and legalism. These need to be avoided, but are there not appropriate uses of characters as examples that would avoid these pitfalls? There are so many New Testament passages where the author uses a character as an example that one should be cautious in condemning all exemplary exegesis.[12] Hebrews 11 uses Abraham as an example of faith in relationship to the sacrifice of Isaac (vv. 17-19).[13]

Further, there may be exegetical reasons in Genesis 22 which support the view that Abraham is being presented as an example of faith. Moberly argues that the story is told in the language of law (torah) so that Abraham can be seen as a model for Israel. Abraham in Genesis 22 embodies the fear of God, which is the response God wants from Israel. He notes that the Genesis text focuses more on the self-offering of Abraham than it does on Isaac, and that the New Testament texts (Heb. 11:17-19 and James 2:18-24) use

---

11. Sidney Greidanus, *Preaching Christ from the Old Testament* (Grand Rapids), pp. 292-305 and *Preaching Christ from Genesis* (Grand Rapids: Eerdmans, 2007), pp. 194-212.

12. Elijah is an example of effective prayer in James 5:17-18 and Abraham is an example of a faith that demonstrates its reality through works in James 2:21-23. Paul calls on believers to imitate him in 1 Corinthians 4:16 and 11:1.

13. Greidanus (*Preaching Christ*, p. 305) would argue that Hebrews is using the example of Abraham for illustrative purposes and is not presenting an exposition of Genesis 22; however, more is going on in Hebrews 11 than mere illustration. The author of Hebrews is drawing out meaning from the text through analogy. Just as God's people in the Old Testament faced difficult situations that required faith or faithful perseverance, so God's people now also face difficult situations that require faith or faithful perseverance (see the article by S. M. Baugh, 'The Cloud of Witnesses in Hebrews 11,' *WTJ* 68 [2006], pp. 113-32, who argues that faith refers to the persevering faith of God's people who are witnesses of the reality of the world to come introduced by Christ).

Genesis 22 as a paradigm for faith, which is the appropriate human response to God.[14]

The point is that texts have primary and secondary levels of meaning. For example, the primary meaning of Matthew 28:19-20 is to make disciples, but it is also appropriate to use this text to argue for the Trinity based on the baptismal formula. Such an approach is not arguing that a text has many meanings. There is one meaning but it is a complex oneness, just as God, who is the author of meaning, is a complex unity (three in one).[15] Thus it is appropriate to approach a text from many different angles. If one approaches this text based on identification with Isaac, then the theme that God will provide a sacrifice becomes prominent (a redemptive historical approach). If one approaches the text based on identification with Abraham, then the response to testing will be emphasized (an exemplary approach). The major systematic theological idea in Genesis 22 is substitutionary atonement so one could focus on that concept and draw in other texts which would support it. There is also the importance of the concept of seed in Genesis 22, which is a major theme in Genesis 15–22, and goes all the way back to Genesis 3:15.[16] Such a theme relates to Christ as the seed (Gal. 3:16) and to God's people today as the seed (Gal. 3:29). These different approaches are not contradictory to each other, and are not necessarily in competition with each other, but are a reflection of the simplicity and the complexity of the God we worship.

---

14. R.W.L. Moberly, *The Bible, Theology, and Faith: A Study of Abraham and Jesus* (Cambridge: Cambridge University Press, 2000), p.83. Genesis commentaries that explicitly argue that Abraham is an example of faith include Waltke and Wenham.

15. See Vern Poythress, *God-Centered Biblical Interpretation* (Phillipsburg, NJ: P & R Publishing, 1999).

16. It is interesting that Greidanus argues that the emphasis on seed, which falls under the promise-fulfillment approach in his analysis, should not be a way to connect to Christ from Genesis 22 because it is not directly related to the theme of the narrative. However, such an approach is too narrow because it sees only one legitimate theme of a text and does not distinguish between primary themes and secondary themes, which are all part of the meaning of a text and thus are fair game for analysis. Greidanus' approach leads to RH (Redemptive Historical) only preaching which argues that there is only one appropriate way to preach a text (see Robert J. Cara, 'Redemptive Historical Themes in the *Westminster Larger Catechism*,' in *The Westminster Confession in the 21st Century* [ed. Ligon Duncan; Ross-shire: Christian Focus, 2009], Vol. 3 pp. 55-76).

STUDY QUESTIONS

1   Why is Sarah concerned with Ishmael's response to the birth of Isaac? Can you think of a modern-day analogy?

2   What does it mean to be in the covenant in a legal sense? What aspect of the covenant relationship is missed if the connection is only legal?

3   In what way is Genesis 22 understood differently if one identifies with Isaac or with Abraham?

4   Why is it inappropriate to condemn all exemplary exegesis?

5   How does understanding God as Trinity help us to understand the meaning of a text? Does that mean you can make a text say anything you want it to say?

I I

The Fulfillment of God's Promise in Faithful Preparation for the Future
(Genesis 22:20–25:18)

Genesis 22:20 begins a new section with the phrase 'Now after these things'. After the great test of Genesis 22 and the confirmation of God's promises to Abraham, the narrative focus begins to shift to the future while at the same time bringing to a close the lives of Abraham and Sarah. The emphasis throughout continues to be on the faithfulness of God's promises, but there is also a focus on what Abraham must do to prepare for the preservation of those promises for the next generation. The promise of land is at the center of the account of Sarah's death and burial (Gen. 23), the promise of a future seed is the emphasis in the account of finding a wife for Isaac (Gen. 24), and the blessings that come from being related to Abraham are emphasized in several passages in this section (22:20-24; 25:12-18).

The Burial of Sarah and the Promise of Land
(Gen. 22:20–23:20)
Genesis 22:20-24 is a transition passage that can be connected to what has gone before but which also looks ahead to what is to follow. It comes right after the confirmation of God's promises to Abraham and reveals God's blessing on Abraham's family. Nahor is Abraham's brother, and his family lineage is given in these verses. Twelve sons were born to Nahor, which is

a significant number in light of the twelve sons who will be born to Jacob. This section also functions as a transition to the following narrative because Rebekah, who will become the wife of Isaac, the promised seed, is a descendant of Nahor.[1]

Although Genesis 23 relates the death of Sarah, most of the chapter covers Abraham's negotiations with the Hittites to obtain a burial site for Sarah. Sarah's life and death are very important. She dies in the land of Canaan at the age of 127 years, which indicates a long life blessed by God.[2] Abraham mourns for his wife and then seeks a burial site for her from the Hittites[3] because he does not own any property in the land. Abraham's negotiations for a burial site demonstrate several things.

First, even though Abraham is a sojourner and a foreigner in the land he is very well respected by the Hittites. He is called a 'prince of God', which can be translated 'mighty prince' if the word for God (*elohim*) is taken as a superlative adjective.[4] The term 'prince' (*naśî*) signifies a leader[5] and Abraham is a distinguished leader in the eyes of the Hittites. Abraham is also called 'my lord' (v. 11) and there is polite interchange between the parties in the negotiations ('listen to me' or 'hear me' in verses 8, 11, 13, 15).[6] Also, Abraham shows humility in bowing to the ground when he first speaks to the Hittites (v. 7) and then to Ephron (v. 12).

Second, Abraham had asked for property to bury Sarah and the Hittites responded by offering Abraham the choicest of their tombs. This may demonstrate reluctance on their part to allow Abraham to acquire permanent possession in the land.[7] But it also would not be suitable for Abraham because he could not be guaranteed permanent access to the site in

---

1. Matthews, *Genesis 11:27–50:26*, pp. 306, 308-09.
2. Matthews, *Genesis 11:27–50:26*, p. 314.
3. There is some uncertainty as to who these pre-Israelite Hittites represent, but Waltke (*Genesis*, p. 317) argues that they are not connected to the Hittite empire which fell in 1200 BC because the Hittites of the patriarchal accounts have Semitic names, not Hittite names. They also do not seem to be connected to the neo-Hittite states of Syria that had contact with Israel during the monarchy (1 Kings 10:29).
4. Waltke, *Genesis*, p. 318.
5. Walter Kaiser, נָשִׂיא, *TWOT*, 2:601. The term 'prince' is used of non-Israelite chieftains (Gen. 17:20; 25:16) and Midianite leaders (Num. 25:18; Josh. 13:21).
6. Matthews, *Genesis 11:27–50:26*, p. 318.
7. Waltke, *Genesis*, p. 318.

the future. A piece of property that he himself owns would guarantee permanent access.

Third, although Ephron offers to give to Abraham the property he has requested, Abraham will not take it as a gift but offers full payment for the property. The point of the narrative is that the transaction is legitimate and permanent so that there is no doubt that Abraham becomes the owner of the property. There are witnesses to the transaction (v. 10) and there is the exchange of money for an agreed price (v. 16). The end of the chapter summarizes what has taken place, which emphasizes that this property in the land of Canaan now belongs to Abraham (vv. 17-20).

Genesis 23 demonstrates Abraham's commitment to the land of Canaan because he does not take Sarah back to Haran to bury her. Ancestral burial grounds were very important because burial in ancestral graves indicated honor and continuity with the family.[8] Abraham has broken ties with his family and pagan background because of his commitment to Yahweh (the LORD). He also demonstrates faith in the promise of God that his descendants will one day possess the land of Canaan. His actions demonstrate his hope for the future. He may only own a cave and a field, but he knows one day the whole land will be given to his descendants. Abraham received a down payment of his inheritance. Even in the Old Testament his focus was on more than the physical land (Heb. 11:10). In light of the coming of Christ, the inheritance for believers in Christ consists of much more than just a portion of land, but consists of the whole world (Rom. 4:13), which will be fully possessed in the new heavens and new earth. However, like Abraham, we have received a down payment of the full salvation God has planned for His people (Eph. 1:11-14).

A Wife for Isaac: Preserving the Future Seed (Gen. 24:1-67)

Abraham is getting old (v. 1), which means that Isaac is also getting older. The time has come for Abraham to ensure the preservation of the future seed by seeking a wife for his son. The importance of this account is emphasized in a number of ways. First, it is the longest single, narrative episode in

---

8. Matthews, *Genesis 11:27–50:26*, p. 310.

Genesis. It is also a beautiful story of the Lord's guidance through perfect timing and the faithful obedience of a servant of Abraham. Second, the servant that Abraham chooses for this mission is presented as one of his most trusted servants. He is the oldest of Abraham's household and he had charge of all that Abraham possessed. Third, the servant of Abraham must take an oath whereby he swears by the LORD, the God of heaven and God of the earth, that he will not take a wife for Isaac from the Canaanites.[9] It is interesting that the non-elect seed of Abraham take wives from the surrounding nations. Ishmael takes a wife from Egypt (21:21) and later Esau will take a wife from the Hittites (26:34). The elect seed of Abraham is to be kept separate from the other nations in order to remain faithful to the covenant and to ensure its future existence. Thus the servant of Abraham is sent back to Abraham's home country and kindred who live in the city of Nahor in Mesopotamia to find a wife for Isaac. Fourth, in response to certain problems that might arise in trying to get a woman to leave her home and come to 'this land' (v. 5), Abraham asserts that the servant is not to take Isaac away from the land where Abraham now dwells (vv. 7-8). This demonstrates a continuing commitment to the promise of land. Land and seed must be kept together so that the promises of God are not forgotten or endangered. The servant also receives the promise that God will assist him by sending His angel before him (v. 7).

The account of the servant's mission to find a wife for Isaac is presented in verses 10-61. The length of the account is partly due to the fact that the servant reviews for Laban and the family of Rebekah his commission and journey (vv. 34-49), which adds some important details about Abraham's greatness and wealth. It also reinforces how God led the servant to Rebekah as the one who will be a good match as a wife for Isaac. Such leading by God will hopefully convince the family to allow Rebekah to accompany the servant to the land of Canaan. Of course, Rebekah herself must be willing to go. Perhaps the

---

9. Abraham tells the servant to put his hand under Abraham's thigh for the swearing of the oath (v. 2). The thigh represents the procreative power and heritage of the patriarch's position as the source of the family (Matthews, *Genesis 11:27–50:26*, p. 326). Some take it as a euphemism for the genitalia that represents the certainty of the future of God's promises (Waltke, *Genesis*, p. 327).

best way to understand this remarkable story is to examine the various characters who are involved.

The servant shows both planning and dependence on God. The planning includes the fact that he goes prepared with 'choice gifts' (v. 10). These gifts will show how much God has blessed Abraham (v. 35), will be used to approach Rebekah to ask about her household (vv. 22-23),[10] and will be an incentive for Rebekah to give assent to the request that she leave her family. There is also planning concerning how the servant will find the young woman. The plan includes asking a young woman for a drink. The right young woman will not only give the servant a drink but will also offer to water the camels. Dependence upon God is evident in the prayer the servant offers to God for success as he develops his plan of action (vv. 12-14). He also worships the LORD and offers a blessing to God for His covenant faithfulness when Rebekah offers hospitality to the servant in her father's house (vv. 26-27).

Rebekah is presented as a woman who would be a good match for Isaac. She is young, attractive, and a virgin (v. 16). Such physical information is fairly uncommon in Hebrew narrative and shows the importance of the description.[11] She is also from the family of Abraham ('born to Bethuel the son of Milcah, the wife of Nahor, Abraham's brother,' v. 15). She passes the test set up by the servant by offering not just the servant a drink, but his camels also. The fact that there are ten camels shows that this is no small act. Thus, she demonstrates character traits associated with hospitality, such as kindness, industry, and generosity.[12] Also, when the family hesitates to send Rebekah away immediately, she understands the urgency

---

10. The account the servant gives to Rebekah's household concerning his commission and journey reshapes the story in order to convince the family and Rebekah that it was God's will that she return with him. A substantive difference appears in his report concerning the order between presenting the gifts and his inquiry about Rebekah's identity. The gifts are mentioned before the servant's inquiry concerning her identity in the narrative account (v.22), yet in the retelling of the story the jewelry is mentioned after her identity is revealed (v. 47). Matthews (*Genesis 11:27–50:26*, pp. 339-341) notes that the two passages may not necessarily be contradictory because two different verbs are used in the two accounts. In the narrative account, the servant 'took' the jewelry and asked about her identity. In retelling the story, the servant states that, after he finds out her identity, he then 'put' the jewelry on her.

11. Matthews, *Genesis 11:27–50:26*, p. 333.

12. Waltke, *Genesis*, p. 328.

of the moment and affirms her willingness to go promptly (v. 58).[13] Here she models Abraham who also was willing to leave his family and homeland. Such a prompt willingness to go may also reflect faith in Abraham's God.[14]

It is understandable that the family of Rebekah would want to seek to delay her departure because they would be likely never to see Rebekah again (v. 55). However, a son of Rebekah will one day cross paths with Laban, Rebekah's brother, and this account gives the reader insight into Laban's character, which will be on full display later in the book of Genesis. The introduction of Laban emphasizes that he saw the ring and the bracelets on the arm of Rebekah before he heard the words of Rebekah concerning the man. In other words, it is the jewelry that excites Laban more than anything else.[15] One can only wonder if Laban and Bethuel[16] give in to the servant's request in hopes of obtaining more gifts (vv. 50-51). Although it is not obvious at this point that desire for gifts is the reason, Laban will be driven by greed in his later interactions with Jacob. They do give their consent to allow Rebekah to go with the servant and they offer a blessing on her that she may have many descendants who will be mighty over their enemies (v. 60). Whether realizing it or not they affirm the promises to Abraham of numerous descendants who will become great. Rebekah will be used by God to bring this about.

There has not been much information up to this point concerning the character of Isaac other than his willingness to submit to his father in Genesis 22. In the concluding account of the servant's mission there is clearly the emergence of Isaac as the new master.[17] Although he does not speak any words, he is the glue that holds the narrative together. Although Abraham is the one who commissioned the servant, the servant brings Rebekah to Isaac and reports to him the success of his journey.

---

13. Matthews, *Genesis 11:27–50:26*, p. 344.

14. Waltke, *Genesis*, p. 325.

15. Matthews, *Genesis 11:27–50:26*, p. 338; Waltke (*Genesis*, p. 325) calls Laban's response greed.

16. This is the only time Bethuel speaks in this passage. He is the important link to Abraham. Although he is the father, his son Laban is more prominent in the chapter, which may indicate that Bethuel is incapacitated in some way (Waltke, *Genesis*, p. 331).

17. Matthews, *Genesis 11:27–50:26*, p. 346.

Thus Isaac is presented as lord and successor to Abraham even as Rebekah is presented as mother and successor of Sarah.[18] The journey is successful. God has provided a wife for Isaac so that the promises of a future seed are secure.

The Death of Abraham: The End of an Era (Gen. 25:1-18)

The end of Abraham's life is presented as being under the blessing of God. The account of the sons of Abraham through his wife Keturah demonstrates the further blessing of posterity in fulfillment of the promise that Abraham will be the father of many nations.[19] However, the special place of Isaac as the true heir is also emphasized in the sending away of the sons of Abraham's concubines (v. 6)[20] and in giving to Isaac all that Abraham possessed (v. 5).

The death of Abraham is presented as the ideal death. Death is always considered an enemy in light of the curse of the fall (Gen. 3), but if one dies in the way that Abraham dies, then one is considered to be very blessed. Abraham lived a long time: 'he died in a good old age, an old man and full of years' (v. 8). In the Book of Proverbs long life is seen as a blessing of wisdom and includes seeing one's grandchildren (Prov. 3:16; 17:6). No doubt this was a reality for Abraham as he lived for 175 years. The phrase 'full of years' is the adjective śabēa', which can mean 'full' or 'satisfied'.[21] This word may not be referring to the length of Abraham's life but to its fullness. Abraham was a wealthy man who had lived a full and satisfying life.

The final phrase in the description of his death is that he 'was gathered to his people'. This phrase occurs after the death of Abraham and before the account of his burial, so that it should not be identified with either event. This phrase cannot be identified with being buried in the ancestral grave because it is used of people who were not buried there

---

18. Waltke, *Genesis*, p. 333.

19. Many of the names listed among the sons of Abraham are connected to people groups who came to live in Northwest Arabia (Matthews, *Genesis 11:27–50:26*, p. 349).

20. These concubines are not identified, but probably include both Keturah and Hagar.

21. There are a few manuscripts, including the Samaritan Pentateuch, the Septuagint, and Syriac, that add the word 'days' to the adjective 'full'.

(Abraham, Moses, and Aaron).[22] The fact that it is stated that he was gathered to his fathers before being buried implies that family solidarity is not broken even in death.[23] It also may signify a belief in a person's continued existence after death. Waltke comments that the phrase refers 'to a belief that despite his mortality and perishability, man possesses an immortal element that survives the loss of life. Death is looked upon as a transition to an afterlife, where one is united with one's ancestors.'[24]

Although both Isaac and Ishmael bury their father, there is a clear focus on Isaac and God's blessing on him (v. 11), which acts as a transition to the Toledot ('the generations') of Isaac, which starts in 25:19. However, the account of the 'generations of Ishmael' is given first in 25:12-18. This passage demonstrates once again God's faithfulness to His promises to Abraham that many nations would come from him (Gen. 17:20) and His promise to Hagar that God would make Ishmael into a great nation (Gen. 21:18). The fact that the sons of Ishmael become twelve princes according to their twelve tribes parallels the blessing that will come to the line of Isaac through Jacob and demonstrates God's blessing of Ishmael. His descendants settle in the general area of northwest Arabia.

Ishmael also lives a long life of 137 years and is said to be 'gathered to his people' (v. 17). One should not read into this phrase that Ishmael joins Abraham as part of the covenant people at his death. He had already been separated from the covenant community and had been described as living 'over against all his kinsmen' (Gen. 16:12).[25] He joins his own people at his death. Although Ishmael may not have received the spiritual blessing, he was blessed because of his association with Abraham, which is seen in the description of the twelve tribes that come from him and in the description of his death.

---

22. The phrase 'was gathered to his people' is used only in the Pentateuch: Abraham (25:8); Ishmael (25:17); Isaac (35:29); Jacob (49:29, 33); Moses (Num. 27:13; Deut. 32:50); and Aaron (Num. 20:24; Deut. 32:50).

23. Hamilton, *Genesis 18–50*, p. 168.

24. Waltke, *Genesis*, pp. 340-41. Others who argue this point include Keil and Delitzsch, 'The Pentateuch,' p. 263; Wenham, *Genesis 16–50*, p. 160; and Currid, *Genesis 1:1–25:18*, p. 435.

25. This is alluded to at the end of the account of Ishmael in Genesis 25:18. The expression '*al-pĕnē* can either mean 'against' or 'the opposite of'. In light of Genesis 16:12 the best meaning is 'against' (Matthews, *Genesis 11:26–50:27*, p. 364).

Study Questions

1   Why is it important that Abraham purchases a burial
    plot for Sarah in the land of Canaan? What parallel is
    there between Abraham's situation and the situation
    of the believer today?

2   Where does Isaac get his wife? Why is the story of
    how the servant found a wife for Isaac important?
    What principles are relevant from this story for
    God's people today?

3   How does Abraham's death exhibit the blessings of
    God? Are all these blessings guaranteed to every fol-
    lower of Christ? Why or why not (see John 15:18-20)?

12

The Family of Isaac: Conflict and Favoritism
(Genesis 25:19–27:46)

The Toledot (Account) of Isaac is found in Genesis 25:19–
35:29. It is not actually an account of Isaac's life but instead
is an account of the life of Jacob, beginning with his birth and
ending with a listing of his twelve sons (Gen. 35:23-26) and the
death of Isaac (Gen. 35:27-29). Only one chapter is devoted to
events in Isaac's life (Genesis 26) apart from his role in seeking
to bless his son Esau (Genesis 27). The rest of the account is
devoted to Jacob and the development of his character. Two
of the obstacles to the fulfillment of God's promises are (1) the
conflict and favoritism in this family and (2) the character of
Jacob. God overcomes family favoritism by working against
the wishes of Isaac and he overcomes the character of Jacob
by changing him from a prayerless schemer into a prayerful
person of faith. There are a series of events that God will use
to bring about this change, including Jacob's interaction with
Laban, but it will culminate in a wrestling match just before
Jacob is reunited with Esau after years of separation.

Family Conflict Based on the Character of the Sons (Gen. 25:19-34)

The Toledot of Isaac begins with a statement of his marriage
to Rebekah and her family connection to Laban (v. 20). This
family connection will be important later in the story. Isaac
is presented positively at the beginning of this account by

praying for his barren wife. Yahweh (the LORD) answers his prayer and Rebekah conceives twins. Even in the womb there is a struggle between the children. The struggle is so intense that Rebekah seeks to inquire of the LORD why this is happening (v. 22). She is answered by an oracle that explains the struggle within her. The two children represent two nations that will be divided or separated from each other. The separation of the two is explained by the statement that one will be stronger than the other. The younger son will be stronger, which means the older son will serve the younger (v. 23). This announcement before birth becomes very important for the way the story unfolds. One must assume that Isaac knows the oracle; it is even possible that Isaac, the patriarch, had a role as the one who received and related the oracle to Rebekah. Isaac has already prayed for the removal of Rebekah's barrenness, a role similar to his father Abraham who is called a prophet in Genesis 20.[1] But even if Isaac does not play such a role at this point in the story, it is a likely assumption that Isaac would have known this statement concerning the future of his two sons. This knowledge will be important for his future actions towards them.

The conflict that began in the womb will continue in the lives of these two sons. This fact becomes evident in the description of the two boys at their birth and then in the description of the character of the two boys. Each parent is going to show loyalty to one of the sons based on their character, which will become the basis for future family conflict. The future character of the two is foreshadowed in the description of the boys at birth and the names given to each.

The first twin comes out looking red and is very hairy, so they call his name Esau. The connection between hairy ($\acute{s}\bar{e}'\bar{a}r$) and Esau ($'\bar{e}\acute{s}\bar{a}w$) is not etymological; rather, there is a sound play between the two with the reversal of the Hebrew consonants $\acute{s}$ and $'$.[2] The colour red anticipates an incident of red stew which will show the character of Esau. Also, the word for red ($'a\underline{d}m\bar{o}n\hat{\imath}$) is a term that is associated with Edom ($'\breve{e}\underline{d}\bar{o}m$). The Edomites are the descendants of Esau.

---

1. Matthews, *Genesis 11:27– 50:26*, p. 387.
2. Waltke (*Genesis*, p. 358) comments that the term 'hairy' symbolizes Esau's animalish nature.

The younger brother comes out of the womb holding the heel of his older brother, so they call his name Jacob. Another wordplay is at work that gives insight into Jacob's character. The name Jacob ($ya'\check{a}q\bar{o}\underline{b}$) is related to the word heel ($'\bar{a}q\bar{e}\underline{b}$), which can be used metaphorically for someone who is a cheat or a deceiver (Pss. 41:9; 49:5). These character traits will be important for the way the story unfolds.

Conflict in this family will revolve around the character of the two sons but will also be increased by the favoritism shown to them by their parents. Esau is described as a skillful hunter and a man of the field (v. 27). He is a rugged outdoors man. The phrase 'man of the field' may stress a preference for open country and separation from the mainstream of society. His descendants settled in Edom, which borders the Arabah (desert region) south and southeast of the Dead Sea, in very rugged terrain.[3] Jacob is described as 'a quiet man, dwelling in tents' (v. 27). The word for 'quiet' is $t\bar{a}m$. Although it can refer to a person who is blameless (Job 1:8), that does not fit the character of Jacob at this point in the story.[4] In this context it may mean someone who is well-cultured or civilized, a fine man. This adjective might emphasize that Jacob is a more complete person than Esau, the rugged outdoors man.[5] The reader is not too surprised when the father is described as loving the older son who is a hunter because he ate of his game and that the mother loves the younger son who kept closer to the tents of the family settlement (v. 28). This preference of each parent for a particular son will be important for how the story develops.

The character of the two sons is shown in an incident where Jacob takes advantage of Esau's hunger (vv. 29-34). Esau comes in from the field exhausted and wants some of the red stew that Jacob has cooked. Jacob is willing to give him some of the stew if Esau will sell his birthright to him.

---

3. Waltke, *Genesis*, p. 391.
4. Waltke, *Genesis*, p. 362.
5. Hamilton (*Genesis 18–50*, pp. 181-82) argues that the meaning of 'quiet' ($t\bar{a}m$) is similar to Job's blameless character (Job 1:1) because he is not specifically condemned in verses 29-34; however, the character of Jacob does not fit such a description at this point in the story (Waltke, *Genesis*, p. 362). Just because Jacob is not specifically condemned for his actions in verses 29-34 does not mean that his actions are 'blameless'. The context supports a negative characterization of Jacob at this point.

The birthright is the right of the firstborn son who had the privileged status of the eldest son and received a double portion of the father's inheritance. Esau views the birthright as trivial in light of the fact that he perceives himself as near death ('I am about to die' in verse 32). He sells the privilege of birthright for a pot of stew and so 'despised his birthright' (v. 34). Esau is a crass man, driven by his passions, who acts on the impulse of the moment. Jacob, on the other hand, is a devious man who takes advantage of his brother's weakness to get the birthright for himself. He is a schemer who will turn a situation to his advantage to get what he wants.

The Blessing of God on Isaac's Family (Gen. 26)

The story of the family of Isaac continues in Genesis 27, so one wonders what the purpose of Genesis 26 is to the unfolding narrative. Genesis 26 focuses on several incidents from the life of Isaac before he is old and his eyes become dim (Gen. 27:1). Isaac follows in Abraham's footsteps, both good and bad. On the negative side, he is like his father in his use of deception. The chapter ends with a note of conflict concerning the marriage of Esau to Hittite women. Both deception and conflict will develop in Genesis 27. On the positive side, Isaac emerges as a powerful force in the region of the Negeb (the southern area of the land of Canaan). This chapter gives evidence of the fact that 'after the death of Abraham, God blessed Isaac his son' (Gen. 25:11). Isaac is the legitimate heir of Abraham who inherits the promises God made to Abraham. In showing how much God blessed Isaac in material wealth, one also sees how large the birthright was that Esau sold for a pot of stew.

Genesis 26 begins with a famine in the land which is going to force Isaac to leave the land. It is made clear that this famine is not the same famine that occurred during the days of Abraham, but the mention of famine, land, and Abraham brings to mind the accounts of Genesis 12:10-20 and 20:1-18. In fact, it seems like Isaac is following in his father's footsteps by heading down to Egypt when God appears to him at Gerar and tells him not to go to Egypt (v. 2). In this appearance to Isaac, God restates all the promises that He had made to Abraham, including the promise that all nations of the earth would be blessed through Isaac's offspring, and that He would fulfill these promises to Isaac and his descendants because of the obedience of Abraham (vv. 2-5). Two things are brought together in the confirmation of God's promises to Isaac.

The first is that God Himself has taken the oath that the promises of God to Abraham will be fulfilled. Thus, there is no doubt that one day in God's timing these promises will come to pass. Hebrews 6:13-20 makes this very point. God had no one greater to swear by, so He swore the oath by Himself. Based on His unchangeable character there is no way His purposes for Abraham will not be fulfilled. Hebrews then points us to the one who fulfills the promises of God and gives the people of God encouragement and hope, Jesus Christ.

Secondly, Genesis 26:5 presents Abraham as one who obeyed God. This verse looks back to Abraham's obedience at the sacrifice of Isaac (the phrase 'obeyed my voice' was used in 22:18). However, the rest of the verse uses phrases that are prominent later in the law of Moses ('my charge, my commandments, my statutes, my laws'). Abraham's obedience is presented as an ideal for Israel, who must observe God's law in the land that God was giving her.[6] Although God's promises are not dependent on Abraham's obedience, God is able to use obedience to further His purposes, a reminder that the way people respond to God is important. God will fulfill His purposes because He has taken the oath, but we pray that He will be able to use the faithfulness and obedience of His people to help accomplish His plan for the blessing of Abraham to come to the nations.

Isaac obeys God by not going down to Egypt; instead, he settles in Gerar. He faces a situation that is virtually identical to what his father Abraham faced and he responds just like his father. In Isaac's case, there is no plan made between Isaac and Rebekah on what they should say about their relationship before they get to Gerar. But when the men of the city ask about his relationship to Rebekah, he responds that she is his sister because he was afraid the men would kill him and take her (vv. 6-7). It is not clear how long this secret was kept but after 'he had been there a long time' (v. 8) Abimelech, king of the Philistines, saw Isaac 'laughing with Rebekah'. The

---

6. Matthews, *Genesis 11:27– 50:26*, p. 405, and Waltke, *Genesis*, p. 368.

verb 'laughing' (ṣḥq) is related to the name Isaac (yiṣḥāq) and in this context it must have the connotation of some kind of 'play' that involved behavior not appropriate between brother and sister. It is not clear exactly what kind of behavior Abimelech observed but he confronts Isaac with, 'Behold, she is your wife' (v. 9). Abimelech is not happy with this deception because people in Gerar would not have known the real relationship between Isaac and Rebekah, and someone might have 'lain with your wife and you would have brought guilt upon us' (v. 10). Abimelech corrects this situation by warning that if anyone touches the man or his wife they shall surely be put to death.

This episode serves two purposes in Genesis 26. It shows, first of all, that Isaac learned from his father how easy it is to use deception instead of trusting in God to be faithful to His covenant promises. God's promises included future descendants and the proper response would have been to trust God to protect their future offspring by guarding their marriage relationship. The fact that there are three episodes that are very similar to each other involving father and son shows how certain sins can easily be passed from one generation to the next.[7] In fact, in the next chapter deception is going to develop in this family.

Another purpose of this episode is to further the development of the character of Isaac. Even though he is following in his father's footsteps in a negative way, there is hope that Isaac can grow in his walk with the LORD as Abraham did. Right before this incident in Gerar is the statement concerning Abraham that he was obedient to God (26:5). Isaac has the same opportunity to grow in obedience that Abraham had. Will the Lord say of Isaac at the end of his life what he said of Abraham, that he 'obeyed my voice'?

The rest of the chapter shows how Isaac becomes powerful, like his father Abraham, among the Philistines and in the land of Canaan. His power stems from his abundant possessions of flocks, herds and many servants (v. 14). He had so many

---

7. See Robert Alter, *The Art of Biblical Narrative* (Basic Books, 1981), pp. 47-62, for a discussion of type scenes, which are similar episodes that occur at a critical juncture in the life of an important character and which are used to teach something important in the development of the narrative.

possessions that the Philistines envied him. This wealth, however, was a blessing from God (vv. 12-13). God was the one who made Isaac wealthy and powerful. In fact, the contrast between Isaac and the Philistines becomes so great that Abimelech asks Isaac to leave their region (v. 16).

The fact that Isaac has so many flocks, herds, and servants makes it difficult for him to live among the Philistines because of the need for resources, especially water. Conflict arises between Isaac and the Philistines over the use of wells. Isaac settled in the valley of Gerar and dug again the wells that his father had dug, and even gave them the same names his father gave them. When Isaac's herdsmen found a well of spring water, the herdsmen of Gerar claimed it as their own; so Isaac named the well 'Esek' (v. 20), a wordplay with the verb 'contend' ('*āśaq*). They also quarreled over another well which he called 'Sitnah', which means 'accusation'.[8] Finally, they dug a well that they did not quarrel over and called its name 'Rehoboth', which means 'broad' or 'spacious'.[9] They offer the explanation that 'now the LORD has made room for us, and we shall be fruitful in the land' (v. 22). Nevertheless, Isaac continues to move on and finally reaches Beersheba, which is in the land of Canaan.

As soon as Isaac reaches Beersheba, the LORD appears to him and reassures him that he will be blessed and his offspring will be multiplied. Although this blessing is for Abraham's sake (v. 24), Isaac is pictured as continuing the legacy of his father Abraham. Like Abraham, Isaac returns to the land promised to him and his descendants after showing benevolence to the Philistines. As he promised Abraham, so God promises to be with Isaac and greatly bless him. Like Abraham, Isaac builds an altar and calls on the name of the LORD. Isaac demonstrates that he accepts his covenant obligations and trusts in the promises of God for his future.

While Isaac is at Beersheba he is approached by Abimelech, along with an advisor and the commander of his army. At first, Isaac sees their coming negatively, feeling that their treatment of him in Gerar was less than acceptable. This response puts them on the defensive, but they understand

---

8. Matthews, *Genesis 11:27–50:26*, p. 410.
9. Matthews, *Genesis 11:27–50:26*, p. 411.

that Isaac has become great through the blessing of God and that if trouble were to break out in the future they would be no match for him. So they seek to make a covenant with him to ensure goodwill between them in the future. The covenant is ratified by both parties and the Philistines depart in peace (v. 31). Isaac has become as powerful as Abraham his father, and the promise to Abraham – that God would bless those who bless Abraham and his descendants – has come to pass (Gen. 12:3). Confirmation of God's blessing comes on the very day that Abimelech leaves in that the servants of Isaac discover another well, which they named 'Shibah' (v. 33), a reference to the sworn oath (*šbʿ*) of the covenant just made.[10] This incident parallels a similar incident between Abraham and Abimelech (Gen. 21:22-32) and further shows how Isaac is following in his father's footsteps of being blessed greatly by God.

Family Conflict Based on Parental Favoritism (Gen. 26:34–27:46)

Although Isaac and his family are greatly blessed by God, there is trouble brewing in the family that is going to develop into heated family conflict. At the heart of this conflict is going to be the character of the two sons of Isaac and Rebekah, but the conflict is going to be fueled by parental favoritism spurred on by deception. Although no one escapes blame in the story, Isaac must take much of the responsibility for how the events unfold.

Although the character of Esau has already been shown in 25:29-34, another glimpse into his life is given in two sections that frame the whole account. Both Genesis 26:34-35 and 27:46 comment on Esau's marriage to two Hittite women. The fact that he marries Hittite women is significant because the line of Abraham is supposed to remain separate from the people in the land of Canaan. Abraham was careful to find a wife for Isaac who was not from the land of Canaan but from his family in Mesopotamia. And now Isaac's older son has not shown any concern about keeping the family line free from Canaanite influence. These marriages indicate that Esau is not

---

10. Matthews (*Genesis 11:27–50:26*, p. 414) comments that finding the well on the very day the Philistines left is not a coincidence but is further evidence of the blessing of God.

concerned about the promises of God made to his forefathers; rather, he shows disdain for the heritage of the covenant. Not only did he sell his birthright for a pot of stew, but his marriages show his lack of spiritual discernment. In essence, Esau rejects the covenant promises and does not live in a way that demonstrates faithfulness to the LORD.

This analysis is supported by the impact of Esau's marriages on his parents. Genesis 26:35 states that 'they made life bitter for Isaac and Rebekah.' The subject of the verb 'they made' is feminine, which means it was the women Esau married who made life bitter for his parents. In Genesis 27:46, Rebekah states, 'I loathe my life because of the Hittite women.' The verb *qwṣ* signifies 'disgust'. The problem is not primarily the Hittite background of the women but that they were not worshippers of the LORD and so would not be true to the covenant promises. Later in Israelite history, a Moabite woman who trusts in the LORD is accepted by God's people (see the book of Ruth). But a woman who worships other gods and does not understand the covenant promises will be disastrous for keeping the descendants of Abraham separate from the people of Canaan. Esau again demonstrates his character in spurning the covenant promises of God.

Genesis 27 begins with the statement that Isaac was getting old and his eyes were dim so that he could not see. He calls in Esau, who is identified as the 'older son' (v. 1), and tells him to hunt game and to prepare some of that delicious food 'such as I love'. Isaac intends to bless Esau before he dies (v. 4). There are two customs that are important to understand in this passage and it is not always clear how these two relate together. The birthright went to the firstborn son and was the inheritance of the father's possessions, which would include a double portion of inheritance and the privileged position within the family. The blessing is a pronouncement that prosperity, potency, and dominion will abundantly be a part of a person's life.[11] It is possible that a blessing could be divided among sons (Gen. 49:28). It is also not clear if the birthright and the blessing must go together, but Esau understands them to be separate because he states that Jacob has cheated him twice,

---

11. Waltke, *Genesis*, p. 377.

once with the birthright (25:29-34) and now concerning the blessing (27:36).

What seems clear is that Isaac's actions are not in accord with the oracle from the LORD before the two sons were born. This oracle clearly stated that 'the older shall serve the younger' (25:23), but when Isaac offers what he thinks is the blessing upon Esau he states the opposite: 'Be lord over your brothers and may your mother's sons bow down to you' (27:29). In other words, Isaac's blessing goes against what the LORD had declared before the two sons were born. The blessing of Isaac also asks for prosperity for the son and reflects the promise of God to Abraham that those who curse him would be cursed and that those who bless him would be blessed (Gen. 12:3). Isaac's favoritism for his older son has blinded his spiritual sight. Even though Esau has demonstrated an unwillingness to follow the covenant by marrying Hittite women, Isaac is still trying to give him the prominent position within the family.

Rebekah overhears what Isaac tells Esau. One can sympathize with her position because she knew that the announcement concerning her two sons had clearly said that the older would serve the younger. Now she fears that her husband is going to do something that will go against what the LORD has declared. Rebekah has the opportunity to trust the LORD to bring about the birth announcement. She could have gone to talk to her husband concerning how his plan to bless Esau was not in accord with the LORD's announcement at the birth of their sons. However, Rebekah's response is to work against the plans of her husband through deception. In fact, in her conversation with Jacob, the conflict in the family and her favoritism toward him become clear. She calls Jacob 'my son' (v. 8), but she calls Isaac 'your father' and Esau 'your brother' (v. 6). Her plan is for Jacob quickly to prepare some food in the way that Isaac loves it and to bring it to him so that he will bless Jacob. However, Jacob sees the problem with this plan because Esau is a hairy man and he is a smooth man. If Isaac detects their deception, he might curse Jacob instead of blessing him. Rebekah assures Jacob that if that happens the curse will fall on her (v. 13).

The food is prepared, and Rebekah places the skins of young goats on the hands and the smooth part of Jacob's neck in order to deceive Isaac. Jacob himself is placed in a precarious position in which he must lie to his father. When Jacob goes before his father, he identifies himself as 'Esau your firstborn'. When Isaac wonders how he was able to catch the game so quickly, Jacob responds that 'the LORD your God has granted me success' (v. 20). Isaac senses that the voice was Jacob's but when he felt the hands covered in goat hair he acknowledged that the hands were those of Esau. Isaac asks Jacob one more time if he is really his son Esau, to which he responds, 'I am' (v. 24). They eat the meal together and right before the blessing, when Jacob comes near to his father, Isaac smells the smell of Esau on the garments that are covering Jacob, and so he blesses him. Although Rebekah is the one behind this deceitful plan, the character of Jacob is further revealed. In order to receive the blessing, he not only has to deceive his father but he also has to tell two or three bold-face lies to his father. After this event, Isaac recognizes the deceitful actions of his son (v. 35) and Esau declares that Jacob has lived up to his name: he is a schemer and a cheat (v. 36). It is possible to paraphrase this as 'Jacob has jacobed me'![12]

Of course, Isaac and Esau are extremely upset when they find out what has really happened. The text even says that Isaac 'trembled very violently' when Esau came in for the blessing. Yet the blessing has been given and there is nothing that can be done about it. As Isaac states, Jacob 'shall be blessed' (v. 33). Esau cries out 'with an exceedingly great and bitter cry', and pleads for a blessing from his father: 'Bless me, even me also, O my father!' (v. 34). He persists by lifting up his voice and weeping loudly. His father offers a statement that could hardly be called a blessing, but it reinforces what has already been stated concerning the relationship between the two brothers. The first declaration from Isaac could be called an anti-blessing because it states the opposite of what the blessing for Jacob had stated.[13] There is no divine

12. Oswald T. Allis, *God Spake By Moses* (Phillipsburg, NJ: P & R, 1951), p. 39.
13. Matthews, *Genesis 11:27–50:26*, p. 435.

invocation and instead of being blessed with the fatness of the earth and the dew of heaven, Esau's dwelling will be away from those things. His relationship to Jacob will be to 'serve your brother', but he will live by the sword, a weapon of war, and will eventually break free from the yoke of his brother (vv. 39-40).

The consequences of favoritism and deception are devastating for the family. Although nothing is said in the text about the relationship between Isaac and Rebekah, the relationship between Esau and Jacob seems irreparable. Esau hates Jacob and decides to bide his time until his father is dead and will then carry out a plan to kill his brother (v. 41). However, Rebekah hears what the intentions of Esau are, so she makes plans to send Jacob away. Her plan includes sending Jacob back to her brother Laban under the pretense that it would be better for him to find a wife from her family than to marry one of the local Hittite women.

No one in the family has acted in an honorable way and no one really wins. The family is torn apart by conflict and favoritism. Although Isaac had emerged in Genesis 26 as blessed by God and a powerful man, he comes across in old age as spiritually blind. He knows Esau's failures but wants to show him favoritism because he is the son who makes the food he loves. Isaac is even willing to act against the oracle of the LORD. Rebekah is willing to act against her husband in order to try to accomplish the LORD's will through her plan of deception. Esau is the son who wants the blessing but is not willing to live a life that honors God so that he could be trusted with the blessing. He is a man of passion who does what he pleases. Jacob lives up to his name. He is a cheating and lying schemer who is willing to manipulate and take advantage of other people's weaknesses. Such is the one through whom the covenant promises will be entrusted. One wonders how secure the covenant promises will be if they are passed on to Jacob. Yet, as with all of us, God is not finished with Jacob yet.

STUDY QUESTIONS

1 Describe the character of Jacob and Esau. How does the character of each one lead to conflict in their relationship?

2 Isaac lies about his relationship to Rebekah just as his father Abraham lied about his relationship to Sarah. What does this teach about how patterns of sin can be passed down to the next generation? Can you give a modern-day example?

3 Explain why each parent might be drawn to a particular son. How does each parent seek the advantage of their favorite son? What negative consequences result from such favoritism?

13

The Crucible of Family Conflict
(Genesis 28–30)

Although Jacob must leave his immediate family, the direction of his life is moving in a spiritually positive direction, which is in contrast to Esau's life. Jacob leaves with the promises of the blessing of Abraham passed on to him from his father and confirmed by God in a dream (Gen. 28). Thus Jacob's journey can be seen as a pilgrimage of faith and there will be the development of his faith through the events of his life. Yet he will meet his match in deceptive Laban, and conflict will be a major part of his life in his marriage to Leah and Rachel and in the birth of their children. In fact, this chapter will show the building of the family of Jacob through intense family struggle.

The Beginning of Jacob's Journey (Gen. 28:1-22)
Jacob is sent away from the land of Canaan so that he would not marry a woman from the land of Canaan. Isaac also comes to accept the fact that Jacob is the one through whom the covenant promises of God will be passed on. Isaac calls Jacob, blesses him, and tells him why he must go back to Paddan-aram where the family of Rebekah lives. The blessing of Isaac includes not just fruitfulness for Jacob's wife in producing many descendants, but also specifically includes the blessing of Abraham that his descendants would inherit the land promised to him by God. The response of Esau reinforces

the fact that he is not the one to inherit the promises. He finally realizes how much the Canaanite women displeased his father and so he takes steps to redeem himself. He may also be trying to imitate Jacob by marrying a woman who is not a Canaanite.[1] He even chooses a woman who is a distant relative, but the woman he chooses is from the rejected line of Ishmael. Although he may be trying to please his father, the family of Ishmael will not inherit the covenant promises given to Abraham. Esau thus seals his own fate by not understanding the spiritual implications of his actions.

Jacob is sent on his way with the blessing of his father Isaac, but he is also sent on his journey with an appearance from God. Jacob left Beersheba and headed toward Haran but stops to spend the night at a certain place (v. 11). He uses a stone for a pillow and while he sleeps he has a dream. In the dream there is a 'ladder' set up on the earth with its top reaching to heaven. Angels of God were ascending and descending on it, and Yahweh (the LORD) stood above it. The Lord identifies Himself as 'the God of Abraham your father and the God of Isaac'. The promises that God had made to Abraham are repeated here to Jacob. His offspring will be like the dust of the earth, they shall inherit the land, and all the families of the earth will be blessed in 'you and your offspring' (vv. 13-14). God also promises Jacob that He will be with him, that He will keep him wherever he goes, and that He will bring him back to this land (v. 15).

Jacob's response to the dream is positive. When Jacob awoke from his sleep, he recognized that the LORD's presence was in that place. God's presence transforms a temporary, nightly camp into a sanctuary. Jacob recognizes that the place is a house of God and the gate of heaven. Unlike the Tower of Babel narrative, God takes the initiative and reveals Himself to Jacob, which leads to the appropriate response of fear and awe (vv. 16-17). He commemorates the event by taking the stone pillow and setting it up as stone pillar, pours oil on top of it to consecrate it,[2] and calls the name of the place Bethel, which means 'the house of God'. Jacob then makes a vow which is the longest vow in the Old Testament. The fact that

---

1. Matthews, *Genesis 11:27–50:26*, p. 441.
2. Waltke, *Genesis*, p 393.

Jacob makes a vow should not necessarily be seen as a negative response because vows were common in the Old Testament. They were made in a crisis and they called upon God to act in a certain way, which would bring forth a response of praise from the one who made the vow. There are two ways Jacob's vow can be translated, depending on where the word 'then' is placed to mark the apodosis.

Many English translations translate the vow in the way the ESV does: 'If God will be with me and will keep me in this way that I go, and will give me bread to eat and clothing to wear, so that I come again to my father's house in peace, *then* the LORD shall be my God and this stone, which I have set up for a pillar, shall be God's house.'[3] This translation could lead one to conclude that Jacob is bargaining with God and that the LORD will not be Jacob's God unless He fulfills what He has promised. However, this does not fit the context where Jacob has been set apart by God to be the one who will inherit the promises even though he is the younger son (Gen. 25:23). God is not sitting by waiting to see if Jacob is going to trust Him. Further, Jacob is not calculating whether he should accept God; rather, Jacob is throwing himself upon God's mercy. Thus, the vow should be translated: 'If God will be with me and will keep me in this way that I go, and will give me bread to eat and clothing to wear, so that I come again to my father's house in peace, and the LORD shall be my God, *then* this stone, which I have set up for a pillar, shall be God's house.'[4]

The seriousness of Jacob's commitment is seen in his willingness to give a tenth to God of all that God gives to him.[5] Jacob also recognizes that he is dependent upon God to bless him.[6] At the moment, he has very little in the way of earthly goods, so that God's blessing will become very evident as the story unfolds. The change in Jacob has begun and will intensify in the next several episodes.

---

3. See also NKJV, NASB, NIV, NRSV.
4. Hamilton, *Genesis 18–50*, p. 248. Hamilton gives both theological reasons and grammatical reasons to support this translation of the vow, which is also the way the NRSV translates it.
5. Waltke (*Genesis*, p. 394) notes that the promise of a tithe shows a change in Jacob's character from grasper to giver.
6. Hamilton, *Genesis 18–50*, p. 249.

The dream of Jacob is alluded to by Jesus in John 1:51, in a passage that describes Him calling several individuals to follow Him. When He calls Nathanael, Jesus identifies him as an Israelite in whom there is no deceit. When Nathanael asks Jesus how He knows this information about him, Jesus responds by demonstrating his full knowledge of Nathanael's life by referring to an incident that occurred before Philip had called Nathanael. Jesus saw Nathanael under the fig tree. Nathanael's response is to declare that Jesus is the Son of God and the King of Israel. But Jesus assures him that he will see even greater things: 'you will see heaven opened, and the angels of God ascending and descending on the Son of Man' (John 1:51).

In the dream of Jacob, the LORD stands at the top of the ladder and the angels ascend and descend from heaven to earth on the ladder. Obviously this scene stresses that there is a connection between heaven and earth. God is not distant from the events that take place on the earth. He is very involved with His creation, which was evident in His appearance to Abraham in Genesis 18. He also uses angels to accomplish His purposes. The dream of Jacob should encourage him that the LORD is able to accomplish all that He has promised him. The allusion in John 1:51 stresses that God is now even more involved with His people because the bridge between heaven and earth is not a ladder with angels on it but is the Son of God Himself. The disciples will have the privilege of seeing for themselves the glory of God through the work of Jesus Christ. Jesus is called both Son of God and Son of Man in this text because He is the bridge between heaven and earth. He has come to fulfill God's promises.

The Humbling of Jacob: Laban's Deceit (Gen. 29:1-30)
In this section of the Jacob story there is presented both the bane (trouble) and blessing of family. Jacob will meet his match in the deceitful, scheming Laban and conflict will be used to build his family with many sons. Jacob for much of the story will be passive, but he will eventually emerge as leader of his family through these difficult events.

Jacob safely arrives at his destination and comes to a well where shepherds are gathered with their flocks. The well has a large stone over it and when all the flocks were gathered the stone would be removed and the flocks would drink from the well. The stone is described as large (v. 2) and it takes several shepherds to remove the stone from the well (v. 3). The shepherds are waiting for more flocks to arrive when Jacob approaches them to find out where they are from and if they know Laban. They are from Haran and they do know Laban. Jacob also wonders why the shepherds do not water the sheep and move on to new pasturage while there is still plenty of light (v. 7).[7] Their answer is that they have to wait for the other shepherds to move the stone so the sheep can be watered. During this conversation, Rachel, the daughter of Laban, arrives with sheep. Jacob is inspired by her presence and removes the stone himself. What three shepherds would not do through laziness or could not do for lack of strength, Jacob accomplishes by himself. Later in the chapter (29:17), Rachel is described as beautiful and one wonders if that is what motivates Jacob at this point. He kisses her, a customary greeting among relatives, and reveals to her his identity. He weeps aloud which may indicate emotional joy for the successful completion of his journey.[8]

Jacob at this point of the story shows boldness and the willingness to take action rather than waiting around for events to unfold. Jacob is no slacker and will turn out to be a dedicated worker.[9] However, if one compares this episode with the earlier episode where Abraham's servant sought to find a wife for Isaac, there are stark contrasts that give insight into the character of Jacob. The servant of Abraham prayed that God would grant him success (24:12), but there is no prayer on Jacob's part. The servant of Abraham tested the character of the woman by the plan of having the woman water the camels (24:14), but there is no indication that Jacob is thinking about the character of the woman. He might just be extremely happy to find someone from Laban's family, but it is also possible that he is smitten by the beauty of Rachel. Although Jacob weeps aloud because he has successfully completed his journey, there is no praise or worship of the LORD as there

---

7. Matthews, *Genesis 11:27–50:26*, p. 462.
8. Waltke, *Genesis*, p. 401.
9. Matthews, *Genesis 11:27–50:26*, p. 462.

was by Abraham's servant (24:26).[10] Although Jacob's journey began well with the restatement of the promises of God and the assurance of God's presence, Jacob still has a lot to learn about trusting in God and not in his own abilities.

Rachel is overjoyed to hear about Jacob's connection to her family. She runs to tell her father Laban, who also runs to meet Jacob. Laban acknowledges that Jacob is his bone and flesh, and Jacob stays with the family for a month (v. 14). In a month Laban would get to know Jacob and Jacob would get to know the family. Laban even puts Jacob to work, but since it would not be appropriate to treat Jacob as a hired laborer because he is family, he asks Jacob what his wages should be (v. 15). Jacob does not yet fully comprehend the character of Laban and so he trusts Laban to act honorably. However, Laban is going to use his relationship with Jacob for his own advantage.[11] Through the deception and scheming of Laban, Jacob is going to get a taste of his own medicine concerning the way he treated his brother and his father.

Jacob requests that Laban give to him his younger daughter Rachel as his wages for working for him for seven years. The narrative stops at this point to describe the two daughters of Laban, which will be important for how the story unfolds. Leah is the older daughter and her eyes are described as 'weak' (v. 16). The Hebrew word for 'weak' ($ra\underline{k}$) can mean tender, sensitive, or delicate. It is possible to take this description in a positive way by stressing that even though Leah was older her eyes were much younger looking.[12] Others argue, however, that the tenor of the passage is to contrast the two women and so the physical description should also be seen as a contrast. In this view, Leah had dull eyes that were feeble or impotent,[13] but Rachel was a beautiful woman in form and appearance. Even if the description of Leah's eyes is positive, there is a contrast with Rachel, whose beauty is not confined to one part of her but encompasses her whole appearance. Jacob asks for Rachel because he loved her (v. 18). Laban

---

10. Waltke, *Genesis*, pp. 399-400.

11. Waltke (*Genesis*, p. 404) notes that if Laban had been a loving relative, he could have helped Jacob get a start on building his own home.

12. Hamilton, *Genesis 18–50*, p. 259.

13. Matthews, *Genesis 11:27–50:26*, p. 468. Waltke (*Genesis*, p. 405) comments that Leah's eyes lacked fire and sparkle.

agrees to this request, but some see his response to Jacob as ambiguous.[14] He agrees to give 'her' to Jacob (v. 19). Certainly Jacob understands 'her' to mean Rachel, and there should be no doubt that this is the agreed-upon deal, but later Laban will feign surprise that Jacob did not understand the custom of having to marry the older daughter first (v. 26).

Jacob works seven years for Rachel and the time passes by quickly because of his love for her. At the end of the seven years, Jacob asks to have Rachel for his wife. But on the wedding night Leah is brought to Jacob instead of Rachel. Jacob does not realize the switch has taken place until the morning. The shock and surprise of the switch are told as 'in the morning, behold, it was Leah' (v. 25). Perhaps we wonder how Jacob did not know until the morning that the switch had taken place. It is not as far-fetched as it sounds. Brides may have been heavily veiled, the tent would be very dark, and Jacob may have been experiencing some of the effects of the feast, perhaps with Laban urging him to have just another drink of wine! Of course, Jacob is outraged that he would be deceived by Laban in this way (v. 25), which is ironic in light of his deception of his own father. Laban acts as if Jacob should have known that this was going to happen according to their cultural custom (v. 26). Jacob has met his match in Laban, who is even more deceptive and scheming than Jacob. Laban comes across as cunning, greedy, and heartless[15] while Jacob is trapped by a similar kind of deceit he used to trick others. All is not lost, however, for Laban offers to give Rachel to Jacob if he will serve him another seven years. Jacob must complete the bridal week festivities for Leah and then he will receive Rachel at the end of the bridal week. Although he receives Rachel as his wife in addition to Leah, he must work another seven years for Laban. Jacob now has two wives. He loves one more than the other (v. 30), and the conflict this sets up in the family is going to be used by God to further refine the character of Jacob. Through deceit and conflict God will bless Jacob and shape his character.

---

14. Hamilton, *Genesis 18–50*, p. 259; Waltke, *Genesis*, p. 405.
15. Waltke, *Genesis*, p. 404.

The Passivity of Jacob: Building the Family through Conflict (Gen. 29:31–30:24)

The growth of Jacob's family is driven by the conflict between Leah and Rachel, who are rival sisters seeking the love of their husband Jacob. The conflict is spurred on by the marital favoritism Jacob shows toward Rachel. Jacob loves Rachel more than he loves Leah (29:30); in fact, the word 'hate' ($\acute{s}\bar{a}n\bar{e}$') is used in verse 31 to describe Jacob's attitude toward Leah. Not all English translations use the word 'hate' to translate this term; but it is a strong term that could express anything from sheer aversion (Deut. 21:15, 17) to vehement animosity (Ps. 25:19; Prov. 19:7; 25:17). It would seem that, at minimum, there is a form of resentment or aversion toward Leah because even though she bears sons for Jacob he does not seem to soften his attitude toward her. Leah, the hated wife, was able to have children but Rachel, the loved wife, was barren. Each wife wants what the other wife has. Leah is seeking to be loved by her husband and Rachel is seeking to have children. Such a dynamic sets up conflict between the two women that leads to a race to see which one can produce more children. God will use this conflict to fulfill His purposes of building the family of Jacob and of continuing the process of changing the character of Jacob.

The pain of conflict between Leah and Rachel is clearly seen in the names that are given to their children. At first, Leah is the only one able to bear children. She names her firstborn son Reuben, which in Hebrew means 'see a son'. She offers the explanation of the name as 'because the LORD has looked upon my affliction; for now my husband will love me' (v. 32). The explanation shows her inferior status of not being loved by her husband. Leah bears another son and calls his name Simeon, which is a wordplay on the Hebrew verb 'to hear'. The explanation for the name Simeon shows the connection, 'because the LORD has heard that I am hated, he has given me this son also' (v. 33). Leah bears a third son who is named Levi, which is a wordplay with the verb 'attached'. The birth of two previous sons has not changed Jacob's attitude toward Leah, but with the birth of a third son she hopes that Jacob's attitude will change: 'Now this time my husband will be attached to me because I have borne him three sons' (v. 34). Only with the birth of the fourth son does Leah move beyond her focus on her unloved status to an attitude of praise to the LORD. The fourth son is named Judah which is a wordplay on the Hebrew verb 'to praise'. Her explanation is, 'This time I will praise the LORD' (v. 35). Leah's response shows development from a focus on what she did not have to how the LORD had blessed her. The births of her first three sons are attributed to the LORD, but she was consumed with Jacob's lack of love toward her. Although her situation is very difficult from a human standpoint, she is finally able to move beyond the focus on herself to give proper praise to God for the blessing of children.

The fertility of Leah and the barrenness of Rachel lead to further conflict in the family. Rachel envies her sister and complains to Jacob concerning her barrenness: 'Give me children or I shall die' (30:1). Jacob does not handle the exasperation of Rachel very well. He does not pray to God for his wife nor does he give her any comfort. Rather, he becomes angry with her as if she is blaming him for her barrenness when the one to blame is God: 'Am I in the place of God, who has withheld from you the fruit of the womb?' (v. 2).

Rachel comes up with a plan very similar to the plan of Sarah when she gave her handmaid to Abraham. She gives her servant Bilhah as a wife[16] to Jacob so she can bear children on Rachel's behalf. Neither Jacob nor Rachel are trusting in the LORD to give them children. The names of the sons born to Rachel through Bilhah also reflect Rachel's conflict with her sister Leah. Rachel is the one who names the sons, which shows that the children are hers.[17] The first son is named Dan, which is related to the Hebrew verb 'to judge'. Rachel gives the explanation that 'God has judged me, and has also heard my voice and given me a son' (v. 6). The verb also has the meaning 'to bring justice' and Rachel's explanation may express that God has vindicated her or brought her justice in relationship to her sister. This aspect becomes clear in the name

---

16. Waltke (*Genesis*, p. 411) points out that the terms 'wife' and 'concubine' are used loosely in the patriarchal period. A concubine would be an auxiliary wife, not a slave, but subordinate to the wife who is her mistress. After the patriarchal period the term 'wife' is never used as a synonym for concubine.

17. Matthews, *Genesis 11:27–50:26*, p. 483.

of the next son. The second son born to Rachel through Bilhah is named Naphtali, which is related to the Hebrew word
group that means 'struggle' or 'wrestle'. In fact, it is possible
that the phrase 'mighty wrestlings' should be translated as
'the wrestlings or struggles of God', which would highlight
that Rachel's struggle with Leah is also a struggle to win favor
with God.[18] The birth of the second son demonstrates her success in this struggle with God and with her sister. However,
her proclamation, 'I have prevailed' may be ill-timed because
more conflict is coming with her sister. Rachel has not yet fully learned to trust God in her struggles.

Leah had stopped bearing children, so she follows in her
sister's footsteps and offers her servant Zilpah as a wife to
Jacob to bear children for her. It seems that Leah does not want
Rachel to have the comfort of thinking she has triumphed
over her, so even though she has children of her own she
offers Zilpah to Jacob in order to have more children.[19] The
names of the two sons born to Zilpah reflect Leah's feelings
of good fortune. The first son born to Zilpah is named Gad,
which is associated with the Hebrew word that means 'luck'
or 'fortune'. Her explanation is, 'Good fortune has come'
(v. 11). There is no overt religious significance to this name.
The name of the second son born to Zilpah is named Asher,
which is related to the Hebrew word that means 'happy' or
'blessed'. The explanation of the name focuses on Leah's state
of happiness in relationship to how she is perceived by other
women because of her fertility: 'Happy am I! For women have
called me happy' (v. 13). Both Leah and Rachel seem more
concerned about their own status in relationship to each other
and about how others perceive them than how God perceives
their attitudes and actions toward each other.

With the birth of these children, one would think that the
conflict between the two sisters would die down. However,
this conflict is always under the surface ready to erupt again.
The situation described in verses 14-18 shows that nothing has
really changed. Reuben, the firstborn son of Leah, finds some
mandrakes in a field and brings them to his mother. Mandrakes
were thought to enhance sexual desire and a woman's fertility.

18. Waltke, Genesis, p. 412.
19. Matthews, Genesis 11:27–50:26, p. 485.

Although there is nothing wrong with using appropriate human means to help achieve a certain result, the mandrakes take center stage as the method to produce children. Each woman must have them! Leah has them in her possession, but Rachel wants them; so they strike a deal. The conversation of the two women shows the deep wounds that each one has experienced. Leah accuses Rachel of taking her husband and now wanting to take her mandrakes. The deal Rachel makes is that Leah can have Jacob for a night in exchange for the mandrakes. When Jacob comes in from the field, Leah's words to him are, 'You must come in to me, for I have hired you with my son's mandrakes' (v. 16). Jacob is compliant and the result is that Leah gives birth to her fifth son. She calls his name Issachar, which sounds like the Hebrew word for 'wages' or 'reward'. Her explanation is that God has 'rewarded' her for giving her servant to her husband (v. 18). She seems to believe that giving her servant to her husband was an unselfish gesture that God rewarded.[20] The name Issachar memorializes the deal that bought Jacob for a night. Jacob is totally passive in these events and is presented as a hired stud (v. 16). He is not a leader in his family but is told what to do by his wives. He does not make any attempt to try to resolve the conflict but rather is controlled by their scheming. Everything that Jacob hopes for is a struggle, but God is bringing him to the end of his ability to scheme and manipulate his way out of this family conflict. The result will be that he will have to trust in God, and then he will come to see that God is ultimately the source of his blessings.[21]

The rest of the account of the birth of Jacob's children completes the family of Jacob. There also seems to be a little more recognition of God's role in the births of the children. Leah bears a sixth son and names him Zebulun, which is related to the Hebrew verb that means 'honor' or 'exalt'. Her explanation is that God has given her a good endowment, so now her husband will honor her because she has borne him six sons (v. 20). Although she is still trying to seek honor from her husband based on her ability to bear children, she also

---

20. Matthews, *Genesis 11:27–50:26*, p. 488.
21. Sailhamer, *Pentateuch as Narrative*, p. 195.

acknowledges that her children are a gift from God. She also gives birth to a daughter named Dinah.

Then, finally, Rachel herself conceives and bears a son. Her conception is not because of the mandrakes but because 'God remembered Rachel, and God listened to her and God opened her womb' (v. 22). She names this child Joseph, with a double pun on the name. In reference to the past, she remarks, 'God has taken away my reproach' (v. 23). The verb 'take away' ($\bar{a}sa\bar{p}$) can be associated with the name Joseph. God has taken away the social stigma of barrenness and the ridicule that may have come with it.[22] The second pun looks to the future with the hope that the LORD would add to her another son. The verb 'add' ($y\bar{a}sa\bar{p}$) can also be related to the name Joseph. It is significant that Rachel here uses the name Yahweh (LORD) and looks to the future with hope that the LORD will act on her behalf in giving her another son. Perhaps through the struggle of conflict God has brought her to a place of looking to the future with hope in what He is able to accomplish.

Study Questions

1 Describe positive spiritual things that occur to Jacob at the beginning of his journey away from his family.

2 How does Jacob demonstrate a lack of spiritual perspective when he first meets Rachel?

3 Make a list of the sons of Jacob and explain the meaning of their names. How do the names of the sons reflect the relationship between Jacob and his wives Leah and Rachel?

4 How does God teach Jacob valuable lessons of trusting in God through Laban and the conflict between his wives?

---

22. Matthews, *Genesis 11:27–50:26*, p. 490.

14

From a Prayerless Schemer to a Man of Faith
(Genesis 30:25–33:20)

Jacob emerges as a bold character immediately after the birth of Joseph. Although he was passive in the earlier narrative, he now becomes active in leading his family to leave Laban. Jacob will come to realize that his own scheming will only go so far and that he needs to rely on God to bless him. Thus there is development in the character of Jacob from a prayerless schemer to a man who depends on God. This will climax in the wrestling match shortly before he meets Esau. God places Jacob in situations where he must trust in God because the situations are beyond his own ability to control.

God is the Source of Jacob's Wealth (Gen. 30:25-43)
It becomes apparent by the birth of Joseph that God is the one who grants conception because He opens the barren womb of Rachel. In this section it will also become apparent that God is the source of Jacob's wealth and that no amount of deception or trickery by Laban can hinder God's blessing of Jacob. In fact, Laban will recognize that he is blessed because of his association with Jacob. As soon as barren Rachel gives birth to Joseph, Jacob emerges as a man who actively begins to take leadership of his family.

The section begins with Jacob requesting that Laban send him away with his wives and children so he can return to his own country. He is seeking dismissal from the service of

Laban based on the fulfillment of his fourteen years of service (seven for each wife). Laban ignores his request and offers him wages for work. His reason to keep Jacob is self-serving. Laban has been greatly blessed by Yahweh (the LORD) because of Jacob (v. 27).[1] It makes sense that Laban would not want Jacob to leave, so he tells him that he can name his wages (v. 28). Jacob agrees with Laban's assessment that he has been blessed because of Jacob. In fact, Jacob states that Laban had very little before Jacob arrived and that his possessions have increased abundantly through God's blessing. However, it is time that he must provide for his own household and so he comes up with a plan. If Laban will agree to this plan, then Jacob will stay with him. Jacob knows Laban's deceitful ways and so he comes up with a plan that will keep Laban, as much as possible, from swindling Jacob out of his real earnings.

The plan relates to the flocks of Laban (vv. 32-33). Jacob is going to go through all the flocks and remove from Laban's flocks every speckled and spotted sheep and goat, as well as the black lambs. Thus any white sheep or goats that are found in Jacob's flock will be considered stolen. In this way there can be a clear division between Laban's flocks and Jacob's flocks. Apparently, sheep are normally white and goats are black or dark brown, so that Jacob is requesting the irregular of the flock.[2] Normally the wages of a shepherd would be about 20 per cent of the flock, but rarely would the speckled portion of a flock be that high of a percentage. So it seems like this would be a good deal for Laban and he agrees to it immediately (v. 34). However, even though the percentages are in his favor, Laban also makes a cunning move to further ensure that the deal will be to his benefit. On the very day that the agreement between Jacob and Laban is reached, Laban removes from his flock all the male and female goats that were speckled and spotted and every lamb that was black. He put these animals under the charge of his sons and separated them from Jacob by a three-day journey. By this action, Laban makes sure that

---

1. Laban comes to the knowledge that he is blessed by the LORD because of Jacob through divination (30:27). Divination is the attempt to find out information through the use of an object, like arrows or a liver from a sacrificed animal, or through the use of a medium. It is a pagan practice that is later condemned in Deuteronomy 18:9-14.

2. Hamilton, *Genesis 18–50*, p. 283.

Jacob's percentage of the flock will be very low. He thus seeks to give himself the advantage.

Jacob also has a plan to increase the percentage of his portion of the flock. He takes fresh sticks from certain trees and exposes the white of the sticks by peeling white streaks in them. He puts these sticks in front of the place where the animals come to water, which is also the place of their breeding. The idea is that the flocks will breed in front of the peeled sticks and will produce striped, speckled, and spotted young. These animals would be Jacob's animals according to the agreement he had made with Laban. He would separate these animals from the rest of the flock and keep them separate. Also, he would only use the peeled sticks when the stronger animals came to breed, which would ensure that his animals were the strong animals and Laban's animals were the weaker animals. In this way Jacob greatly increased the size of his flock. However, it is also clear that not only did his flock increase but his servants, camels, and donkeys increased. Thus Jacob became very wealthy.

So what does Jacob's plan mean? First, the character of Jacob is still developing and this plan shows that he is still trying to get ahead based on his own planning, rather than trusting in God. Second, the plan reflects a common view of that day that prenatal impressions affected the unborn.[3] The Bible itself does not teach this view but it describes those who did accept it. Jacob is seeking by his scheming to increase his own flock, but the true source of Jacob's blessing will be acknowledged before the story is finished.

A significant development of Jacob's character occurs in Genesis 31 where he separates himself from Laban and begins the return to the land of his kindred. It becomes apparent to Jacob that Laban and his sons no longer regard Jacob with favor because they believe that he has become wealthy by taking the possessions and flocks that belonged to them. The LORD appears to Jacob and tells him to return to the land of his fathers.

Jacob calls together Rachel and Leah to the field in order to explain to them why they must leave. In his explanation,

---

3. Waltke, *Genesis*, p. 420.

it becomes clear that God is the one who is the real source of Jacob's wealth. God has protected Jacob from Laban's schemes. Jacob tells his wives that 'your father has cheated me and changed my wages ten times' (v. 7). However, even though the odds have been stacked against Jacob, God protected him. Also, Jacob acknowledges that God is the true source of his wealth and not his own planning. In other words, Jacob did not boast to his wives how he had outsmarted their father Laban. Rather, he acknowledges that God is the one who gave him the plan to take as his own the spotted and striped animals (v 8), and in this way God took away the livestock of Laban and gave them to Jacob (v. 9). This fact is confirmed by Rachel and Leah in their response to Jacob. They also feel estranged from Laban because he has treated them as foreigners by not leaving them any inheritance. They specifically acknowledge that God has taken wealth away from Laban and given it to them and to their children. Thus they agree that Jacob should do what God has told him to do. They believe the veracity of Jacob's God and are willing to return with him to the land of his fathers.[4]

A change in Jacob's character is seen in the fact that he acknowledges that God is the one who has blessed him with wealth rather than attributing the acquisition of his wealth to his own clever planning. Also, Jacob is no longer passive, nor does he speak just a few words, but he gives a full speech to his wives in 31:4-16. He takes leadership of his family in order to separate from Laban. He is also acting promptly to obey God because God has told him to return to his own land. However, Jacob is still fearful of Laban and so he plans to leave while Laban is away shearing sheep. In fact, Jacob 'tricks' Laban by not telling him of his plans and by trying to leave secretly. Jacob and his family do not fully trust in the LORD to protect them and bless them. Also, Rachel steals her father's household gods (v. 19). There is debate as to the size, shape, and function of these household gods ($t^e r\bar{a}p\hat{i}m$).[5] Rachel may have stolen them because they were made of costly metal. She would have reasoned that they would make up for how

---

4. Matthews, *Genesis 11:27–50:26*, p. 510.

5. See Matthews, *Genesis 11:27–50:26*, pp. 518-19, for a discussion of the form and function of the household gods.

Laban had mistreated her and short-changed her in terms of what was her due (v. 15), which is perhaps a reference to her bridal gift.[6]

Jacob has a three-day head start before Laban hears that he has left with all his possessions. Laban pursues Jacob for seven days and overtakes him in the hill country of Gilead. In the confrontation between Jacob and Laban, God protects Jacob from the further schemes of Laban and ensures a valid separation between the two men. Laban confronts Jacob over his trickery in leaving secretly without giving him the opportunity for a proper send-off and without the opportunity of saying goodbye to his daughters (v. 28). He warns Jacob that he could do him great harm but that Jacob's God (the God of your father) warned Laban not to say anything to Jacob either good or bad (v. 29). He also confronts him with the accusation of taking his household gods.

Jacob explains that he had left secretly because he feared that Laban would take away his daughters from Jacob by force. In light of the character of Laban and his statement that the daughters are his daughters, the sons are his sons, and the flocks are his flocks (v. 43), Jacob's fear is well-grounded. Many times he has experienced the deceitful character of Laban. Jacob then denies that anyone among his family had stolen the household gods because he was not aware that Rachel had taken them (v. 32). God again protects the family of Jacob by not allowing Laban to find the household gods that Rachel had stolen. They were hidden in a camel's saddle in Rachel's tent. She sat on them and feigned that it was her monthly cycle, and that she was ill and could not rise. Thus, the man who was the master of deceit was deceived by his own daughter.

Jacob responds with righteous indignation at the false accusation of Laban when the household gods were not found (vv. 36-42). He gives a full justification of all the years he worked for Laban. He worked hard in the heat of the day and in the cold of the night, many times going without sleep in order to take care of Laban's flocks. He also bore the burden of loss himself when an animal from the flock was stolen or taken

---

6. Matthews, *Genesis 11:27–50:26*, p. 516.

by wild beasts. For twenty years he served Laban and, even though Laban kept changing the terms of their agreement, God had protected Jacob from Laban's deceitful plans.

Laban's hands are tied and he offers to enter into a covenant with Jacob (v. 44). They gather together a heap of stones as a witness to their agreement. The agreement includes that the LORD would watch each of them so that they would keep the terms of the agreement. Jacob is not to oppress the daughters of Laban or to take other wives (v. 50), and Laban promises not to cross the boundary of the heap of stones in order to do Jacob any harm (v. 52).

The agreement emphasizes the different loyalties of Laban and Jacob. When Laban states that 'the God of Abraham, and the God of Nahor, the God of their father judge between us' (v. 53), he is not equating the God of Abraham with the God of Nahor, but is showing the difference among the deities between the two families. Thus, the phrase could be translated 'the God of Abraham and the god of Nahor, the gods of their father judge between us.'[7] Laban may have used the name of Yahweh (LORD) in the covenant agreement because Jacob's God had appeared to him to warn him not to harm Jacob.

Jacob uses the phrase 'the Fear of Isaac' twice in the context of speaking of 'the God of my father, the God of Abraham' (vv. 42, 53). This could be translated 'the Awesome One of Isaac' who inspires fear and dread.[8] Jacob may have used this name not only as a warning to Laban that his God is not a God to trifle with, but also to emphasize that the promises of God have been passed down from Abraham to Isaac. When Jacob swears by this name, he is also affirming this God as his God.

Jacob and Laban depart from one another in peace. So far, God has been faithful to the vow that Jacob had made (Gen. 28:20-22).

Prayerful Planning to Meet a Crisis (Gen. 32–33)

Jacob's greatest challenge is staring him in the face and it will result in his greatest struggle from which he will emerge as a changed man. After peacefully separating from Laban, Jacob receives some encouragement when he is met by the

7. Waltke, *Genesis*, p. 434.
8. Waltke, *Genesis*, p. 432.

angels of God (32:1). He recognizes that this particular place represents the 'camp of God', a phrase which can have military connotations (1 Chron. 12:22). He calls the name of the place Mahanaim, which means 'two camps'. There may also be a connection with his plan to divide his family into two camps as he prepares to meet Esau.[9] This incident should encourage Jacob that God will protect him from any danger as he returns to the land of his father.

Jacob knew that a meeting with Esau was inevitable, so he sent out messengers to try to prepare the way. The relationship between Jacob and Esau was not good when Jacob left home; in fact, Esau wanted to kill him because he had taken away Esau's blessing. The report from the messengers leaves the reader with an ominous sense of dread: 'we came to your brother Esau, and he is coming to meet you, and there are four hundred men with him' (v. 6). There is no indication whether Esau comes in peace or in revenge. Jacob is 'greatly afraid and distressed' (v. 7). This is a major crisis for Jacob because he and his family are vulnerable before the power of Esau. God's promises for the future are also at stake. Although Jacob puts together a plan that seeks to both appease Esau and to protect his family, it is not the planning that is the key point. Rather, it is Jacob's praying that shows his changed character and his dependence on God. The interaction between the planning and the praying is seen in the flow of the narrative:

Jacob Plans	32:7-8
Jacob Prays	32:9-12
Jacob Plans	32:13-21
Jacob 'Prays'	32:22-32
Jacob Plans	33:1-3

The planning of Jacob includes dividing his people into two camps, so that if Esau attacks one camp the other camp can escape (vv. 7-8). He also puts together a present for his brother Esau hoping to win his favor (vv. 13-15). The gift is a very

9. Waltke (*Genesis*, p. 441) points out that the number two is prominent throughout the account: two camps, two families, two meetings (with God and Esau), and two brothers.

sizeable one and includes valuable livestock.[10] However, it is more than just a gift; in addition, it is Jacob's attempt to restore what he had taken from Esau and to show that he is a changed man. Jacob calls Esau 'lord' and refers to himself as 'servant' (vv. 4, 18). In this way, he hopes his brother will accept him (v. 20). Even the planning of Jacob shows that he is a different man from when he left Esau.

The prayer of Jacob in verses 9-12 demonstrates the kind of changes that have occurred in his life. He prays to the God of his father Abraham and the God of his father Isaac. He accepts the God of the covenant and all that such a covenant relationship includes. He confesses his own unworthiness of the covenant faithfulness that God has shown to him in blessing him. He specifically prays that God would deliver him and his family from Esau. Jacob's prayer demonstrates that he is now trusting God's power to save and not in his own planning. In his prayer for deliverance, Jacob also appeals to the covenant promises that God would make his offspring as numerous as the sand of the sea. Jacob is facing a situation beyond his ability to control. He acknowledges that his life is in the hand of God and that God must be the one to deliver him.

The change of Jacob culminates in a wrestling match that typifies in many ways his whole life of striving with others, except this time he strives with someone who is more than a human being. Jacob had sent his wives and children ahead, so he was left alone on the night before his meeting with Esau. Mysteriously, Jacob has a wrestling match with someone who is at first identified as a 'man' (*'îš*). They wrestled until the break of day, but the man could not prevail against Jacob.

It becomes clear, however, that this individual is more than a man. After the wrestling is over, Jacob names the place Peniel, which means 'the face of God'. He also gives an explanation for the name when he states, 'for I have seen God face to face, and yet my life has been delivered' (v. 30). This may also be the reason why the person would not divulge his name to Jacob. But since this individual is more than a human being, how does one explain that he could not prevail in the

---

10. Matthews, *Genesis 11:27–50:26*, p. 553.

wrestling match with Jacob? Also, even though he could not overcome Jacob in the wrestling match, he is able to dislocate Jacob's hip joint by touching the socket of his hip (v. 25).

One way to explain these anomalies is that God humbled Himself and met Jacob on his own terms for the purpose of bringing him to the end of his own strength. Even though Jacob is physically broken because of the dislocated hip, he continues to strive with God in order to obtain a blessing. Striving to obtain a blessing has been the pattern of Jacob's whole life, but this time he strives with God to receive a blessing (v. 26). Jacob seeks a blessing not by his own scheming but through a relationship with God.

The change in Jacob is reflected in the change of his name. No longer will he be called Jacob, which reflects his old way of deception and scheming (Gen. 27:36), but from now on he will be called Israel. This name is a combination of the word God (El) and the word 'struggle' (śārāh). Normally the meaning would be 'God struggles' or 'May God struggle',[11] but this is reversed in the explanation of the name given to Jacob: 'you have striven with God and with men and have prevailed' (v. 28). Jacob has learned to wrestle with God and he emerges broken, but blessed. His deliverance in this situation (v. 30) is a foreshadowing of his deliverance from Esau.

The meeting of Jacob and Esau is told in Genesis 33. It is a wonderful meeting of reconciliation. It is evident that Esau's attitude toward Jacob has changed because when he saw Jacob 'he ran to meet him and embraced him and fell on his neck and kissed him, and they wept together' (v. 4). At some point over the years Esau had let go of the desire to kill his brother. Jacob's character has also changed, which is shown in how he approaches Esau and responds to him. Although he has sent delegations to meet Esau, Jacob takes the lead with his immediate family by going before them. He also shows humility and deference to Esau by bowing down to the ground before him seven times.[12] He shows true repentance by seeking to make amends for cheating his brother by offering him a large gift. He even calls it 'my blessing' (v. 11), which

---

11. Matthews, *Genesis 11:27–50:26*, p. 559.
12. Matthews (*Genesis 11:27–50:26*, p. 566) points out that the number seven may indicate a sense of complete humility before Esau.

is a reminder of the very thing that Jacob had taken away from Esau.[13] In explaining the reason for the gift, he alludes to the incident the night before when he wrestled with the messenger of God: 'I have seen your face, which is like seeing the face of God, and you have accepted me' (v. 10). What a relief that Esau comes in peace, but more, what a marvelous indication of God's protective presence in Jacob's life in order to ensure that the covenant promises will be fulfilled!

The spirit of reconciliation continues between the two brothers as Esau offers to accompany Jacob on his return journey (v. 12), which also may be an offer to ensure that Jacob's family has a safe trip.[14] Jacob, however, courteously refuses the offer by explaining that his group must move at a much slower pace than Esau's. When Esau offers to leave behind some of his people to accompany Jacob, again probably for protection, Jacob declines by explaining there is no need for such a plan (v. 15). Although reconciliation has taken place, Jacob seeks to separate himself from Esau. It is apparent that the offer to travel together includes the common destination of Esau's home of Seir, a city in Edom (v. 14). According to the vow that Jacob had made to God, he had promised to return to his father's house (28:21). By distancing himself from traveling with Esau he had the freedom to go where he needed to go. It is also important that Jacob separate his family from Esau in order to keep the promised line separate from the rejected line. The covenant community must not intermingle with those outside the community in case they will lose their distinct relationship to the God of the covenant. Jacob does not need the protection of Esau because he has the protection of God.

Jacob travels to Succoth, on the east side of the Jordan river, where he builds booths for his animals. This stop is not permanent because he has not yet reached the land of Canaan.[15] Then he comes to Shechem in the land of Canaan. He

---

13. Jacob is not here trying to reverse the blessing his father had given but is showing repentance through his willingness to surrender to Esau the wealth that had come with the blessing.

14. Matthews, *Genesis 11:27–50:26*, p. 571.

15. Matthews (*Genesis 11:27–50:26*, p. 572) notes that part of the purpose of the stop at Succoth may have been to make a staging area to prepare to cross the Jordan river.

buys a piece of land from the Shechemites, where he pitched his tent and erected an altar (vv. 18-20). He names the altar El-Elohe-Israel, which means 'God, the God of Israel'. This episode ends with Jacob arriving safely in the land of Canaan. He keeps his distance from the Canaanites by setting up camp outside the city. His purchase of land seems to parallel the action of his forefather Abraham, who also purchased land. It is possible that Jacob purchased this land for the purpose of providing a place of burial.[16] He also gives honor to God by building an altar. However, trouble is lurking in Shechem. One wonders what pain could have been avoided if Jacob had returned to Bethel, only a day's journey away, instead of settling near Shechem. It is not until Genesis 35 that he finally makes it back to the place of his vow.

STUDY QUESTIONS

1   How does Jacob begin to take leadership of his family?

2   Describe the character of Laban. How would you characterize Jacob's attempt to establish his own wages, including the breeding plan? How is it clear that God is the source of Jacob's wealth?

3   What is the relationship between planning and prayer as Jacob prepares to meet Esau? How can planning and praying work together in a believer's life? Why are they both important?

4   How would you describe the person with whom Jacob wrestles? How is Jacob's whole life represented in the wrestling match? What evidence is there that Jacob is a changed person after the wrestling match?

---

16. Waltke, *Genesis*, p. 461. Waltke also notes that the Canaanites may have been seeking to intermarry with Jacob's clan in order to absorb them as part of their people and culture, a constant danger for the covenant people of God.

15

Transition from One Generation to the Next Generation
(Genesis 34:1–37:1)

The next several chapters bring to an end the story of a period by recounting the deaths of Rachel and Isaac and by giving a summary of the generations of Esau. There is also a summary of God's promises and blessings to Jacob and it reveals that the promises of the covenant are given to him and his descendants. But before this, one is given a glimpse into the character of the family of Jacob through an incident at Shechem. This is the family through whom the covenant promises are given. Just as their father Jacob had some character flaws that needed to be refined by God, so this family has character flaws that God will need to change. These flaws are very similar to the flaws of their father and they will not be fully addressed until the story of Joseph.

A Glimpse into the Character of Jacob's Family (Gen. 34:1-31)
Although Jacob had made his camp outside of Shechem, Dinah seems drawn to the city of Shechem. She leaves the protection of her own household and ventures out 'to see the women of the land' (v. 1). For a girl of marriageable age to leave a rural encampment and go unchaperoned into an alien city was not a wise thing to do.[1] This story demonstrates the lure of

---

1. Waltke, *Genesis*, p. 461. Matthews (*Genesis 11:27–50:26*, p. 590) is correct

the Canaanite way of life and the problems that come when God's covenant family intermingles with the Canaanites. Dinah is seen by Shechem, son of Hamor the Hivite, who is an important ruler of the land. The actions of Shechem are briefly described: 'he saw her, he seized her and lay with her and humiliated her' (v. 2). It is clear that Shechem forces himself on Dinah and rapes her. However, he also has feelings for Dinah, which is expressed by three verbs that counter the three verbs of the rape. He was 'drawn to' Dinah, he 'loved the young woman', and he 'spoke tenderly to her' (v. 3).[2] These verbs may express natural emotion or even lustful passion.[3] He wants to possess what he had wrongfully taken. However, there is no hint of remorse for doing something wrong or any evidence of repentance. He charges his father with the command, 'Get me this girl for my wife' (v. 4). Shechem displays the true character of a Canaanite. He takes what he wants and shows no remorse for the effect his actions have on others.

The response of Jacob and his sons to this incident gives a glimpse into the character and dynamics of the family. Jacob himself is passive throughout the chapter and only speaks at the end of the chapter. Although he hears what has happened to his daughter Dinah, he takes no action. When he does speak, he is more concerned about his reputation in the community than the humiliation of his daughter, and he expresses fear that the inhabitants of the land might gather together against them to destroy them (v. 30).[4] It is interesting that Jacob is not called by his name Israel in this passage, for he is acting more like the old Jacob than the new Israel. Jacob's passive response is highlighted by its contrast to the response of his sons. They were 'indignant and very angry' (v. 7). They express moral outrage. Their anger is justified because their sister has been violated and humiliated. There is an appropriate desire for justice to be done. Yet they come up with a plan that shows that they have learned the art of deception well from their father.

---

to point out that even though Dinah's actions show a lack of wisdom she should not be blamed for the rape.

2. Waltke, *Genesis*, p. 462.

3. Waltke (*Genesis*, p. 463) mentions the former and Matthews (*Genesis 11:27–50:26*, p. 593) mentions the latter.

4. Waltke, *Genesis*, p. 467.

Hamor and Shechem approach the clan of Jacob to request that Dinah be given to Shechem for a wife (vv. 8-12). The reasons given by Hamor include the fact that his son longs to have Dinah for a wife. Hamor also lays out the benefits to the family of Jacob if this marriage takes place. They will become a part of the community by intermarrying with them and the opportunities for acquiring property will increase because of their peaceful cohabitation. Shechem adds that he is willing to pay whatever they ask for a bride price.[5] They try to make the deal sound appealing to Jacob's family, but there is no apology or recognition of any harm caused by Shechem's treatment of Dinah.

The response to the request is given by the sons of Jacob who set out a deceitful plan to take revenge for the defilement of their sister Dinah (vv. 13-17). They use the rite of circumcision as a ploy to carry out their scheme of revenge. They are not able to give Dinah to Shechem because it would be a disgrace for them to give their sister to one who is uncircumcised. The only condition they require is that all of the men of Shechem should be circumcised. If they are willing to fulfill that condition, then the sons of Jacob promise that they will give Dinah to Shechem, they will intermarry with them, and they will dwell with them as one people. If they will not carry out the condition of circumcision, then the sons of Jacob will leave and be gone. This is a deceitful plan because the sons of Jacob have no intention of giving Dinah to Shechem or dwelling as one people with them. This is a plan to carry out revenge.

Hamor and Shechem are pleased with this arrangement and set out to convince the men of the city of Shechem to go along with it. The circumcision of adult males would not have been an easy thing to sell because it is a very painful procedure! However, the standing of Shechem in the community is important – he is identified as 'the most honored of all his father's house' (v. 19). He also appeals to the benefits such an arrangement with the family of Jacob will bring to the city of Shechem. They will be able to acquire 'their livestock, their property, and all their beasts' (v. 23). This explanation works and the men of Shechem agree to

---

5. Waltke (*Genesis*, p. 465) points out that the bride price refers to a sum of money paid by the bridegroom to the bride's family at the time of the betrothal. From that point forward the couple were understood to be legally married even though the marriage had not yet been consummated.

be circumcised. With each group, Hamor and Shechem appeal to self-interest. They tell the sons of Jacob how they will benefit by acquiring more land and property, and they tell the men of Shechem how they will benefit by acquiring more possessions. Be careful when a ruler or politician comes to you and declares that he has a good deal for you!

Specifically, two of the sons of Jacob carry out the revenge. They are identified as Simeon and Levi, Dinah's brothers. In other words, they had the same mother, Leah.[6] Just as Shechem had originally taken ('seized') Dinah, they took swords, came against the city and killed all the males of the city, including Hamor and Shechem, and also took Dinah from the house of Shechem.[7] They also plundered the flocks, herds, and wealth of the city and captured the women and children of the city. When Jacob confronted Simeon and Levi with the trouble such actions would cause for their family with the inhabitants of the region, they ask a rhetorical question that speaks up for the honor of their sister (v. 31): 'Should he treat our sister like a prostitute?'

Neither Jacob nor his two sons act appropriately in Genesis 34. Jacob is silent concerning the defilement of his daughter, reacts out of fear rather than faith, and seems more concerned about his standing and reputation in the community than the honor of his daughter. However, if nothing were done the clan would look weak because they are not able to protect their women. Simeon and Levi are justified in their anger concerning how their sister was treated, but they express their anger through deception in order to execute revenge.[8]

---

6. Why the other brothers of Dinah who are sons of Leah do not participate (Reuben, Judah, Issachar, and Zebulun) is not stated. There is some ambiguity in the phrase 'sons of Jacob' in verse 27, which describes who participated in the plunder of the city. The phrase could include the other sons of Jacob. Although Jacob only speaks to Simeon and Levi after the deed is carried out (v. 30), he may be speaking to them as the ones who came up with the plan and made sure it was carried out.

7. It seems that Shechem had kept Dinah in his house after he raped her, which means that in the negotiations with the sons of Jacob he may have had an upper hand. Waltke (Genesis, p. 467) comments that the negotiations between the two groups were never honest because of this fact.

8. An appropriate response would have been to appeal to the unjust actions of Shechem against Dinah and to call for justice to be done. Even unbelievers have a sense of justice. Although the city of Shechem might have rejected a call for justice, it would place the family of Jacob in the right and allow God the opportunity to work in a way that would show His covenant faithfulness. The approach of deception short-circuits an honorable outcome.

Deception has been a part of this family for generations. The seeds of deception were sown by their forefather Abraham (Gen. 12 and 20) and deception became a character trait of Jacob. Although Jacob has given evidence of a change in this area of his life, his sons have learned from him. God intervened in the deception of Abraham in Genesis 20 and made Abraham a source of blessing to Abimelech by praying for his barren household, but Jacob and his sons are not a blessing in Genesis 34. The danger of associating with the Canaanites is clearly part of the message. When you associate with them, it is easy to begin to act like them.

Covenant Blessings at Bethel (Gen. 35:1-15)

Jacob finally returns to Bethel, the place where God first revealed Himself to him (Gen. 28:10-22). He does not return to Bethel on his own initiative, but because God tells him to go to Bethel, dwell there, and build an altar (v. 1). Bethel is significant because of the vow that Jacob had made to God. A return to Bethel would confirm to Jacob God's covenant faithfulness. Jacob recognizes the importance of Bethel by preparing his family for the trip. Specifically, he tells the members of his household that they must put away the foreign gods that are among them, they must purify themselves, and they must change their garments (v. 2).[9] In explaining the move to Bethel, Jacob acknowledges God's faithfulness by confessing that he is the God 'who answers me in the day of my distress and has been with me wherever I have gone' (v. 3). This passage shows the spiritual state of Jacob's household. Jacob himself acknowledges God's role in his life, but some in his household still harbor idols. Thus it is possible that the altar Jacob built at Shechem fell short of full allegiance to God because Jacob then reacted in fear in Shechem and was not a blessing to those around him.[10]

The consecration of Jacob's household to God and the move to Bethel bring immediate changes in the family's relationship

---

9. Matthews (*Genesis 11:27–50:26*, p. 618) notes that the rings in their ears that they give to Jacob may have been plunder from Shechem. He also notes that the rings might have had pagan associations, or could be used to make idols.

10. Waltke, *Genesis*, p. 471. He also comments that in Shechem Jacob worships according to his own agenda.

with God. On the journey there, a terror from God fell upon the cities that they passed, so that the inhabitants did not pursue the sons of Jacob (v. 5). In other words, God protected the household of Jacob from any retaliation from the Canaanites because of what happened at Shechem. This protection by God shows that Jacob's first response should have been to trust in God.

Jacob returns to Bethel, builds an altar, and calls the place El-bethel, with the explanation that it was at this place that God had revealed Himself to him when he fled from his brother (vv. 6-7). God then appeared to Jacob a second time at Bethel and blessed him. Several things are confirmed to Jacob at Bethel. First, there is confirmation of Jacob's new name Israel (v. 10), which is a reminder of his change of character and the need to be fully committed to God. Second, there is confirmation of God's character in the name 'God Almighty' (El Shaddai); this name for God connects with Jacob's ancestors (Gen. 17:1) and emphasizes God's power to fulfill His promises. Third, the promises are also confirmed: the descendants of Jacob will become a great nation, kings will come forth from him, and the land that God had promised to Abraham would be given to Jacob's descendants. Jacob responds by worshipping God in fulfillment of his vow. The stone pillar is a memorial that is set apart by a drink offering and oil. Such actions parallel the actions when Jacob was first at Bethel, the house of God (Gen. 28:18-19). Jacob should be assured of the great things God will do if he will only trust Him and follow Him.

The End of an Era (Gen. 35:16-29)

No reason is given for why the household of Jacob leaves Bethel, but they head toward Ephrath (Bethlehem) on their way to Hebron, which would complete Jacob's safe return to his father's house.[11] The deaths of several people are recorded, which brings to a close a generation, even as the next stage of the story is set forth in the completion of the family of Jacob in twelve sons. While they were at Bethel Deborah, who was Rebekah's nurse, had died. Deborah had

---

11. Matthews, *Genesis 11:27–50:26*, p. 624.

accompanied Rebekah from Haran when she returned with Abraham's servant to marry Isaac (Gen. 24). It is not known how Deborah now came to be with Jacob's household, but Rebekah had promised to send for Jacob in Haran when it was safe for him to return (Gen. 27:45). Jacob may have developed a close relationship with his mother's nurse as he was growing up, which explains Jacob's heartache at her death. This grief is expressed in the name given to the site of her burial. The name 'Allon-bacuth' means 'oak of weeping' (v. 8).[12] Deborah represents the older generation, as does Isaac, whose death is recorded at the end of the chapter. Jacob had safely returned to his father at Hebron before Isaac died (v. 27). Isaac was blessed with a long life of 180 years and the description of his death parallels the description of Abraham's death. In fact, Abraham is specifically mentioned in verse 27, so that at the end of Genesis 35 Abraham, Isaac, and Jacob are all mentioned. Although both Esau and Jacob bury their father Isaac, the promise of covenant blessing that began with Abraham will go through the family of Jacob.

Although the deaths in this chapter signify the end of an era, the future comes into view in the completion of Jacob's family. Rachel gives birth to her second son, but she dies in giving birth. This tragic event takes place on the way from Bethel to Bethlehem and she is buried along the way. The last son of Jacob is born in the land, and Rachel is also buried in the land that God had promised to give to Abraham's descendants. The last son was originally named Ben-oni, which means 'son of my sorrow' (v. 18).[13] This name would emphasize Rachel's difficulty in the birth, but Jacob renames the son with a more positive name. Benjamin means 'son of my right hand'. The right hand indicates the place of power or favor. This son becomes a special son of favor to Jacob as the story of this family unfolds.

---

12. Matthews, *Genesis 11:27–50:26*, p. 621.

13. The Hebrew *'ôn'* comes from the word for 'sorrow' (*'āwen*), but the connection to *'ôn*, which would yield 'son of my strength' has also been suggested. The latter name might indicate that the child depletes Rachel of her vitality or that the child possesses Rachel's strength. However, Matthews (*Genesis 11:27–50:26*, p. 625) points out that when the word for 'strength' is applied to a parent's vigor it refers to the father's strength or virility.

The completion of the family is set forth with the listing of the twelve sons of Jacob (vv. 23-26). The sons are presented based on the social ranking of the wives of Jacob, with the sons of Leah listed first, then Rachel, then Rachel's servant Bilhah, and finally Leah's servant Zilpah. The list not only emphasizes the faithfulness of God to Jacob in giving him many sons, but it also sets up the conflict and rivalry that will take place in this family in the last section of the book of Genesis. Reuben is specifically identified as the firstborn (v. 23), but he will fall short of providing leadership in the family as the story unfolds. In fact, a significant incident is recorded in verse 22 concerning Reuben. After the death of Rachel, Reuben, the son of Leah, has a sexual relationship with Bilhah, his father's concubine and the mother of his brothers Dan and Naphtali. There may be several reasons for this act. He might have been afraid that, after the death of Rachel, her servant Bilhah would supplant his mother Leah as the chief wife. He also might have been trying to seize leadership of the family. Nevertheless, he will be condemned for this act against his father and will forfeit his privileged place as the firstborn son. Jacob, called Israel, at this point remains silent, but later speaks against Reuben for what he has done (Gen. 49:3-4). The reader waits to see which son will emerge as leader of the family and how God will fulfill His promises through this family.

The Generations (Toledot) of Esau (Gen. 36:1–37:1)

It is rather remarkable that a whole chapter is devoted to the descendants of Esau. The chapter can be divided into two parts, with each part beginning with 'these are the generations of' (vv. 1 and 9). The first part of the chapter reviews the immediate family of Esau (36:1-8). The wives of Esau and the sons born to them are named. Also, the reason for Esau's move to the country of Seir (Edom) is given. God had blessed both Jacob and Esau with so many cattle that the land could not sustain them both. In this way, Esau is separated from the land of promise and settles in the place where his descendants will become a nation.

The rest of the chapter sets forth Esau's descendants as a developing nation. The first section focuses again on Esau's sons and grandsons (vv. 10-19), including those among his sons who became chiefs, which may designate a clan or tribal leader.[14] The second section lays out the sons and chiefs of Seir the Horite (vv. 20-30). Seir was the ancestor of the Horite clans. Although the descendants of Esau intermarried with them, they also dispossessed the Horites from their land (Deut. 2:12, 22). The third section lays out the kings of Edom (vv. 31-39). The comment in verse 31, 'These were the kings who reigned in Edom before any Israelite king reigned,' is a comment that highlights the relationship between Edom and Israel.[15] Although Edom had kings before Israel, Edom eventually became subject to David and, for the most part, to David's dynasty of kings. The last section returns to the chiefs of Edom descended from Esau by their clans and regions. Thus the emphasis on chiefs frames this section (vv. 15-19 and 40-43).

There are several reasons why it is important to show the development of the descendants of Esau. First, this account shows how God blessed Esau. Even though Esau and his descendants were not partakers of the promise of covenant blessings (Gen. 12:1-3), they were blessed by God in a remarkable way. This is partially a fulfillment of the promise to Abraham that kings would come forth from him.

Second, the description of the descendants of Esau and where they settled is important for the rest of the history of Israel. The relationship between Israel and Edom is at times rocky (see the prophecy of Obadiah). During much of the history of Israel, Edom was under the yoke of the kings of Israel, but when Israel would become weak Edom would revolt (2 Kings 8:16-24). Eventually Edom became very weak and was displaced by an Arabian tribe, the Nabateans, late in the fourth century B.C. In fact, Malachi uses Edom as an example of a nation that does not have any future because they are separated from the covenant and not loved by God (Mal. 1:1-5). Thus to be outside the covenant is to be without hope of an enduring future.

14. Matthews, *Genesis 11:27–50:26*, p. 652.
15. The comment about kings reigning in Edom before there were Israelite kings comes from a later scribe. Moses had committed what he wrote to the Levites for preservation of the text and future reading of the text (Deut. 31:9-11, 24-26). For a discussion of Mosaic authorship and minor textual changes made by the scribes, see the Introduction to this commentary.

Finally, there is a contrast between Esau and Jacob in this section. Esau intermarried with the people of the region but Jacob took wives from outside the land. Esau also moved from the land to settle in the area of Edom, while Jacob was heir to the promise God made concerning the land. Thus the concluding verse of this section (37:1) has Jacob dwelling in the land of Canaan. Just like his ancestors, he is a sojourner in the land waiting for the promises of God to be fulfilled. A major step in the fulfillment of those promises will come in the next section of Genesis, which focuses on the story of Joseph.

STUDY QUESTIONS

1   How do the actions of Shechem and Hamor demonstrate the character of the Canaanites?

2   Is there anything positive in the response of the sons of Jacob to the rape of their sister Dinah? What plan do they come up with? What is wrong with the plan? What would have been a better way to respond? What family character flaw is illustrated in their plan?

3   What is the purpose of the story of the rape of Dinah? What would the message be to the Israelites in the Old Testament and to the church today?

4   Why is it important for Jacob to return to Bethel? What are the positive results?

5   Why is there so much emphasis on the descendants of Esau? What significance should this have for God's people today?

16

The Beginning of the Story of Joseph:
Major Problems among Brothers
(Genesis 37:2–38:30)

The last major toledot section begins at Genesis 37:2 and covers the rest of the book of Genesis. It is called the 'generations (Toledot) of Jacob' (37:2–50:26) and is the story of what happens to the family of Jacob. It also describes how the family of Jacob ended up living in Egypt. The story focuses on Joseph, so this toledot section could be called the story of Joseph. Yet it is more than the story of Joseph; it is also a story of how God takes a troubled family and works to bring the family together. God works on this family to bring unity out of conflict and in the process the leader of the family emerges.

The theme of this story is that God is able to fulfill His promises in spite of the evil intentions of people who act in ways that would hinder His promises. There is a significant change of focus in this section of Genesis. The difficulties Abraham faced centered on the circumstances of his life and whether he would trust in God to fulfill His promises. The story of Jacob focused on the problems of Jacob's character and how God had to work on Jacob to change him. The problems encountered in Joseph's life emphasize the adverse circumstances that he faced. These circumstances arose because of opposition to Joseph, but God worked providentially in those adverse circumstances to accomplish His purposes.

Joseph was severely tested through the evil intentions of other people, but God was able to make Joseph prosper even in the midst of those difficult situations.

Conflict among the Sons of Jacob (Gen. 37:2-36)

Joseph is immediately introduced in verse 2 because the story will focus on him. He is now seventeen years old and is pasturing the flock with his brothers. He is described as 'a boy with the sons of Bilhah and Zilpah, his father's wives' (v. 2). The emphasis is upon the youth of Joseph and his lower status among his brothers because of his youth. The problem that drives the plot of Genesis 37 is the hatred that Joseph's brothers feel toward him; in fact, they hate him so much they are willing to act on their hatred. The reason for their hatred of Joseph is due to a number of factors which demonstrate the dysfunctional nature of this family.

First, part of the problem is that Jacob showed favoritism to Joseph over against his other sons. Jacob loved Joseph more than his other sons because he was the son of his old age (v. 3), and he showed that love to Joseph by making him 'a robe of many colors'. This description of the robe is based on the Septuagint,[1] but in light of the Hebrew term used (*kutōnet*) a better description might be of a robe that was long and flowing, reaching to the palms and soles of the feet.[2] The important thing is that Jacob's favoritism was clearly evident to his other sons. They knew that their father loved Joseph more than any of them (v. 4), which produced in them a searing hatred for Joseph. In fact, they hated him so much that they could not even speak peacefully to him. This attitude showed the depth of their hatred. The sad thing is that Jacob should have understood how such favoritism would impact the family, for it was parental favoritism in his own family that led to his deception of his father. Favoritism also produced hatred from his brother Esau that was so intense that he planned to murder Jacob, with the outcome that Jacob had to leave his family.

---

1. Waltke, *Genesis*, p. 500.
2. John D. Currid, *Genesis 25:19–50:26* (Darlington: Evangelical Press, 2003), p. 186.

Second, the bad relations among the brothers were also due to Joseph's actions. He previously brought a bad report of his brothers to their father (v. 2). The content of this report is not stated, but it is clear that the report was not good. Apparently, Joseph observed things his brothers were doing while he was pasturing the flock with them and told his father about it. Later in the chapter, it becomes clear that Jacob sends Joseph to check up on his brothers and to bring him word of how they are doing (v. 14). This 'reporting' no doubt adds to their hatred of him because no one likes a tattle-tale little brother.

Further, Joseph showed immaturity by relating his dreams to his brothers. In light of the hatred they had for Joseph, the dreams would be fuel of the fire of that hatred because the dreams assert the priority of Joseph over his brothers. In the first dream, Joseph's sheaf in the field stood upright and the sheaves of his brothers bowed down to his sheaf (vv. 5-8). The response of his brothers raises a key question for the rest of the story: 'Are you indeed to rule over us?' Little did they know that one day they would bow down to Joseph! In the second dream,[3] the sun, the moon, and the stars bow down to Joseph (vv. 9-11). He told this dream to his brothers, but then also to his father. In light of his father's response, it appears that the sun may refer to Jacob, the moon to Rachel, and the eleven stars to his brothers: 'Shall I and your mother and your brothers indeed come to bow ourselves to the ground before you?' Although he questioned Joseph in this way, Jacob seemed to take the dream more seriously than his sons, for it is stated that 'his father kept the saying in mind' (v. 11). Jacob himself knew from his own experience the mysterious ways of God because he was the younger brother who was given preference by God in his family. The dreams, however, feed the hatred that the brothers of Joseph already have for him (vv. 5, 8). They are also extremely jealous of Joseph's favored treatment (v. 8).

The opportunity for the brothers of Joseph to express their hatred for Joseph occurred when Jacob sent Joseph to check on the brothers and the flock. Neither Jacob nor Joseph seemed

---

3. Waltke (*Genesis*, p. 501) notes that the dreams in the Joseph story come in pairs. An isolated dream can be misinterpreted but two dreams with the same meaning confirm the interpretation.

aware or concerned about the hatred of Joseph's brothers toward him. They were pasturing their flocks near Shechem, a place which should produce negative associations in the mind of the reader.[4] At first Joseph was not able to find his brothers (vv. 15-17). He was found by 'a man' wandering in the fields. Joseph's wandering highlights his vulnerability.[5] The fact that he was helped by 'a man' reminds one of the incidents involving Jacob, who wrestled with 'a man' (Gen. 32:24) who turned out to be more than just a man. There is no indication that the man who helps Joseph is more than human, but the incident is encouraging because it is an indication that God will help Joseph even in the bad circumstances that are going to come. The unseen hand of God was at work even in Joseph's wandering.[6] The man informed Joseph that his brothers had gone to Dothan and Joseph eventually found them there.[7]

The extent of the hatred of Joseph's brothers toward him becomes clear in the events that unfold. When they saw Joseph coming to them they began to conspire against him in order to kill him (vv. 18-24). They specifically called him 'a dreamer' and mentioned his dreams. If they killed him, his dreams would come to nothing. They came up with a plan to kill Joseph and threw him into a pit. They were willing to deceive their father by saying a fierce animal had devoured him. However, Reuben exhorted them not to kill Joseph. His motivation was to rescue Joseph from the other brothers and to restore him to his father. It is likely that Reuben was trying to get back into the good graces of Jacob after the incident described in Genesis 35:22 when he had sexual relations with Bilhah. He was willing to set his own interests above those of his other brothers so as to make himself look good at their expense. So when Joseph arrived, they stripped him of his robe and cast him into a pit.

---

4. Matthews (*Genesis 11:27–50:26*, p. 694) notes that because the brothers can pasture near Shechem, it shows that the times were peaceful. It also may indicate how far the brothers must go to get sufficient grazing areas, perhaps an early indication of the coming famine.

5. Matthews, *Genesis 11:27–50:26*, p. 694.

6. Matthews, *Genesis 11:27–50:26*, p. 695.

7. Waltke (*Genesis*, p. 502) points out that Dothan is thirteen miles northwest of Shechem.

Reuben's plans come to naught. While he was away, Joseph was sold to a caravan of Ishmaelites[8] on their way to Egypt to sell goods (gum, balm, and myrrh). Judah took the initiative in selling this plan to his brothers (vv. 25-28). They would not have to kill Joseph, so his blood would not be upon their hands and they could make some profit in the sale. So they sold Joseph for twenty shekels of silver, which was the typical price for a slave at that time.[9] When Reuben returned, he was distraught that Joseph had been sold because his plan to rescue him had been undermined (vv. 29-30). However, his response to his brothers was feeble and cowardly: 'The boy is gone, and I, where shall I go?' Instead of confronting his brothers and pursuing Joseph to rescue him, he offered a statement that showed he was more concerned about his plan to get back into the good graces of his father than he was concerned about Joseph. He participates in the deceptive cover-up by remaining silent. The brothers took Joseph's robe, dipped it in the blood of a goat, and brought it to their father. They asked Jacob to identify the robe and he drew the conclusion that a fierce animal had devoured Joseph. Jacob mourned his son's death and he refused to be comforted by the family. In fact, the deception and hypocrisy continued as 'all his sons and daughters rose up to comfort him' (v. 35). The brothers participated in a charade of mourning because they knew that Joseph was not really dead. They allowed their father to mourn the death of a son who was really alive. Not one of them broke ranks and told the truth. They participated in these deceitful activities because of their intense hatred for Joseph.

The family of Jacob was dysfunctional in their relations with each other. Deceit and favoritism were passed down from one generation to the next as Jacob carried on the tradition of showing favoritism to one of his sons. Also, the tension between Leah and Rachel, and the favored status of Rachel, would have made an impact on these boys as they grew up. They learned from their parents as the same dynamics continued in their own lives. They hated Joseph because of

---

8. Waltke (*Genesis*, p. 502) comments that the names 'the Ishmaelites' and 'the Midianites' are alternative designations for the same group of traders (Judg. 8:24).

9. Matthews, *Genesis 11:27–50:26*, p. 699.

the favoritism he was shown by their father. They were even willing to act on their hatred when the opportunity presented itself. Joseph himself was not completely free of blame but his own father does not set him up for success with his brothers. Jacob not only showed favoritism to Joseph, but he also sent him to check up on his brothers and to report back to him. Joseph's immaturity was seen in making public the content of his dreams.

Two of the brothers emerge as leaders in this account. Reuben acted selfishly by trying to use the situation to his own advantage, but his plan failed. Judah acted to spare Joseph's life but gets rid of Joseph by persuading the brothers to sell him to a caravan on their way to Egypt. They all profit from the sale and participate in the deception of their father. It is interesting that Jacob had deceived his father with goat's skins and Esau's clothing, and now he is deceived by his sons with a goat's blood and his son's robe.

Although this chapter shows the dysfunctional condition of this family in their evil actions and attitudes toward one another, God was going to work in this family to bring unity and the willingness to sacrifice for each other. Joseph will learn wisdom and grow in maturity. Jacob's mourning will be turned to joy. Reuben and Judah will both step forward as possible leaders of the family, but only one will emerge as a wise leader. Even though the situation appeared hopeless, God was able in His providence to coordinate events to bring change in this family. Change will begin with Judah, while there are hints of Joseph's well-being in Egypt as he is sold to Potiphar, the captain of the guard, an officer of Pharaoh, a man of responsibility (v. 36).

The Development of the Character of Judah (Gen. 38:1-30)
Some scholars question the purpose of Genesis 38 at this point of the narrative because it seems to interrupt the story.[10] One can read Genesis 37:36 and then jump to Genesis 39:1 without missing a beat. However, Genesis 38 creates suspense for we

---

10. Gerhard von Rad, *Genesis* (Philadelphia: The Westminster Press, 1962), pp. 351-53. E. A. Speiser (*Genesis* [New York: Doubleday, n.d.], p. 299) states that this narrative is a completely independent unit that has no connection with the drama of Joseph.

are left wondering what will happen to Joseph in Egypt.[11] It will also be seen that there are thematic connections between Genesis 38 and the story of Joseph.[12] Genesis 38 focuses on the development of the character of Judah, who will play a major role later in the story of Joseph, and it explains the events which lead to the births of Perez and Zerah by Tamar.

The beginning of Genesis 38 reveals possible tension between Judah and his brothers because Judah separates from them. There is also an indication of the spiritual state of Judah because he marries the daughter of a Canaanite. Here Judah acts more like Esau, the non-elect line, by not keeping separate from the Canaanites. This act of intermarriage should cause great concern for the future of Judah who may be forfeiting his role in the family by acting in this way. The name of the Canaanite woman is not even given; she is identified only as the daughter of Shua. However, she bears Judah three sons who are named Er, Onan, and Shelah.

Judah arranges for Er, the firstborn, to marry Tamar. The character of Judah and his sons becomes apparent in the events that follow. Er is described as 'wicked in the sight of the Lord' (v. 7). His wickedness is not detailed but he is put to death by the Lord. Judah then tells the second son, Onan, to perform 'the duty of a brother-in-law' to Tamar and raise up offspring in place of his brother Er. This is an early indication of the practice of levirate marriage (Deut. 25:5-10). The son that would result from the union of Tamar and Onan would carry on the name of Er and receive his inheritance. If such a son is not produced, then Onan and Shelah would receive more inheritance. Onan understands this and so refuses to complete the act of sexual union by wasting his semen on the ground. Such an act is wicked in the sight of the Lord and so the Lord also puts Onan to death. Judah then tells Tamar to remain a widow in her father's house until Shelah, the youngest son, grows up. However, Judah is spiritually blind to the wickedness of his sons and fears that his sons are dying because of Tamar (v. 11).

---

11. Wenham, *Genesis 16–50*, p. 363.
12. See Hamilton, *Genesis 18–50*, pp. 431-32, for a discussion of why Genesis 38 must occur here in the story and for the linguistic and thematic parallels with the surrounding chapters.

The promise by Judah to give Shelah to Tamar never materializes. Time passes and the wife of Judah dies. Tamar has been biding her time in her father's house but nothing happens. She realizes the promise Judah made will not be fulfilled (v. 14). After Judah mourns the death of his wife, Tamar takes matters in her own hands. She is told that her father-in-law is shearing sheep at Timnah. She takes off her widow's garments, covers herself with a veil, and sits at a prominent place on the road. Her intention is to deceive Judah, and it works because he thinks she is a prostitute (v. 15). In arranging payment for services, Tamar protects herself by receiving as a pledge Judah's signet ring, cord, and staff to ensure that he would later send a young goat from the flock. Tamar becomes pregnant by Judah and then puts on again her widow's garments. When Judah tries to send payment to the prostitute and get his property back, Tamar is nowhere to be found because she had gone back home to her father's house. When inquiry is made concerning the whereabouts of the cult prostitute, the men of the place deny that a cult prostitute has been in the area.[13] Judah drops the issue to keep from looking foolish and being ridiculed (v. 23). The fact that Judah would entertain a prostitute shows he is living like the Canaanites around him.

Three months later, Judah hears that Tamar is pregnant and he is outraged, partly because this would be an act of unfaithfulness to the family and partly because her pregnancy is the result of immorality (*znh*), a word that stresses prostitution and harlotry (v. 24). Judah orders her to be brought out to be burned because of her immorality. As she is being brought out, she sends word to Judah that she is pregnant by the man who owns the ring, the cord, and the staff. Of course, Judah identifies them as his own and then declares, 'She is more righteous than I, since I did not give her my son Shelah' (v. 26). Judah confesses his own guilt and is able to acknowledge the righteous actions of Tamar. Perhaps one wonders how the actions of Tamar

---

13. The word 'cult' here refers to activities related to worship. A cult prostitute offers herself as a representative of a fertility god and the payment given to her for her services goes to support a local temple.

can be seen as righteous since she deceives her father-in-law by acting as a prostitute. However, she remains loyal to the family of Judah instead of abandoning the family by marrying a Canaanite. She becomes known in history because she gives birth to Perez, an important son of Judah, whose house is invoked in an exemplary way in the story of Ruth (4:12). Tamar also becomes a part of the messianic line, which not only leads to David (Ruth 4:18-22), but also to Christ (Matt. 1:3).

The birth of the twin sons of Tamar is significant (vv. 27-30). The fact that there are twins reminds one of the births of Esau and Jacob. There also seems to be a struggle between the two boys in the womb in this birth. One boy puts out his hand from the womb and the midwife ties a thread around it, identifying the son that came out first. However, when he drew back his hand, the other boy comes out. His name is called Perez with the explanation, 'What a breach (*pāraṣ*) you have made for yourself.' The other son, Zerah, 'broke through' asserting himself ahead of his brother. It is the younger son Perez who will become prominent in the history of Israel (Ruth 4).

Genesis 38 is a significant turning point in the character of Judah. He separates from his brothers and shows a lack of spiritual discernment by marrying a Canaanite woman. Such a marriage also demonstrates callousness toward the covenant. He is spiritually blind to the character of his sons and his life reflects the Canaanites among whom he lives by paying for the services of a prostitute. His confession of guilt and recognition of the faithfulness of Tamar to his own family is a turning point in his character, which will be significant for his role later in the Joseph story. In the birth of Zerah and Perez, the younger son prevails, which parallels the Esau and Jacob story and may be a subtle reminder that God is able to cause the younger son to have prominence if it is His will. In other words, no matter what the brothers of Joseph do to Joseph, they will not be able to hinder his rise to a position over them.

STUDY QUESTIONS

1   List the reasons why the brothers of Joseph hate him. How could each of the members of the family have acted differently to alleviate some of the tension?

2   Compare Reuben and Judah in Genesis 37. Does either one of them act in an appropriate way?

3   What evidence is there in Genesis 38 that Judah is spiritually blind? How can his response to Tamar be seen as a change of character?

4   What principle does the birth of Zerah and Perez illustrate?

17

Joseph's Rise to Power in Egypt
(Genesis 39–41)

The story of Joseph's rise to power in Egypt is a wonderful story of the providence of God. Several times in the story it seems as if his life is ruined and that there is no hope for his future; however, the purposes of God cannot be hindered by the evil actions of others or by circumstances that appear to be devastating. Joseph's faithfulness and his God-given abilities are used by God in each situation to accomplish His purposes.

God's Abundant Blessings in Adverse Circumstances (Gen. 39:1-23)

What a shock it must have been to Joseph to be betrayed by his brothers and callously sold to traders on their way to Egypt. In Egypt he is sold as a slave to Potiphar, an Egyptian, who is identified as 'an officer of Pharaoh, the captain of the guard' (v. 1). The success of Joseph in this man's house is recounted in verses 3-6. Although Joseph must have had great administrative abilities because everywhere he goes he is put in charge (39:22), his success is directly tied to the fact that Yahweh (the LORD) was with Joseph. In fact, Potiphar himself recognizes that 'the LORD caused all that he did to succeed in his hands' (v. 3). The LORD's blessing falls on everything that Potiphar possessed for the sake of Joseph. Thus Joseph is made overseer of Potiphar's house and he had charge of everything that belonged to Potiphar. He so trusted Joseph that he had no concern about anything in his house 'but the food that he ate' (v. 6).

Joseph was not only a young man blessed by God but he was also 'handsome in form and appearance' (v. 6b). Joseph catches the eye of his master's wife and she propositions him to have a sexual relationship with her (v. 7). In this incident the character of Joseph becomes clear. He refuses her advances with two solid reasons as to why such an act would be wrong. First, it would be a betrayal of the trust that his master has placed in him. Joseph has been put in charge of everything and he has won the trust of his master; therefore, his master has no concern about anything in his house. In other words, Joseph has demonstrated loyal service so that the master has entrusted everything he has to the charge of Joseph, except for his own wife. Thus Joseph calls such an act of betrayal wickedness (v. 9). Secondly, he also calls such an act a sin against God. Joseph's refusal is not just the prudent thing to do but it is the right thing to do according to the standards of the God that he serves. In this story the character of Joseph is in contrast with the character of Judah in Genesis 38. Judah lived like a Canaanite among the Canaanites but Joseph honors God as he lives among the Egyptians.

The wife of Potiphar is persistent in her request. Each day she tries to convince Joseph to sleep with her. Joseph seeks to run from the temptation by not listening to her, by not lying beside her, and by not being with her. However, the master's wife makes use of an opportunity when Joseph is in the house and there are no men around. She catches him by his garment, seeking to persuade him to lie with her. Joseph flees the situation but his garment is left in her hand. She uses this incident to pay Joseph back for the scorn of his refusal of her desires. She falsely accuses Joseph of trying to seduce her by using the garment he had left behind as evidence of the truthfulness of her charge against him. Of course, Joseph's master, the husband of this woman, is angry at this violation of trust and has Joseph thrown into the prison where the king's prisoners are confined. Some commentators point out that attempted rape was a capital offense in Egypt and the fact that Joseph was thrown into prison may indicate that

Potiphar is not totally convinced of Joseph's guilt.[1] Although Potiphar is angry, the focus of his anger is left unstated. Is he angry at Joseph? Is he angry for losing the competent services of Joseph? Does Potiphar know the character of his wife and the character of Joseph and is not convinced of Joseph's guilt? Must he do something to save face, so he throws Joseph into prison? Although certainty concerning these matters is not possible, a scenario whereby Potiphar does not completely believe the charges against Joseph makes sense in light of the clear recognition by Potiphar earlier in the chapter that God was blessing his house because of Joseph.

Joseph is clearly innocent and is falsely accused by Potiphar's wife. He is ruined by these false accusations and finds himself in prison. However, the LORD was still with Joseph and demonstrated his 'steadfast love' to Joseph by blessing him even in the prison. He found favor from the keeper of the prison and was put in charge of all the prisoners. Joseph's responsibilities were broad because 'whatever was done there, he was the one who did it' (v. 22). Joseph was so trustworthy that the keeper of the prison paid no attention to anything that was under the charge of Joseph. Although there is no doubt that Joseph had administrative and organizational abilities, his success is directly related to the fact that the LORD was with him. Even in prison, God blesses Joseph. The evil intention of Potiphar's wife and the adverse circumstances of prison could not separate Joseph from the LORD's presence or from His blessings.

Faithfulness in Prison: Preparing the Way for the Future (Gen. 40:1-23)

The events of Genesis 40 demonstrate Joseph's God-given wisdom to interpret dreams which will be the method through which he will come to the attention of Pharaoh. Genesis 40 also clearly shows God's providence which coordinates all that happens in order to work out His purposes. Joseph has fallen from overseer of his master's house to prisoner, but

---

1. Waltke (*Genesis*, p. 522) and Hamilton (*Genesis 18–50*, p. 471) argue this point; however, Currid (*Genesis 25:19–50:26*, p. 224) notes that although there is some evidence that in Egypt adultery leads to death, there is no official state-enforced sanction of the death penalty for adultery, so it is not unusual that Potiphar would send Joseph to prison for adultery.

even in prison Joseph rises to a place of responsibility. He is faithful to use his God-given gifts in whatever situation he finds himself.

In Genesis 40, two of Pharaoh's officers are thrown into prison. The chief cupbearer and the chief baker have important roles because of their access to the food of the king. Kings feared being poisoned, so they entrusted their lives to such men and sometimes close relationships would develop between the king and these officers.[2] Although the text is not specific on details, these men had committed an offense against the king of Egypt which had made him angry with them. Thus they both were in prison and Joseph is appointed to attend to their needs (v. 4). One night the cupbearer and the baker each dreamed a dream which left both of them troubled. Joseph could see that their faces were downcast and so he asks them why they are looking sad. Dreams could be omens of good things or bad things. The fact that these two men dream a dream on the same night probably added to their anxiousness over what these dreams might mean.[3] In the court of the king there would be professionals who would study and interpret dreams, but these prisoners do not have access to such means. However, Joseph recognizes that dreams and their interpretations belong to God and so he requests that they tell him their dreams (v. 8).

The dream of the chief cupbearer is given in verses 9-15. He sees a vine with three branches. The vine buds, blossoms, and produces clusters of ripened grapes. The cupbearer takes Pharaoh's cup, and presses the grapes into the cup and gives the cup to Pharaoh. Joseph gives the interpretation of the dream. The three branches are three days, and in three days the cupbearer will be restored to his office and place Pharaoh's cup in his hand as formerly. Joseph then requests that when the cupbearer is restored to his position he would mention him to Pharaoh so that he could get out of prison. Joseph tells the cupbearer of his plight of being stolen from his land and that he is now in prison for something that he did not do. His faithful service in prison would have supported his claims of

---

2. Waltke, *Genesis*, p. 525.

3. Matthews, *Genesis 11:27–50:26*, p. 747.

innocence. He was also hoping that one good turn would lead
to another.

The chief baker sees that the interpretation is favorable for
the cupbearer, so he also wants Joseph to interpret his dream
(vv. 16-19). In his dream there are three cake baskets on his
head and in the uppermost basket were all kinds of baked
food for Pharaoh; however, the birds were eating food out
of the basket. Joseph also interprets this dream. The three
baskets are three days, and Joseph states that in three days
the head of the baker will be lifted up, but not in the sense of
being lifted up in favor. Rather, the head of the baker will be
lifted up negatively – from you![4] His body will be hung on
a tree and the birds will eat his flesh.

Joseph's interpretations of the dreams are fulfilled
(vv. 20-23). The third day was Pharaoh's birthday and at the
birthday feast 'he lifted up the head of the chief cupbearer and
the chief baker among his servants' (v. 20). There is suspense
in the way this is stated because to lift up the head could be
a very positive thing but, as was evident in the baker's dream,
it could also be very negative. The cupbearer's head is lifted
up in favor and he is restored to his position, but the baker's
head is lifted up in the negative sense, for he is hanged.
Joseph's wisdom is clearly manifested in the fulfillment of the
dreams, but the chief cupbearer forgot all about Joseph (v. 23).
Nothing seems to be going right for Joseph. He was sold as
a slave to Egypt, falsely accused and thrown into prison, and
now the one opportunity to have his situation made public
passes without anything changing for Joseph. One wonders
if he thought he was only spinning his wheels and getting
nowhere. But the events of our lives are significant to God and
He even uses what seem to be lost opportunities to accomplish
His purposes. Joseph's faithfulness in carrying out his duties
in prison will one day be rewarded by God in a way that not
even Joseph could imagine.

---

4. Matthews (*Genesis 11:27–50:26*, p. 751) points out that the phrase 'from upon
you', translated 'from you', does not have to refer to a literal decapitation but is a rhetorical
play on the lifting of the head that occurs in the two dreams.

'God's Purposes Shall Ripen Fast' (Gen. 41:1-57)

Joseph remained in prison 'two whole years' after his interpretation of the dream of the cupbearer, which must have seemed like an eternity to him. But God's timing is not our timing. The events in prison laid the foundation for Joseph's rise to power. Pharaoh has two dreams. In the first dream (vv. 1-4) Pharaoh is standing by the Nile river and there come up out of the Nile seven cows that are 'attractive and plump'. They feed in the reed grass. But then seven more cows come up out of the Nile and they are ugly and thin. The ugly and thin cows eat up the attractive, plump cows. Pharaoh also has a second dream (vv. 5-7). In this dream seven ears of grain were growing on one stalk. These seven ears were 'plump and good'. Then there sprouted seven other ears that were thin and blighted by the east wind. The thin ears swallowed up the plump ears. After the dream Pharaoh is troubled in spirit and sought to have the meaning of the dreams told to him by the wise men in Egypt. However, none of the wise men of Egypt could interpret the dreams (v. 8).

At this point in the story, the cupbearer remembers how his dream had been interpreted by Joseph. He reminds Pharaoh of how he and the baker were placed in prison. He tells Pharaoh that they each had a dream and how Joseph was able to interpret their dreams accurately. He identifies Joseph as a young Hebrew who was captain of the guard (v. 10). This information lets Pharaoh know that Joseph is not an Egyptian, but also that Joseph had a prominent place in the prison even though he was not an Egyptian. Pharaoh immediately calls for Joseph and they bring him out of prison. He is made presentable to the king by shaving his beard and by changing his clothes. These changes give hope of a possible change in Joseph's status, but no one could have guessed how high Joseph would rise in power through God's providence.

In verses 17-24 Pharaoh recounts his two dreams to Joseph. The information of the two dreams is the same as what was given in verses 1-7, except that Pharaoh comments concerning the seven thin cows that they are the ugliest and thinnest cows he has ever seen. Also, when the seven thin cows eat the seven plump cows, they remained thin and ugly as if they had not eaten anything. Before Joseph interprets the dreams, he reminds Pharaoh that the interpretation of the dreams does not come from his wisdom but from God (v. 16). The two dreams mean the same thing and they are a revelation to Pharaoh of what God is about to do (v. 25). In other words, the dreams will lay out the purposes and plans of God for Egypt and for the surrounding world.

The interpretation of the dreams, along with some advice on how to respond to the dreams, is given in verses 25-36. The seven good cows and the seven good ears represent seven years of great plenty throughout all the land of Egypt. The seven thin cows and the seven empty ears represent seven years of famine. The seven years of plenty will come first and they will be followed by seven years of famine that will be so severe that the seven years of plenty will be forgotten. The famine will be so severe that it will consume the land. The fact that Pharaoh had two dreams means that these events are fixed by God and that they will shortly come to pass. In light of the severity of the famine that is coming, Joseph advises Pharaoh to put a discerning and wise man in charge of Egypt, along with the appointment of overseers over the land, to gather one-fifth of the produce during the seven plentiful years, so that there will be food during the seven years of famine.

Joseph's plan pleases Pharaoh who puts Joseph in charge of the plan by making him second in command in Egypt. Pharaoh acknowledges that Joseph is a wise and discerning man because God has shown him what is to take place shortly. He also comments that Joseph is the right man for the job because he has the *rûaḥ* of God. It is unclear from Pharaoh's polytheistic perspective exactly what he means by this phrase. The NASB translates it 'a divine spirit'. However, since Joseph is able to do what no Egyptian could do by their magical powers, and since the source of this wisdom is from the God that Joseph worships, even Pharaoh may recognize the special nature of this 'spirit' from God. Certainly, the Israelites would recognize that it is God's Spirit who is the source of Joseph's wisdom.[5]

The power that Joseph now possesses is remarkable. Pharaoh states that 'only as regards the throne will I be

---

5. In Waltke's discussion of this passage he translates *rûaḥ* as S/spirit (*Genesis*, pp. 532-33).

greater than you' (v. 40). He is now over the house of Pharaoh and the people of the land of Egypt, so that they must obey Joseph's command. The extent of Joseph's power is seen in Pharaoh's comment that no one shall lift up hand or foot in all the land of Egypt without Joseph's consent. This new position of power that Joseph receives is accompanied by external benefits. Pharaoh's investiture of Joseph includes transferring his signet ring to Joseph's finger, dressing him in fine linen, putting a gold chain around his neck, and having him ride in the second chariot, with people bowing before it.

The change in Joseph's status also brought with it a new name and a new wife. Joseph's new Egyptian name is Zaphenath-paneah (v. 45), which probably means 'God speaks and lives'. Although there is debate concerning the meaning of the name,[6] it fits the situation just described where God is the one who speaks to Joseph concerning the interpretation of the dream. Joseph is also given a new wife, Asenath, who is the daughter of Potiphera, the priest of On.[7]

One day Joseph is in prison, and the very next day he is second in command of Egypt, with all the power of the world at his fingertips. Although not every believer will know the same reversal of fortunes in the way that Joseph experienced it, it is encouraging to know that God is able to work even in the midst of the most difficult circumstances of our lives to accomplish His purposes for our good. Joseph experienced what many believers know:

> His purposes will ripen fast,
>
> unfolding ev'ry hour;
>
> the bud may have a bitter taste,
>
> but sweet will be the flow'r.[8]

The reversal that Joseph experienced is similar to what every believer will one day experience when they will be transported from the struggles of this world to the glorious freedom of

---

6. See Hamilton, *Genesis 18–50*, p. 506, for a discussion of the different possibilities of the meaning of Joseph's new name.

7. It is possible that Joseph is elevated to nobility through this marriage.

8. This line is from the hymn 'God Moves in a Mysterious Way', written by William Cowper.

the children of God in the new heavens and the new earth. Although different from what Joseph experienced in many ways, the change will be even more wonderfully far-reaching as we put on our new resurrection bodies.

Joseph is no longer a Hebrew slave but is now an Egyptian lord.[9] Not only is his rise to power remarkable, but he is only thirty years old when he enters the service of Pharaoh (v. 46). Joseph is very young, yet he has power, status, a new Egyptian name, and a new Egyptian wife, who happens to be the daughter of an Egyptian priest. One wonders if his change of status will change his Hebrew identity. In other words, will Joseph remain faithful to God with all these changes?

Some Jewish people also asked this question, which they answered in the work *Joseph and Asenath*.[10] In this account, Joseph does not marry Asenath until she converts to Yahweh (the LORD). However, there is no evidence in Genesis 41 that Asenath becomes a convert; the text is silent on the matter. There is evidence, however, that Joseph remained faithful to God even with his change of status. Two sons were born to Joseph and Asenath. The names of Joseph's two sons are a testimony to where his true allegiance lies. They are Hebrew names.

The first son is named Manasseh, which is derived from the word 'forget' (*nāšāh*). The reason for this name is, 'God has made me forget all my hardship and all my father's house' (v. 51). The name Manasseh praises God for delivering him from the hardship that he had experienced from his own family.[11] The way his brothers treated him no longer has a hold on him. Joseph is able to move beyond bitterness because he can now see the sovereign providence of God at work in his life.

---

9. Joseph's rise to power is not impossible in the history of Egypt. Semitic rulers, known as the Hyksos Pharaohs (1720–1550 B.C.), took over existing Egyptian bureaucratic administration and appointed naturalized Semites to high office while at the same time observing Egyptian customs (Waltke, *Genesis*, p. 533).

10. There is doubt concerning the date of this work, but it probably comes from the first or second century A.D. The story can be read in James H. Charlesworth, ed., *The Old Testament Pseudepigrapha* (2 vols.; New York: Doubleday & Company, 1985), 2:177-248.

11. Waltke, *Genesis*, p. 535.

The second son is called Ephraim, which is derived from the word 'fruitful' (*pārāh*). The explanation of this name is that 'God has made me fruitful in the land of my affliction' (v. 52). This explanation fits the theme of the Joseph story. God is able to work through the evil intentions of other people and adverse circumstances to accomplish His purposes.

Joseph's faith in the promises of God is also seen at the end of Genesis when he makes his brothers swear not to leave his bones in Egypt but to take his remains with them to the land God promised to give to Abraham (Gen. 50:24). Joseph recognizes that Egypt is not his final home by expressing faith in the fulfillment of the promises of God.

The rest of the chapter sets the stage for the brothers of Joseph to come to Egypt because of the severe famine. Joseph institutes his plan to store food during the seven years of plenty. He was able to store grain in great abundance, like the sand of the sea. So much grain was stored that it could not be measured (v. 49). The seven years of plenty is followed by seven years of famine. When people cry to Pharaoh about the lack of food, he sends them to Joseph.[12] Joseph opened all the storehouses where grain had been stored and sold it to the Egyptians. Thus in the land of Egypt there was food during the famine. However, the famine is so severe that it affected areas outside of Egypt, so that 'all the earth' came to Egypt to buy grain from Joseph (v. 57). It is only a matter of time before the brothers of Joseph will be in Egypt because of the famine. God's purposes will continue to ripen fast in the molding of this family so that they can be instruments of His blessing.

---

12. Hamilton (*Genesis*, p. 513) comments that Pharaoh here refers to Joseph by his Hebrew name instead of his Egyptian name, which indicates that Joseph's Egyptian name plays no significant role in the narrative.

STUDY QUESTIONS

1   In each situation of this chapter God blesses Joseph in a special way. How is God's blessing of Joseph evident in Potiphar's house? How is his character revealed in his response to the request of Potiphar's wife?

2   What kind of abilities does Joseph demonstrate in prison? Although Joseph was thrown into prison unjustly, what lesson is there in how he responds in prison?

3   Contrast Joseph's lowly position in prison with his exalted position of second in command of Egypt. What kinds of temptations would come with such power? What evidence is there that Joseph remained faithful to God?

4   Review how Joseph is blessed by God in each situation, but then how adverse circumstances brought him low again. What does this teach God's people concerning God's ways?

18

The Testing of Joseph's Brothers
(Genesis 42–44)

The story of Joseph now changes to focus on Joseph's brothers. In God's providence, they will appear before Joseph without knowing his identity. He will use this opportunity to test his brothers in order to observe their character. Are they the same brothers who selfishly sold him to Egypt? Do they look out for their own interests or are they willing to sacrifice for each other? How do they treat their youngest brother Benjamin? God uses these events to expose the guilt of the brothers for what they did to Joseph and to change their relationships to each other. Through this process of testing the brothers will be reconciled with Joseph, and one of the brothers will emerge as the leader of the family.

The First Trip to Egypt: 'You are spies' (Gen. 42:1-38)
The severe famine that Egypt experienced was also prevalent in the land of Canaan (42:5). Jacob learns that there is grain for sale in Egypt. He makes an interesting statement to his sons, 'Why do you look at one another?' This comment gives a hint that the sons are indecisive, blind to what is obvious, and unwilling to do what is necessary to remedy the situation.[1] There is unwillingness among the sons to band together to help each other out in this common problem that they all face.[2]

---

1. Matthews, *Genesis 11:27–50:26*, p. 774.
2. Waltke, *Genesis*, p. 544.

So Jacob suggests that they go down to Egypt to buy grain. Ten of the brothers go, but Jacob will not let the youngest son, Benjamin, go to Egypt for fear that harm would come to him. He has lost Joseph and he does not want to lose Benjamin, the other son of his wife Rachel.

The test of Joseph's brothers is set up in verses 6-11: they appear before Joseph but do not recognize that the governor of the land is their brother. Joseph has grown up from a lad of seventeen, when they sold him to the Midianites, to a man thirty years old. Also, at this time, he dressed and looked like an Egyptian, which would mean that he did not have a beard.[3] Further, the last person in the world the brothers expected to see as the governor of Egypt was their brother Joseph.

In partial fulfillment of Joseph's dream (Gen. 37:5-8), ten of the brothers bow down to him with their faces to the ground. Joseph recognizes his brothers but does not reveal himself to them. Rather, he treats them like strangers and speaks harshly to them. He even accuses them of being spies who have come to search out the land. Joseph is not seeking revenge against his brothers but is seeking information about the family. Is his father still alive? Is Benjamin well? The first response of the brothers is to deny that they are spies. They identify themselves as a family when they state, 'We are all sons of one man' (v. 11). In other words, they do not represent a government and they are not mercenaries sent to spy out the land.[4] They claim to be honest men and call themselves 'your servants'.

In response to Joseph's continued accusation that they are spies, the brothers reveal more about their family. They are twelve brothers of one man in Canaan. The youngest brother is at home with their father and one of their brothers 'is no more' (v. 13). This information told Joseph that Benjamin was still alive and that the brothers thought that he was dead,[5] or at least they had no idea where he was.

Joseph sets up a test which will allow the brothers to prove that they are not spies. He first tells them that he is going to keep all the brothers in Egypt, except one, who will return

---

3. Waltke, *Genesis*, p. 545.
4. Currid, *Genesis 25:19–50:26*, p. 283.
5. Waltke, *Genesis*, p. 546

to Canaan and bring back their youngest brother. If they bring back Benjamin, the truth of what they are saying will be established. He then puts them in custody for three days. This confinement places them in the 'crucible of transformation' and gives the brothers time to discuss among themselves who would stay in prison and who would return to Egypt.[6]

Joseph, however, suggests a different plan that will allow all the brothers except one to return to their father in Canaan. This plan works out better for the family, which is in need of the grain that the brothers have purchased in Egypt (v. 19). Joseph is fairly certain that they would have to come back to Egypt for more grain because the famine will last for seven years, but he ensures that they will return by keeping one of their brothers in custody in Egypt. He also tells them that to prove their innocence and to verify that they are not spies they must not return to Egypt without bringing their youngest brother Benjamin.

At this point of the story we are given insight into the thinking of the brothers. They speak freely in front of the Egyptians because they do not think they can be understood. Communication with Joseph has been through an interpreter (v. 23). The brothers confess their guilt over what they had done to Joseph and believe that they are now experiencing the consequences of divine retribution for their sinful deed. Further insight is given into the callousness of their actions against Joseph when they state, 'we saw the distress of his soul, when he begged us and we did not listen' (v. 21). Reuben is the only brother whose comments are identified. He is the firstborn of the brothers and the one who has the potential to emerge as leader of the family. Perhaps for the first time, Joseph finds out that Reuben tried to save him. However, Reuben's words also sound self-justifying as he separates himself from his brothers by not speaking in terms of 'we' but speaking in terms of 'you' (plural). Yet, he was just as guilty as the brothers in participating in the cover-up of what had happened through the deception of his father. It is interesting that Joseph binds Simeon to keep him in custody in Egypt. Simeon is the second brother. One wonders if the

6. Matthews, *Genesis 11:27–50:26*, p. 779.

reason Joseph did not keep Reuben in custody is because of his attempt to deliver Joseph from his brothers.[7]

Although it would be easy for Joseph to seek revenge against his brothers for what they did to him, his actions are not motivated by revenge. The name of his son Manasseh showed that Joseph had forgotten the hardship of his father's house in the sense that it no longer had a hold over him (Gen. 41:51). In addition, insight is given into Joseph's motivation in these events.

First, it is clear that while Joseph is testing his brothers to discover more about his family, he also wants to discover more about their character. Thus, he places them in a situation where they must choose between acting selfishly for themselves or acting on behalf of their other brothers. When Joseph sends the nine brothers back to the land of Canaan, he puts the money they had paid for the grain back into their sacks. When one of them discovers the money in his sack, they all react with great distress because when they return to Egypt they could be accused of stealing the grain (vv. 26-28). They face the dilemma of saving their own skins by abandoning Simeon or putting their lives in danger by going back to Egypt to rescue Simeon. These tests are meant to reveal the character of the brothers.

Second, when Joseph announces his change of plans and that only one brother will have to stay behind, he introduces the plan with the statement, 'Do this and you will live, for I fear God' (v. 18). This statement must have sounded strange coming from an Egyptian through an interpreter, but the concept of the fear of God is at the heart of how someone who is in covenant with God should respond to Him (Gen. 20:11; 31:42). On one level, this statement asserts the integrity of this Egyptian governor who is standing before them. In fact, he has more integrity than they do in light of their confession of sin in their treatment of Joseph.[8] But also, the fear of God is a clear indication that Joseph is not acting out of revenge but is acting in a way that would honor God. It should also be a hint to the brothers that the one standing before them is more than just an Egyptian governor.

---

7. Waltke, *Genesis*, p. 548.
8. Matthews, *Genesis 11:27–50:26*, p. 779.

Third, when Joseph hears the confession of his brothers concerning their bad treatment of him, he turns aside and weeps (v. 24). His heart is not full of self-vindication but it is broken over the remorse of his brothers. Joseph is able to see the big picture of God's sovereign purposes, which does not excuse the actions of the brothers, but recognizes that God can even use the evil intentions of others to accomplish His greater purposes.

The brothers return to their father Jacob and they tell him all that happened in Egypt, including the fact that when they return they must take Benjamin with them (vv. 29-34). They also discover that the money has been returned in each of their sacks of grain. It is hard to conceive what else could go wrong. Earlier, when one of them discovered the money in his sack of grain, they all questioned what God was doing through these events. The brothers are beginning to see that the hand of God is at work. They also respond with fear because they recognize the possibility that they could now be accused of being thieves as well as spies.

There are two responses to these events recorded at the end of Genesis 42. The first is by Jacob, who responds out of fear and despair. He accuses his sons of being the reason that he lost Joseph and Simeon, and that they would also be the reason that Benjamin is being taken away from him. These events do not draw Jacob closer to his sons. Jacob seems willing to abandon Simeon to the same fate of Joseph because he says of Simeon what he had said of Joseph, 'Simeon is no more' (v. 36). Jacob will not only have to learn to trust God, but he will have to learn to trust his sons.

The second response is given by Reuben, the oldest son (v. 37). As the oldest son, Reuben should be the leader of the family, but he always falls short of true leadership. He tries to assure his father that he can take care of Benjamin if they have to go back to Egypt, but his comments do not help relieve Jacob's anxiety. He says to his father, 'Kill my two sons if I do not bring him back to you.' Reuben does not courageously offer to sacrifice himself for the sake of Benjamin, but he cowardly offers his two sons, which frees himself of responsibility for what happens to Benjamin. Killing his two sons is not a solution that helps the situation; rather, it would only further jeopardize the family.[9] Jacob recognizes this by refusing to allow Benjamin to go to Egypt. Thus tensions still remain within the family between the brothers and between Jacob and his sons. The consequences of their sin have not yet been fully resolved, but God is not finished with this family yet.

Second Trip to Egypt: Sacrifice for the Family (Gen. 43–44)
It is just a matter of time before the grain that they have bought in Egypt is consumed. They really have no choice but to return to Egypt for more food. At Jacob's suggestion that they go again to Egypt to buy grain, Judah reminds his father of the warning they had received in Egypt not to return without their youngest brother. Jacob reacts defensively by raising questions concerning why they had had to divulge so much information about the family. He even states, 'Why did you treat me so badly as to tell the man that you had another brother?' Jacob is overprotective of Benjamin because he fears losing him as he lost Joseph.

However, instead of the brothers hating Benjamin, Judah steps forward to take responsibility for protecting him. Judah lays his own life on the line as a pledge of safety to bring Benjamin back. He is also willing to bear the blame if something happens to Benjamin. In other words, Judah will do everything in his power to protect Benjamin from harm, even if it means giving his life for the sake of Benjamin. Judah no longer wants to get rid of the favorite son by selling him (Gen. 37:26) but is willing to put his own life on the line for the sake of the favored son. Judah's character has changed and he clearly emerges as the leader of the family who is willing to take responsibility for it. Reuben's comments to Jacob about Benjamin had earlier failed to convince Jacob to entrust Benjamin to him, but Judah's comments convince Jacob that he can send Benjamin with him to Egypt.

God uses these events to bring Jacob to a place where he must trust his sons. Jacob feels that he does not really have a choice in the matter because they desperately need grain from Egypt and the only way they can get grain is if they

9. Waltke, *Genesis*, p. 550.

take Benjamin with them. Thus, he comments, 'If it must be so, then do this' (v. 11) and 'if I am bereaved of my children, I am bereaved' (v. 14). His willingness to allow Benjamin to go comes after Judah's willingness to pledge the safety of Benjamin.

Then Jacob offers the plan for how they should appear before 'the man'[10] in Egypt in order to show that they did not steal the grain. They will take with them for 'the man' choice fruits, some presents (honey, gum, myrrh, pistachio nuts, and almonds), and double the money to show their sincerity in wanting to pay for the grain. They are hoping it was just an oversight that they had their money returned to them (v. 12). Jacob also tells them to take Benjamin, and he offers the prayer that God Almighty would grant them mercy so that they may be able to return with Simeon and with Benjamin (v. 14). Jacob is able to put aside his fears and commit Benjamin to the care of his sons because he trusts in God.

When Joseph sees that Benjamin has returned to Egypt with his brothers, he sets up another test in order to observe how the brothers treat Benjamin. The plan includes bringing the men to Joseph's house for a meal (v. 16). When Joseph's brothers are brought to his house, they fear that it is a ploy to get them away from everyone else so that they can be assaulted and seized as slaves. They approach the steward of the house and try to explain that they did not steal the money for the grain on their first visit (vv. 19-22). They do not know how the money got into their sacks and they have brought it with them to show that they are honest men.

The reply they received from the steward must have both relieved them and astounded them. The steward tells them not to be afraid because he had received their money, and that their God and the God of their fathers must have put treasure in their sacks. Although this answer does not tell the whole story, it is true that the steward had received their money, and that the God of their fathers, the very same God that Joseph served, had sovereignly through Joseph provided this treasure. The brothers are also reunited with Simeon (v. 23). Instead of being seized as slaves, they receive their

---

10. In Genesis 42:30, Joseph is called 'the man, the lord of the land' by his brothers, and throughout the story he is referred to as 'the man'.

brother, who is released from custody. In God's providence the fortunes of this family may be changing for the better.

When Joseph comes home, they present to him their gifts and bow their heads to the ground by prostrating themselves before him. Little did the brothers realize that this act was a fulfillment of the earlier dream of Joseph in which the brothers' sheaves bowed down to Joseph's sheaf (Gen. 37:5-8). Also, the question that they asked is here answered, 'Are you indeed to reign over us?'

Joseph seeks information concerning their welfare and the welfare of their father. The brothers tell him that their father is still alive. Joseph also asks them whether Benjamin is their youngest brother. After pronouncing a blessing on Benjamin, 'God be gracious to you, my son!' (v. 29), Joseph is so over-whelmed with compassion and warmth for his brother, 'his mother's son,' that he must excuse himself from their presence in order to weep. Both Joseph and Benjamin are sons of Rachel, and they must have been close before Joseph was sold to Egypt because Benjamin would have been too young to be with the other brothers pasturing the flocks.

When Joseph returns, they serve the food but Joseph does not eat with his brothers because the Egyptians could not eat with the Hebrews. In fact, eating with the Hebrews is called an abomination to the Egyptians (v. 32). This practice may be rooted in the Egyptian notion of ethnic and cultural superiority.[11] It also may be related to the fact that the Israelites sacrificed cows, which the Egyptians considered sacred animals.[12] When Jacob's family eventually comes to Egypt, there will be no danger of being integrated into the Egyptian culture. How different from the problem of being assimilated into the Canaanite culture which had been a distinct danger during their time of living in Canaan!

The test in this meal comes as they sit down together to eat. They are seated around the table according to the order of their birth. This seating arrangement symbolically recreates the tension of sibling rivalry that had led to the crimes against Joseph.[13] Of course, the brothers are amazed at this seating

11. Waltke, *Genesis*, p. 556.
12. Matthews, *Genesis 11:27–50:26*, p. 791.
13. Matthews, *Genesis 11:27–50:26*, p. 792.

arrangement, which should have given them some clue that something strange is taking place in God's providence. Did they ever wonder who this strange Egyptian was who feared God, who was so concerned about their father and youngest brother, and who was able to set them at table according to their birth order?

They are served portions from Joseph's table and the test is that Benjamin's portion of food was five times as much as any of their portions. How would they react to this favoritism? Would they respond with stingy complaint that their brother was receiving more than they received? Certainly Joseph was watching to see if the same dynamics are driving his brothers that caused them to sell him into Egypt. But the brothers pass this test. No one complains about Benjamin's larger portions; rather, 'they drank and were merry with him' (v. 34). God had used hardship to begin to bring this family together, but here they show their change in character in how they handle the blessing of abundance. God demonstrates His sovereign purposes in providing for this family in a remarkable way.

Joseph has one more major test for his brothers which will clearly show their attitude toward their younger brother Benjamin (44:1-34). Joseph wants to see how they will react with Benjamin's life on the line. Will they abandon Benjamin like they abandoned Joseph? So Joseph tells the steward to fill their sacks full of grain, to put each man's money in the mouth of his sack, and to put Joseph's silver cup in the mouth of the sack of the youngest. Not long after the sons of Jacob have left Egypt, the Egyptians pursue them and accuse them of returning evil for good by stealing the silver cup of the lord of Egypt. This cup is identified as the cup with which 'he practices divination' (v. 5).

The practice of divination includes the use of an object to find out hidden information concerning the future; for example, the king of Babylon later uses divination when he must decide which road to take as he marches to conquer regions of Canaan (Ezek. 21:20-22). The different practices include the use of arrows or the reading of the liver of a sacrificed animal. In Genesis 44, the use of a cup for divination refers to pouring water into oil (hydromancy) or oil into water (oleomancy) and reading the configuration of the liquids as they mingle together.[14] Such practices are later condemned in Deuteronomy 18:9-14 because God will speak to His people through the prophets.

The statement in Genesis 44:5 that this is the cup with which Joseph practices divination could be seen as part of the ploy.[15] The cup they have allegedly taken is an important cup. The statement about divination also hints at the impossibility of getting away with such an act because the Egyptians would be able to discern through such practices what they have done. However, the irony to the reader is that the Egyptian practices could not reveal the meaning of Pharaoh's dreams. Only God could reveal that information and He revealed it to Joseph. It is not necessary to conclude that Joseph really used this cup for divination purposes. In fact, Joseph does not call this cup a cup for divination but only calls it 'my cup, the silver cup' (v. 2).

The sons of Jacob are astonished at this accusation and testify to their honest character by recounting how they had brought back to Egypt the money that they had earlier found in their sacks. It would be ludicrous for them to do such a thing. They are so confident of their innocence that they boldly volunteer the worst of punishments. The culprit who has done this thing shall die and the rest of them will become slaves (v. 9). Their response shows corporate responsibility for the actions of one of them because they offer that all of them will become slaves, even if only one of them has committed this theft. The trials they have experienced through these events have brought them closer together as brothers. The steward, however, tempers the punishment by suggesting that the one found with the cup will become a servant and the others will be innocent (v. 10), which suggests that the rest of the brothers can go free. What a shock it was to them that the cup was found in the sack of their youngest brother Benjamin! The worst-case scenario has played out in front of them. What their father feared has come to pass.

The brothers are brought back to Egypt and they appear before Joseph. Judah takes the lead, not only in the narrative account, which states that 'Judah and his brothers came to

---

14. Waltke, *Genesis*, p. 560.
15. Matthews, *Genesis 11:27–50:26*, p. 799.

Joseph's house' (v. 14), but also in the response to Joseph's inquiry concerning what they have done and why they thought they could get away with such a deed (v. 15). Judah is at a loss to explain what has happened and he does not know how they can clear themselves. His only explanation is that God's hand is behind these events because of their guilt. He does not specify what that guilt means, but everyone, including Joseph, knows that Judah is referring to the way they treated Joseph. Judah sees no other option but that they will become servants to 'my lord' (v. 16).

However, Joseph, the lord of Egypt, looks at the situation differently. Only the one who is guilty, the one in whose sack the cup was found, shall be a servant. The rest of the brothers can return in peace to their father. Of course, this is the test to see whether the brothers will act for their own self-interest and abandon Benjamin like they abandoned Joseph.

Judah continues to take the lead in responding to Joseph. He recognizes Joseph's position by calling himself 'your servant', by addressing Joseph as 'my lord', and by acknowledging that 'you are like Pharaoh' (v. 18). Judah explains to the lord of Egypt the situation with his father and his two younger brothers (vv. 20-32). One brother is dead and the father loves the youngest brother; in fact, he loves him so much that he did not want him to return to Egypt with them. If something happens to the youngest son, it will devastate their father to such an extent that he will die a sorrowful death. Judah is willing to fulfill the pledge he made to his father to bring the youngest son back safely to him. So he offers to take the place of his youngest brother (v. 33). Judah is so concerned for his father's health that he is willing to remain as a servant in Egypt so his youngest brother can be reunited with his father. Judah is willing to sacrifice himself for Benjamin for the sake of his father.

There is a clear change in the brothers' relationship to each other, even though it does not appear that their father has changed very much in his preferential love for the youngest son.[16] When Joseph's brothers sold him into slavery, Judah and his brothers were willing to get rid of Joseph and to deceive

---

16. Waltke, *Genesis*, p. 562.

their father into thinking that Joseph was dead. In fact, it was Judah's idea to sell Joseph to a caravan going to Egypt, rather than kill him. The animosity the brothers felt toward Joseph is not the way they are responding to Benjamin, even though Jacob still shows him preferential treatment. Rather, Judah is willing to sacrifice himself for the sake of his brother. God has used this crucible of testing to expose the guilt of the brothers in reference to Joseph and to bring about a change in the way they treat each other. It remains to be seen what impact this impassioned plea that Judah makes for Benjamin has on Joseph, their brother, the lord of Egypt.

STUDY QUESTIONS

1   How do the brothers first respond to the famine? What does this show about their character?

2   Describe how Joseph tests his brothers when they first come to Egypt. What information does he learn from them? What dilemma do they face when they discover that the money they paid for the grain is back in their sacks?

3   What evidence is there in the story that Joseph is not acting out of revenge toward his brothers? What does this show about the character of Joseph?

4   Why does Joseph use Benjamin to test his brothers? Compare and contrast Reuben's words to his father Jacob concerning the safety of Benjamin and Judah's words. Why are Judah's words more helpful? What evidence is there that the character of the brothers has changed through these events?

19

The Reconciliation of a Family

(Genesis 45–47)

A Stunning Revelation: God's Hand at Work (Gen. 45:1-28)
Genesis 45 is one of the great narrative scenes in the Bible.
It is full of drama. Judah's impassioned plea for his brother
Benjamin made a great impact on Joseph. He is the lord, the
one in charge, but he could not control himself before all those
who stood by him (v. 1). He makes everyone leave the room
except for his brothers. He wept so loud that the Egyptians
heard it, and even the house of Pharaoh heard it.[1] One
wonders what the brothers must have been thinking during
these moments, but when Joseph reveals to them who he is
they are not able to answer him. No doubt they experience
stunned disbelief in finding out that the lord of Egypt, the one
next to Pharaoh, is really Joseph, but they also 'were dismayed
at his presence' (v. 3). The verb *bhl* can express 'terror', which
describes the panic that seizes a person when surprised by
obvious doom.[2] However, Joseph assures them that they have
nothing to fear. They should not be distressed or angry with
themselves because they sold him to Egypt because God was
at work through these events.

God's sovereignty is not an excuse for the brothers' im-
proper actions toward Joseph; otherwise, Joseph would not

---

1. Waltke (*Genesis*, pp. 562-63) points out that in the Egyptian wisdom literature
a cool, controlled spirit was held up as the goal, but Joseph allows his true emotions
for his brothers to be expressed.
2. Matthews, *Genesis 11:27–50:26*, p. 812.

have been so concerned to test their character. Rather, God is able to work through the evil actions of people to accomplish His purposes. In reality it was God who sent Joseph to Egypt (v. 8) in order to preserve general human life because of the famine and to preserve the family of Jacob as a remnant. The land is only two years into the famine, with five more years to go. God sent Joseph to Egypt as a part of His covenant faithfulness to His people in order to provide for them.

The privileged position of Joseph as father to Pharaoh and ruler over all the land of Egypt (v. 8) means that he has the power to take care of his family without anyone intervening. He tells them to go back to their father and report all that has happened, so that the whole family, including their father Jacob, can come to Egypt to live in the land of Goshen.[3] The account ends with Joseph embracing Benjamin first, but then he embraces all his brothers with much weeping.

One can only wonder what they talked about after finding out that the lord of Egypt was their brother (v. 15). This is a marvelous scene of reconciliation. Joseph has seen that the character of his brothers has changed from selfishness to sacrifice. He also does not hold a grudge against them because he sees the bigger picture of the hand of God at work. The God that they serve not only rules the nations, but He also rules the actions of people. He can use the evil actions of people to accomplish His purposes. In fact, God rules over everything in order to fulfill His covenant promises to His people and to provide what they need. A similar thought is expressed in Ephesians 1:22 where Christ is said to be head over all things for the sake of the church. The events of this world are not haphazard or governed by chance, but the God of this universe is working out all things for the benefit of His people.

The abundant way that God provides for the covenant family is seen in verses 16-24. When Pharaoh hears that Joseph's brothers have come to Egypt, he is very pleased. He invites the family to move to Egypt and promises them the

---

3. Although the exact location of Goshen is disputed, many believe it was located in the eastern Delta area. Two things are significant about Goshen (Gen. 45:10). It was near Joseph and it had plenty of room for pasturing their flocks (Waltke, *Genesis*, p. 564, and Matthews, *Genesis 11:27–50:26*, p. 815).

best of the land of Egypt. He even seeks to make their journey to Egypt less difficult by offering to send wagons to transport Jacob's father, their wives, and their little ones. They do not even need to worry about their goods because the best of all the land of Egypt is theirs.

Joseph makes sure that these commands of Pharaoh are carried out. He also sends abundant provisions for the journey back to Egypt, which include ten donkeys loaded with the good things of Egypt and ten female donkeys loaded with grain and bread. Joseph also gives to his brothers a change of clothes, but to Benjamin he gives three hundred shekels of silver and five changes of clothes. The gift of clothing demonstrates that reconciliation has taken place between Joseph and his brothers. They had stripped Joseph of his robe but now Joseph supplies them with new clothes.[4] Benjamin, the natural brother of Joseph, who did not have a part in selling Joseph to Egypt, is given more than his brothers.

Joseph's parting words to them as they begin their trip back to Canaan is that they should not quarrel on the way. Perhaps Joseph is concerned that the extra gifts given to Benjamin will cause trouble among the brothers, or that they will assign guilt among themselves over the selling of Joseph into Egypt. But those days are past and the brothers truly have experienced change in how they relate to each other. Joseph is second in command of Egypt and the best of the land of Egypt lies before them. The future looks bright because God has demonstrated His power to provide above and beyond anything they could have imagined.

When the brothers return to Canaan, they must tell their father that Joseph is not really dead but that he is alive. And even more, Joseph is not only alive but he is ruler over all the land of Egypt. Nothing is said about how the brothers explain to their father their deception about Joseph's death and how they sold him to Egypt. Jacob did not at first believe his sons. For so many years he had thought that Joseph was dead. Also, 'his heart became numb' (v. 26), which may express that he was emotionally depleted. The word 'numb' (pwg) can also mean 'weak'.[5] The news is almost too good to be

---

4. Waltke, *Genesis*, p. 572.
5. Matthews, *Genesis 11:27–50:26*, p. 820.

true. However, the evidence is staring Jacob in the face in the wagons and all the provisions they brought back from Egypt. Jacob is convinced[6] that Joseph is alive, with the result that his spirit is strengthened and he is resolved to go to Egypt to see his son before he dies (v. 28).

The Family of Jacob Moves to Egypt with God's Blessing (Gen. 46:1-30)

On the way to Egypt, Jacob stops at Beersheba and offers sacrifices to the God of his father Isaac. Beersheba is on the border of the land, and Jacob recognizes that the destiny of his descendants will be fulfilled in the land of Canaan and not in Egypt. However, God assures Jacob that this trip to Egypt has His blessing. In Egypt, God will make the family of Jacob into a great nation. God's presence will go with them to Egypt and God will bring them up out of Egypt, but Jacob will die in Egypt (v. 4). In contrast to Abraham, who went down to Egypt in fear (Gen. 12:10-20), Jacob goes to Egypt with the confidence of God's presence and blessing.

The arrival of Jacob and his family in Egypt is described in verses 5-7. The emphasis of these verses is that the whole household of Jacob comes to Egypt, including his sons, his sons' sons, his daughters, and his sons' daughters, even all his offspring. Also, the name Israel is used in the phrase 'the sons of Israel'. There is a hint here of an embryonic nation.[7] The family of the twelve sons of Jacob which goes down to Egypt will come out of Egypt as a nation of twelve tribes. A genealogy of the twelve sons of Jacob is given in verses 8-25 to show the number of people who migrated to Egypt. Those who went to Egypt with Jacob were sixty-six people, a number which includes only his descendants and does not include Jacob's sons' wives (v. 26). If one adds Joseph and his two sons, the number of the house of Jacob in Egypt was seventy, but there is some debate over whether the seventieth person is Jacob, Dinah or some other person.[8] The number seventy is a modest

---

6. The Hebrew word *raḇ* (v. 28) means 'much' or 'many' and is used here in the sense of 'enough (said)', which the NIV translates as 'I am convinced' (Matthews, *Genesis 11:27–50:26*, p. 820).

7. Matthews, *Genesis 11:27–50:26*, p. 827.

8. Matthews, *Genesis 11:27–50:26*, p. 836.

number and will later be contrasted with the great increase of the sons of Israel while they live in Egypt (Exod. 1).

The reunion of Jacob and Joseph is told in verses 28-30. Judah's leadership role in the family is emphasized as he is sent ahead of Jacob to prepare for the arrival of the family in Goshen, where Joseph is reunited with Jacob. One can only imagine the emotions of that reunion. They embraced 'a good while' (v. 29), with Joseph weeping on his father's neck. This reunion brings a sense of closure to Jacob for he is now ready to die even though he will live seventeen more years.[9] The wound of his heart can begin to heal because the longing to see his son has been satisfied.

The Sons of Israel in Egypt: Separation not Assimilation (Gen. 46:31–47:12)

There are several reasons why God brought the family of Jacob to Egypt. One reason becomes clear at the end of Genesis 46 and is developed in the first section of Genesis 47. The family has come to Egypt with Pharaoh's blessing but there are cautions that need to be observed in the relationship between the sons of Israel and the Egyptians (46:31-34) and in the right diplomatic steps that need to be taken before Pharaoh (47:1-12). The occupation of the Israelites could cause a problem because 'every shepherd is an abomination to the Egyptians' (46:34). It is unclear exactly what this statement means because the Egyptians also had livestock. The difference could be in the way the animals were treated because the Egyptians associated animals with their gods, which was not a view held by the Israelites. Thus, to sacrifice certain animals was an abomination to the Egyptians. Perhaps something else is behind this attitude, such as cultural superiority, racial exclusivity, or dislike of certain foreign peoples.[10] What is clear is that there will be little opportunity for the Hebrews to interact with or become assimilated to the Egyptian culture. They will remain separate from the Egyptians, which separation God will use to preserve the distinctive character of His people in preparation for His future plans.

---

9. Hamilton, *Genesis 18–50*, p. 602.
10. Hamilton, *Genesis 18–50*, p. 604, and Currid, *Genesis 25:19–50:26*, p. 306.

Joseph explains the situation of his family to Pharaoh and presents them to him in 47:1-12. Part of the purpose of this meeting with Pharaoh is to acquire the land of Goshen for the family and to let Pharaoh know that the family of Joseph has no desire to cause trouble or seek power while in Egypt. He first presents to Pharaoh five of his brothers who explain their occupation and why they have come to Egypt. They are in Egypt to dwell in the land because of the famine, which has made pasturing flocks in Canaan difficult. They specifically request from Pharaoh his permission to live in the land of Goshen. Pharaoh is favorable toward their request and grants it. He even gives opportunities for competent men among Joseph's family to be put in charge of Pharaoh's livestock. This offer shows how much Pharaoh is pleased with Joseph. Perhaps he believes that the same competence and blessing which he has seen in Joseph's life would also be found among his brothers.[11] Deception has been so much a part of this family's history, but Joseph is honest with Pharaoh concerning the nature of his family and that honesty is rewarded by receiving the favor of Pharaoh.

Joseph then presents his father Jacob to Pharaoh (vv. 7-12). Pharaoh asks Jacob how old he is, which reflects the value placed on those who were aged.[12] Jacob compares his own age with those of his ancestors whose lives had preceeded his own. Jacob is 130 years old at this time and will live another seventeen years, but Abraham lived 175 years (Gen. 25:7) and Isaac lived 180 years (Gen. 35:28).[13] Jacob also recognizes that his days have been difficult. He uses the word ra^ς, which can mean evil or full of trouble and tragedy. Although the ESV translates the word as 'evil', a better translation would be 'unpleasant' (NASB) or 'difficult' (NIV). Jacob's life has been full of intrigue and treachery, some of it caused by his own actions and some of it caused by others.

Yet, as Jacob stands before Pharaoh he blesses him twice, once when he was brought in to Pharaoh and once when he went out from his presence. These blessings are more

---

11. Waltke (*Genesis*, p. 585) notes that Egyptian inscriptions frequently mention superintendents over the royal cattle who are foreigners.

12. Matthews, *Genesis 11:27–50:26*, p. 846.

13. Matthews, *Genesis 11:27–50:26*, p. 847.

than a formal greeting or farewell, but they have religious significance. Jacob is grateful to Pharaoh for his kindness to his family, but he also pronounces a blessing upon Pharaoh. This is remarkable because the one who gives the blessing is usually considered to be in a superior position (Heb. 7:7). Although no one has more power in Egypt than Pharaoh, the one who is in a covenant relationship with God is greater because the God of the covenant is greater than the gods of Egypt. God's power over the Egyptian gods, and even over Pharaoh himself, will be demonstrated later in Israel's history when God redeems His people from Egypt through the ten plagues. But for now, the relationship of goodwill between Jacob and Pharaoh is itself an indication that God is with Jacob as he has been with Joseph.

So even in Egypt God provides a refuge for His people. He is able to sway the heart of kings. He is able to raise the humble prisoner to a position of power and might. He is able to reconcile a family. He is able to give them a land in a foreign country and he is able to provide food in the midst of a severe famine. No other god is as great as the God of Abraham, Isaac, and Jacob.

The Administration of Joseph: A Savior in Egypt (Gen. 47:13-31)

Most of this section gives an account of the severity of the famine and what steps are taken to make sure the people have food. The famine is so bad that there is not any food left in Egypt or Canaan. At first, people had come to Joseph to buy grain with money, but things became so bad that the people did not have any money left (v. 15). Joseph suggests that they bring their livestock in exchange for food, and so people brought horses, donkeys, and animals from their flocks and herds (v. 17). The following year they still do not have money, and their livestock is gone as well. All they have left are their bodies and their land. The people suggest to Joseph that they sell themselves to Pharaoh as servants and that they exchange their land for food. They also request that they be given seed to plant. Otherwise, the people of the land believe they will die because of the shortage of food (v. 19). Joseph accepts their suggestion and buys up all the land of Egypt for Pharaoh. In this way, the people of Egypt become servants of Pharaoh. Only the priests of Egypt were exempt from the selling of their land because of an arrangement they had with Pharaoh of a fixed allowance from him (v. 22). Also, in exchange for seed the people would keep for themselves four-fifths of the crop and they would give a fifth of the crop to Pharaoh (v. 24).

During the worst days of the famine, the Egyptians sell all their livestock and land to Pharaoh to become his servants. The people became tenant farmers to Pharaoh. These policies seem oppressive and they seem to take advantage of the people's condition of poverty. However, one must be careful not to judge Joseph and these policies by modern sensibilities. Debtor's slavery was common in the context of that day.[14] The one-fifth that was to be given to Pharaoh from the crops, with the people keeping four-fifths, was very generous compared to the normal amount of one-third that would be paid in such a situation.[15] Further, the people themselves are very grateful to Joseph because these policies saved their lives (v. 25). Joseph is not an oppressive overlord but is considered by the people as a savior.

On one level, this arrangement will parallel the arrangement that Israel will experience later in the land of Canaan with Yahweh, instead of Pharaoh, as the one who owns the land and who gives it to His people to use for His benefit. The problem with human kings, however, is that they do take to themselves more power and authority than they should, which many times leads to oppression, but Yahweh always acts in justice and for the benefit of His people.

Joseph is a savior for the Egyptians but he also provides refuge for his own family (vv. 27-28). The Egyptians become indentured servants to Pharaoh, but the family of Jacob lives in freedom and is provided for, without becoming servants to Pharaoh. They were separated from the Egyptians in the land of Goshen, gained possessions in the land, and multiplied greatly during the whole time that Jacob was alive. For seventeen years the sons of Israel enjoyed this time of blessing in the land of Goshen. However, Jacob knew that Goshen was not their final destination or the place that God had promised

---

14. Matthews, *Genesis 11:27–50:26*, p. 851.
15. Waltke, *Genesis*, p. 591.

to give to his descendants. Thus he made Joseph promise that he would not be buried in Egypt, but that he would be taken out of Egypt to be buried with his ancestors in the land of Canaan (vv. 29-31). Joseph swore to his father that he would carry out his request. Jacob understood that Egypt was not their final home because he had faith in the promises of God. The bliss of Egypt would not last forever.

Study Questions

1   What theological principle does Joseph use to assure his brothers that they do not have to be afraid of him because of what they had done to him when they sold him to the Midianites? Can you see examples of this principle in your life or the world around you?

2   In the past when patriarchs sought to go to Egypt, either the results were not good (Gen. 12:10-20) or they were not allowed to go to Egypt (Gen. 26:2). Why is Jacob's going down to Egypt different?

3   What are some benefits for the family of Jacob in going to live in Egypt?

4   Why do the people of Egypt see Joseph as a savior?

20

Looking to the Future through Faith in the Promises of God
(Genesis 48–50)

The last three chapters of Genesis bring an era of Biblical history to an end. Jacob, the last patriarch, dies and his son Joseph, second in command of Egypt, also dies. Significant changes will take place for the family of Jacob in Egypt. They will increase from the seventy that went down to Egypt into a great multitude. No longer will they be the family of Jacob but they will become the sons of Israel, numerous enough to be a nation (see Exodus 1 for this transition). A Pharaoh will yet arise who does not know Joseph and he will make it hard for the Israelites by making them slaves (Exod. 1:8).

Yet, before the hardship of bondage, there are important changes that take place in the family of Jacob during this time of peaceful tranquility at the end of Genesis. Joseph's two sons are incorporated into the family of Jacob (Gen. 48) and Jacob proclaims a prophecy concerning the future of his sons (Gen. 49). Genesis ends with a clear statement of the purpose of God in the Joseph story and the promise of God concerning the land of Canaan (Gen. 50). It is clear that the promises of God to Abraham are being fulfilled in this family, but all the promises of God have not yet been fulfilled. God is still at work to accomplish His purposes.

The Adoption of Joseph's Two Sons (Gen. 48:1-22)

The end of Genesis 47 mentioned that Jacob's death was drawing near (47:29). In chapter 48, Jacob is ill and Joseph takes his two sons, Manasseh and Ephraim, to his father so that he can bless them. The seriousness of the illness is seen in the fact that Jacob must summon strength to sit up in bed (v. 2). Jacob briefly reviews God's appearance to him at Bethel (Luz), and states again the promises of God that he would have many descendants and that they would be given the land of Canaan (vv. 3-4).

Jacob then turns to the two sons of Joseph who were born in Egypt. He declares that Ephraim and Manasseh belong to him, just as Reuben and Simeon belong to him. In other words, Ephraim and Manasseh are full recipients of the inheritance that will be passed down from Jacob to his other sons. They are also inheritors of the promises of God and become a part of the covenant family. This adoption of Ephraim and Manasseh,[1] which gives them full status as sons, does not apply to any other offspring of Joseph, whose inheritance will fall under the inheritance of Ephraim and Manasseh (v. 6). Jacob then recounts the premature death of Rachel (v. 7), which may be part of the rationale for his adoption of the two sons of Joseph, because Joseph is Rachel's son.[2]

When Joseph brings his two sons to Jacob, he responds with the question, 'Who are these?' This question seems strange in the context because Jacob has just been talking about these two sons. However, Jacob's eyesight is very poor and the purpose of the question may be to assure Jacob that the two sons are present. The question also parallels the incident when Isaac blessed Jacob. Isaac asked the question, 'Who are you?', before he blessed Jacob. Although there is no deception in this account, the parallel shows that this blessing is very important for the future of this family.[3] The blessing

---

1. Waltke (*Genesis*, p. 596) describes the adoption ritual as it is presented in Genesis 48 and gives evidence from documents of the ancient Near East of intrafamily adoptions. The two sons of Joseph are about twenty years of age. They are placed on Joseph's knees, not because they are young children but because this act may symbolize the birth and descent of the sons. They are from Joseph and will become part of the family of Jacob, not the Egyptian family of Asenath.

2. Matthews, *Genesis 11:27–50:26*, p. 875.

3. Matthews (*Genesis 11:27–50:26*, p. 876) mentions the possibility that the question is a formal preface to an official utterance.

of Jacob will change the future of this family like the blessing of Isaac changed the future of Jacob and Esau. The joy of this occasion is seen when Jacob embraces the two sons of Joseph and tells Joseph that he never expected to see his face again, much less to see his children (vv. 10-11). The solemnity of the occasion is seen when Joseph bows before Jacob, a surprising act of humility by an Egyptian ruler, which acknowledges the superiority of Jacob as the mediator of the covenant promises of God.[4]

Joseph presents his two sons to Jacob for a blessing, which is given in verses 15-16. Although verse 15 reads that Jacob blessed Joseph, the blessing is for the two boys who are the sons of Joseph.[5] The invocation of the blessing gives a description of God's care and protection of Jacob and his forefathers. The spiritual heritage, which began with Abraham and Isaac, was passed down to Jacob, who passes it on to his sons. For one to walk with God is to live in a way that is pleasing to God, an idea that goes all the way back to Enoch in Genesis 5:22. Jacob also experienced the care and presence of God through his angel, who redeemed him from all evil. Jacob requests that the God who is faithful to His covenant promises will continue His faithfulness in blessing the two sons of Joseph by allowing them to carry on the heritage of Jacob and his forefathers. He also requests that the two sons of Joseph would grow to be a multitude on the earth, a request in line with the covenant promise of God for many descendants. Ephraim and Manasseh are now in covenant with God, which will mean both blessing and covenant responsibility.

Joseph placed Ephraim, the younger, at the left hand of Jacob and he placed Manasseh, the older, at the right hand of Jacob (v. 13). This placement of the sons fits the cultural expectation of the prominence of the firstborn son. However, Jacob crossed his hands and placed his right hand on the younger son Ephraim and his left hand on the older son Manasseh. This move displeased Joseph and he tried to switch the hands of Jacob so that the right hand would fall on the older. Jacob refuses to uncross his hands, but gives the explanation that the younger son would be greater than the

---

4. Matthews, *Genesis 11:27–50:26*, p. 878.
5. Matthews, *Genesis 11:27–50:26*, p. 878.

older son because his offspring would be more numerous (v. 19). In the future, the blessing of God will be so evident that Ephraim and Manasseh will be used as standards of God's blessing: 'God make you as Ephraim and Manasseh' (v. 20). To confirm the promise of God in relationship to the land of Canaan, Jacob grants to Joseph a choice piece of land for an additional inheritance (vv. 21-22).

The significance of the adoption of Ephraim and Manasseh as sons of Jacob is that they become co-heirs with the other sons. They are considered full sons with all the privileges that come with that status. Reuben and Simeon are specifically mentioned in verse 5 because they are being bypassed to give the double portion to Joseph. The reasons for this will be given in Genesis 49 (see also 1 Chron. 5:1). The fact that Joseph is Rachel's firstborn means that Rachel's firstborn son supersedes Leah's firstborn son.[6]

This adoption ceremony partly explains the future twelve tribes of Israel. If Joseph is removed as a tribe because his two sons will each receive a full inheritance, and if Levi is removed as a tribe because they will not receive an inheritance of land (see Genesis 49), then the twelve tribes will consist of Reuben, Simeon, Judah, Ephraim, Manasseh, Zebulun, Issachar, Dan, Gad, Asher, Naphtali, and Benjamin. Judah has risen as a leader of the family and his descendants will emerge as a significant tribe. Joseph has become prominent as a leader of the family through the providence of God in elevating him to a high position, and his descendants will become important through the tribe of Ephraim, which later will become the major tribe of the northern kingdom of Israel. God is laying a foundation in Genesis for the future history of His people. The providence of God in people's lives today has significance for His purposes in the future.

---

6. Waltke, *Genesis*, p. 596. Waltke (p. 600) also points out that the combined population of Ephraim and Manasseh forty years after the Exodus was 85,200. By contrast, the combined population of Reuben and Simeon at the same time of history was only 65,930. In fact, during the wilderness period the tribes of Ephraim and Manasseh increased in number but the tribes of Reuben and Simeon decreased in number (see Numbers 26).

The Future Significance of the Sons of Jacob (Gen. 49:1-28)
Genesis 49 is different from most other chapters in Genesis. The genre is Hebrew poetry instead of Hebrew narrative and it looks to what will happen in the future, 'in days to come' (v. 1). This phrase literally reads 'in the latter days', which refers to what will take place in the distant future. The general future time period in view is when the twelve tribes of Israel settle into the land of Canaan, but some of the statements go beyond the period of the settlement and have messianic significance (vv. 8-12).[7] Jacob reflects on the character of his sons and uses that as a basis for declaring what will happen to the sons and their descendants in the future.[8]

Reuben is the firstborn son and Jacob begins with him (vv. 3-4). Majestic terminology is used of Reuben because he is the firstborn son. There is an importance that comes with that position, which is described as being pre-eminent in strength, might, and honor. However, Reuben forfeits his pre-eminent position by acting in an unstable way by defiling his father's bed, an event that is described in Genesis 35:22. The word 'unstable' (*paḥaz*) can also mean proud, insolent, uncontrollable, and undisciplined.[9] The character of Reuben causes him to forfeit his place of privilege. In fact, every time Reuben has attempted to take leadership in the family, his leadership has fallen short (Gen. 37:29-30; 42:37). Historically, the tribe of Reuben received land in the area on the east of the Jordan and faded from significance in historical importance.

Simeon and Levi, also sons of Leah, are cursed because of their anger, violence, and cruelty against the Shechemites (Gen. 34:25-7). Jacob distances himself from their actions by rejecting their 'council' or plans and by separating his 'glory' or honor from their actions. In other words, he abhors what they did. The curse is that they would be divided or scattered in Israel. Historically, Simeon is the smallest tribe in the census of Numbers 26. They receive land in the desert region in the vicinity of Judah and become integrated into the tribe of Judah (Josh. 19:1, 9). The descendants of Levi, on the other hand, did

7. Waltke, *Genesis*, p. 605.
8. Ross, *Creation and Blessing*, p. 697. Waltke (*Genesis*, p. 605) regards Jacob's words in Genesis 49 as prophecies.
9. Waltke, *Genesis*, p. 606.

not receive an inheritance of land and were scattered among the other tribes. However, the curse of being scattered was turned into a blessing because of the actions of the sons of Levi in supporting Moses in the incident of the golden calf (Exod. 32:28-29). They actually went throughout the camp of Israel and put to death by the sword those who were participating in the idolatry. They did this without regard for whether those involved were their brothers, companions, or neighbors. Moses blessed them by setting them apart for the service of the Lord to assist the priests in their work. Although they did not receive land as an inheritance, they did receive forty-eight towns and pasturelands scattered throughout the tribes. Faithful actions in honor of God can even turn a curse into a blessing.

In the story of Joseph, Judah has emerged as a leader among his brothers and so it is not surprising that his descendants will also play a major role in the history of Israel (vv. 8-12). Judah is praised by his brothers and is given a place of prominence among them. They bow down before him because of his victory over his enemies (v. 8). Judah is described as like a lion that conquers his prey. He is majestic in power and strength so that no one dare rouse him. The lion imagery fits well with the kingly language that is used to describe the future of Judah. The scepter, which is used in parallel with the ruler's staff, is a symbol of kingship.[10] The picture in verse 10 is of a king sitting on his throne with his scepter resting on his shoulder and lying between his feet. The scepter will remain with Judah until something designated *šîlōh* comes to him, which will also in some way include the obedience of the peoples. There is debate concerning what the term *šîlōh* means. It is translated a number of ways.[11]

Some identify the term with the proper name Shiloh and translate the phrase as 'until Shiloh comes' (KJV, NKJV, NASB). However, nowhere else in the Hebrew Bible is Shiloh spelled *šîlōh*. It is normally spelled *šilô* and occurs for the first time in Joshua 18. It is possible to take *šîlōh* as several small Hebrew particles that together make up an adverbial phrase. The

---

10. Waltke, *Genesis*, p. 608.
11. See Matthews, *Genesis 11:27–50:26*, pp. 893-896, for further discussion of the views of *šîlōh* in Genesis 49:10.

three particles are *šî* ('which'), *l*('to'), and *ōh* ('him'), which if read together mean 'which is/belongs to him'. The NIV (1984) translates the phrase as 'the scepter will not depart from Judah ... until he comes to whom it belongs and the obedience of the nations is his.' This would mean that the right to rule would remain in the tribe of Judah until the one comes to whom that right to rule belongs. The main problem with this view is that for the first particle to mean 'which' it should be *še* instead of *šî*.

Some Hebrew manuscripts have the alternate reading *šellô*, which is supported by many ancient manuscripts (Qumran text 4Q252, Septuagint, Syriac, and the Targums).[12] Also, Ezekiel 21:27 [32] may allude to Genesis 49:10 when it uses *'ăšer-lô*, a similar phrase with identical meaning.[13]

A third possibility is to change the vowel of the first particle *šî* from an 'i' vowel (*ḥiriq-yod*) to an 'a' vowel (*pataḥ* followed by a *yod*) which yields the phrase *šay lōh*, which means 'tribute to him'. The translation would be 'the scepter would not depart from Judah ... until tribute come to him, and to him shall be the obedience of the peoples' (ESV, NRSV, NJPS). This view sets up a good parallel between 'tribute' and 'obedience'.

Although there are differences concerning how to understand *šîlōh*, all three views agree that Genesis 49:10 is referring to a future ruler who will arise from the tribe of Judah. When that ruler arises, 'the peoples' will be obedient to him. The word 'peoples' (*'ammîm*) refers to more than just the descendants of Abraham; it can also refer to foreign nations (Deut. 32:8). Thus, this verse has in view worldwide dominion.

Also, this ruler will bring abundant prosperity (vv. 11-12), which is represented in the abundance of grape vines and wine. Grape vines are protected because they take several years to bear fruit and the fruit they bear is highly valued. One would never bind a donkey to a vine, but there will be so many vines that people will bind their donkeys to them. The multitude of vines is also expressed by the abundance of wine. In fact, there is so much wine that it is being used like

---

12. Matthews, *Genesis 11:27–50:26*, p. 895.
13. Waltke, *Genesis*, p. 608.

water in the washing of garments.[14] Such prosperity leads to health, with dark eyes and white teeth.[15]

Although King David is a partial fulfillment of this passage, the universal reign over all the earth and the abundant prosperity await a future, eschatological figure, who is David's greater son. This one will crush the head of the serpent (Gen. 3:15) and will bring in the full restoration of what was lost in the fall. There has been a progression in Genesis concerning the identity of this coming one from son of Adam, to son of Abraham, to a descendant of the tribe of Judah, and later in Scripture to son of David. Worldwide obedience to the son of David is becoming a reality today as peoples from all nations and tribes submit their lives to King Jesus. The full restoration of prosperity will take place when He comes again and defeats Satan and the powers of evil.

The next several statements concerning the sons of Jacob are much shorter. Zebulun is Leah's sixth son and chronologically Jacob's tenth, but he is listed here before Issachar, Leah's fifth son.[16] Zebulun is the more energetic and prosperous of the two. Jacob's words place Zebulun near the seashore (v. 13), which is difficult to understand because Zebulun was virtually land-locked, with Asher and Manasseh in the west and Naphtali and Issachar in the east (Josh. 19:10-16). Several explanations have been offered to explain this verse. Perhaps the verse refers to the tribe's Solomonic borders which extended to the Mediterranean Sea. It is also possible that Zebulun and Issachar shared territory (Deut. 33:18-19 speaks of a mountain sanctuary in dual possession), which would make the sea to be the Sea of Galilee and Sidon to be a reference to the Phoenician occupation of Accor on Zebulun's western flank.[17] Another possibility is that a major thoroughfare for trade passed through Zebulun, which connected it to the sea nearby.[18]

---

14. Waltke (*Genesis*, p. 609) points out that the phrase 'the blood of grapes' may also connote the violent trampling of enemies.

15. Matthews (*Genesis 11:27–50:26*, p. 897) interprets Genesis 49:10 in light of the effect of the abundance of wine, with eyes darker than the wine and white teeth against red-stained lips.

16. Waltke, *Genesis*, p. 609.

17. Waltke, *Genesis*, p. 609.

18. Matthews, *Genesis 11:27–50:26*, p. 898.

Issachar is presented as a strong donkey, which suggests the attribute of hard work. The phrase 'crouching between the sheepfolds' could refer to rest from a heavy load. The land allotted to Issachar was good and pleasant, but this tribe became forced laborers to the Canaanites in order to remain in her fertile territory.[19]

Dan is the first son of Bilhah and the fifth son of Jacob. There is an emphasis in Jacob's words concerning Dan on deliverance, which frame the stanza (vv. 16-18). Dan delivers his people by judging (dîn), a wordplay on the name Dan. But ultimately deliverance comes from God: 'I wait for your salvation, O LORD' (v. 18). Dan is described as a serpent that bites the horse's heels so that the rider falls backward. There is tension between the comparison of Dan to a snake and the statement that salvation comes from the Lord. The snake is an aggressive and dangerous animal that strikes unexpectedly.[20] It is also the one animal used in the comparisons of Genesis 49 that lives alone.[21] This same tension is seen in the actions of the descendants of Dan. They sought an inheritance other than the one allotted to them and struck the unsuspecting inhabitants of Laish to take over the city (Judg. 18). Also, Samson is from Dan. He is the one judge who acted alone in fighting against the Philistines rather than gathering together an army (Judg. 13–16). It seems that only when he was brought to his knees and in the last act of his life did he look to the Lord for his 'salvation' even in death.

The next three sons of Jacob are handled with a verse each. Gad is the first son of Zilpah and the seventh son of Jacob.[22] The description of Gad in verse 19 includes words that sound like the name Gad (the noun 'raiders' and the verb 'raid'). This tribe will be attacked by marauding bands but will fight back and become proven warriors. Gad settled in the area east of the Jordan and endured attacks by the Ammonites

---

19. Waltke (*Genesis*, p. 610) characterizes Issachar as lazy and willing to submit to the Canaanites for peace. Hamilton (*Genesis 18–50*, pp. 666-68) offers a different view of Issachar as a strong worker, based on a different translation of verse 15b.

20. Waltke, *Genesis*, p. 611. Matthews (*Genesis 11:27–50:26*, pp. 901) points out that the second word for snake refers to a viper (a horned snake), which is a small, obscure snake that strikes unexpectedly. This illustrates lethal stealth.

21. Matthews, *Genesis 11:27–50:26*, p. 900.

22. Waltke, *Genesis*, p. 611.

(Judg. 10–12), the Aramaeans (1 Kings 22:3; 2 Kings 10:32-33), and the Assyrians (2 Kings 15:29). The fact that raiders raid at their heels emphasizes that these raids are more like guerrilla tactics than full-scale wars or battles.[23]

Asher is Jacob's eighth son and the second to Leah's handmaid Zilpah.[24] The statement concerning Asher (v. 20) stresses the abundance of food. Asher settled on the fertile land of the western slopes of Galilee, northwest of the Sea of Galilee.

Naphtali is the sixth son of Jacob and the second son of Rachel's maid Bilhah. He is described as a doe let loose that produces beautiful fawns (v. 21). This description is a symbol of sure-footedness and security. Naphtali could roam where it pleases, which may describe the unrestricted northern frontier where the descendants of Naphtali settled.[25]

Jacob's blessing of Joseph is the longest statement in Genesis 49 (vv. 22-26). It falls into three parts. The first part describes Joseph's prosperity through the image of a fruitful vine (v. 22). The second part shows God's protection of Joseph, even though he was bitterly attacked and severely harassed (vv. 23-24). No doubt this describes the hatred and animosity that Joseph's brothers felt toward him, leading to their selling him into slavery, but it could also include the troubles he experienced in Egypt. Joseph was able to overcome these attacks and prosper because of the help of God. God is described as a God of strength ('the Mighty One of Jacob'), who was so faithful that Joseph could rely on Him in danger ('the Stone of Israel'), and who intimately cared for Joseph in every challenge of life ('Shepherd'). Joseph prevailed in every danger through the help of his God.

This same God also blessed Joseph (vv. 25-26) in every possible way from the heavens above to the deep below. This blessing includes help from God, the fruitfulness of many children (breasts and womb), and the inheritance of the blessings of his forefathers. Joseph is no longer set apart from his brothers because of hatred but is now set apart because of blessing. The one sold into slavery became the distinguished

23. Waltke, *Genesis*, p. 611.
24. Waltke, *Genesis*, p. 612.
25. Matthews, *Genesis 11:27–50:26*, p. 902.

brother, the one who ascended to become ruler in Egypt by the help of God. These blessings will be passed on to Ephraim and Manasseh, the double portion of blessing given to Joseph, whose descendants will play a major role in the history of Israel. Ephraim especially will be fruitful in fulfillment of the name that means 'fruitfulness'.

Finally, Benjamin, the second son of Rachel and the twelfth and youngest son of Jacob, is described as a ravenous wolf who in the morning devours the prey and in the evening divides the spoil (v. 27). The Benjamites became known for their bravery and skill in war (Judg. 3).

The pronouncements of Jacob end with verse 28, which makes clear that his statements are blessings concerning the future of the sons as the twelve tribes of Israel. Although some of the statements were negative (Simeon and Levi), the future for each tribe was open for blessing if each tribe would trust in God. Thus, even the negative statements about Levi being scattered were fulfilled as a blessing because Levi trusted God in a later moment of decision. From a human standpoint, the future is open to God's blessing if each tribe will remain faithful to God. The same is true for God's people today. A sinful past does not have to be held against anyone and even some of the consequences of sin which cannot be removed can ultimately be turned into a blessing by God if faithfulness to God becomes the number-one priority of a person's life.

God's Purposes and His Future Promises (Gen. 49:29–50:26)
The last section of Genesis looks to the future in light of the promises of God. While Jacob was still alive he commanded his sons that they must bury him in the cave that Abraham had purchased in the land of Canaan. This cave in the field of Machpelah is where Abraham, Sarah, Isaac, Rebekah, and Leah were buried. Burial in this cave would not only show family solidarity but it would demonstrate that God's promise to give the land of Canaan to the descendants of Abraham was still a promise that the sons of Jacob should embrace. When Jacob finished giving these instructions to his sons, he died (v. 33).

The first part of Genesis 50 describes the sons of Jacob carrying out the instructions of their father. Joseph takes the lead, and so his actions are highlighted. He mourns for his father and commands his servants to embalm Jacob. Embalming was an Egyptian practice that honored the dead and assisted the journey of the dead in the afterlife. The fact that Jacob was embalmed shows the prestige with which he was held among the Egyptians. Although the Israelites did not normally embalm their dead, embalming would make it easier to journey to the land of Canaan with a dead body. With Pharaoh's permission a great company went with Joseph to Canaan. Not only his own family and brothers went, but also his Egyptian family, servants of Pharaoh's, elders of Egypt, and chariots and horsemen accompanied Joseph. The small children of the Israelites, along with their flocks and herds, were left behind in Egypt, which assured Pharaoh that Joseph would return as he had promised (50:5). This entourage was a great funeral procession which did not go unnoticed by the Canaanites (v. 11). When the caravan arrived in the land, there was a period of mourning for seven days, which must have included the Egyptians, for the Canaanites renamed the place of mourning 'the mourning of the Egyptians' ('Abel-mizraim'). Jacob in his death is showing the way out of Egypt to the land promised to his descendants.

After the death and burial of Jacob, the brothers of Joseph are worried that Joseph will harbor revenge in his heart and pay them back for what they did to him (vv. 15-21). So they send a messenger to Joseph with a message from their father Jacob, which he gave while he was still alive, that Joseph should forgive the sin and the evil actions of his brothers against him. The brothers also identify themselves as 'servants of the God of your father' (v. 17), which indicates that they are now willing servants of the God that Jacob served. They are stressing to Joseph the change of their character from the days when they sold him into Egypt. They demonstrate this change of character by bowing before Joseph and proclaiming that they are his servants. Joseph weeps at their request, perhaps because after seventeen years of kindness they still do not trust him.[26] But Joseph assures them that they do not have to fear and that he will provide for them.

---

26. Waltke, *Genesis*, p. 622.

This response of assurance is based on the theology of
the sovereignty of God. Joseph asks the rhetorical question,
'Am I in the place of God?' In other words, although Joseph
is a powerful man in Egypt, he is not in control of the events
of history. God is in control and He was able to take what the
brothers meant for evil and use it to bring about His good
purposes. This is not only a summary of the Joseph story,
but it is also a summary of the theology of the Bible. The
sinfulness of human beings cannot hinder the good purposes
of God to restore His good creation (Gen. 1–11). The lack of
faith in Abraham and Sarah did not stop God from fulfilling
His wondrous promise of a child. God was able to transform
the greedy character of Jacob into a man who trusted in the
promises of God. Not even a powerful ruler like Pharaoh will
be able to destroy the people of God (Exodus). The ultimate
example of this principle is that the wicked opposition
toward Jesus that led to His crucifixion was used by God to
accomplish the redemption of His people (Acts 2:23). On this
basis, God's people can live in confidence that His purposes
will be accomplished for their good.

The book of Genesis ends with the death of Joseph
(vv. 22-26). God's blessing upon Joseph's life is evident in that
he lives a long life of 110 years, that he sees his grandchildren
of the third generation (Prov. 17:6; Ps. 128:6), and that he is
able to count the sons of Machir as his own.[27] Joseph dies in
Egypt, is embalmed and placed in a coffin in Egypt, but he had
requested that his bones be carried up from Egypt when the
sons of Israel leave Egypt in the future. Joseph confirmed by
faith that one day God would visit His people and bring them
to the land of Canaan. Joseph realized that the final home of
God's people is not in Egypt.

The book of Genesis ends, however, with God's people
still in Egypt. Yet there is hope that the promises of God will
be fulfilled because God has been active in carrying out His
promises to Abraham (Gen. 12:1-3). God has made Abraham's
name great through the rise of Joseph to power as second in

---

27. The evidence that this is a legal adoption comes from the phrase in 50:23
which literally reads 'were born upon the knees of Joseph' (ESV: 'were counted as
Joseph's own'). The word 'knees' also occurred in Genesis 48:12 in the adoption of
Manasseh and Ephraim by Jacob.

command of Egypt. This foreshadows on an earthly level the position of one who will come as Lord of all of creation, and before whom every knee will bow (Phil. 2:10-11).

God has made the descendants of Abraham a blessing to others through the wisdom He gave to Joseph in providing for people during the years of famine. Just as Joseph saved the world on an earthly level, so one will come from Abraham who will be a greater blessing because He will save the world through the complete restoration of all things, spiritual and physical (Col. 1:19-20).

God had promised Abraham that nations would come forth from him, which has been fulfilled on an earthly level by the Edomites, the descendants of Esau, but will also be fulfilled as people from every nation and tongue become children of Abraham (Gal. 3:29).

God's promise of blessing on others through His people is seen in God's blessing on Laban, Potiphar, and the land of Egypt. God's promise of curse to those who mistreat His people will be demonstrated when Israel experiences trouble in Egypt. God takes seriously how His people are treated by individuals and nations, which should be an encouragement to the persecuted and a warning to all who would harm the people of God (Luke 18:6-8; Rev. 6:9-11).

Finally, the promise of land is still the future for the sons of Israel, for God will surely visit them in Egypt and bring them to the land which was promised to them by God. Although in the coming of Jesus Christ many of the promises to Abraham have been fulfilled, the people of God still await the day when those promises will be completely fulfilled. God will yet one day visit the people of God and bring them to their final home in the new heavens and the new earth. May we live by faith in the promises of God until that great and glorious day!

STUDY QUESTIONS

1   What significance does the adoption of the two sons of Joseph have for the family of Jacob (Gen. 48)? What does it mean for the future of these two sons that Jacob crosses his hands when he blesses them?

2   How do the actions of Reuben, Simeon, and Levi affect their descendants (Gen. 49:1-7)? How is the curse of Levi turned into a blessing?

3   Summarize what is said about Judah (Gen. 49:8-12). Reflect on how these words are fulfilled.

4   How does Genesis 50:20 summarize the theology of the Joseph story? How does that verse summarize the message of the whole Bible? Can you see that principle at work in your life?

5   How have the promises that God made to Abraham in Genesis 12:1-3 been fulfilled by the end of Genesis? How should this give encouragement to God's people?

Subject Index

Scripture Index

Other Commentaries in the Focus on the Bible Series

Christian Focus Publications
publishes books for all ages

Our mission statement –

STAYING FAITHFUL
In dependence upon God we seek to impact the world through literature faithful to His infallible Word, the Bible. Our aim is to ensure that the Lord Jesus Christ is presented as the only hope to obtain forgiveness of sin, live a useful life and look forward to heaven with Him.

REACHING OUT
Christ's last command requires us to reach out to our world with His gospel. We seek to help fulfil that by publishing books that point people towards Jesus and help them develop a Christ-like maturity. We aim to equip all levels of readers for life, work, ministry and mission.

Books in our adult range are published in three imprints:

Christian Focus contains popular works including biographies, commentaries, basic doctrine and Christian living. Our children's books are also published in this imprint.

Mentor focuses on books written at a level suitable for Bible College and seminary students, pastors, and other serious readers. The imprint includes commentaries, doctrinal studies, examination of current issues and church history.

Christian Heritage contains classic writings from the past.

Christian Focus Publications Ltd,
Geanies House, Fearn, Ross-shire,
IV20 1TW, Scotland, United Kingdom.
www.christianfocus.com